THE HUMAN FOOTPRINT
CHALLENGES FOR WILDERNESS AND BIODIVERSITY

SERIES PRODUCER
CEMEX BOOKS ON NATURE
PATRICIO ROBLES GIL

ERIC W. SANDERSON • PATRICIO ROBLES GIL
CRISTINA G. MITTERMEIER • VANCE G. MARTIN • CYRIL F. KORMOS

PREFACE BY
STEVEN E. SANDERSON

FOREWORD BY
JARED DIAMOND

CEMEX

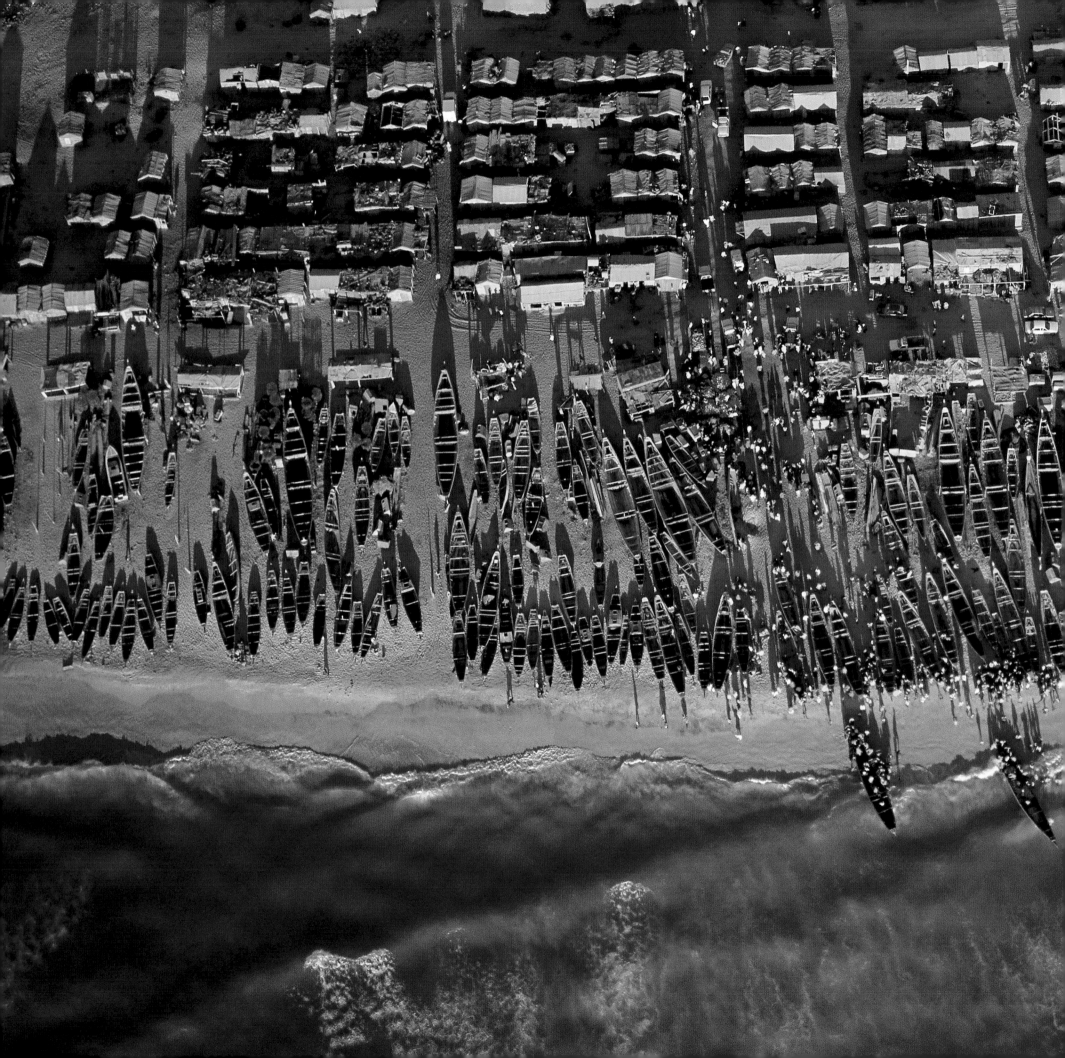

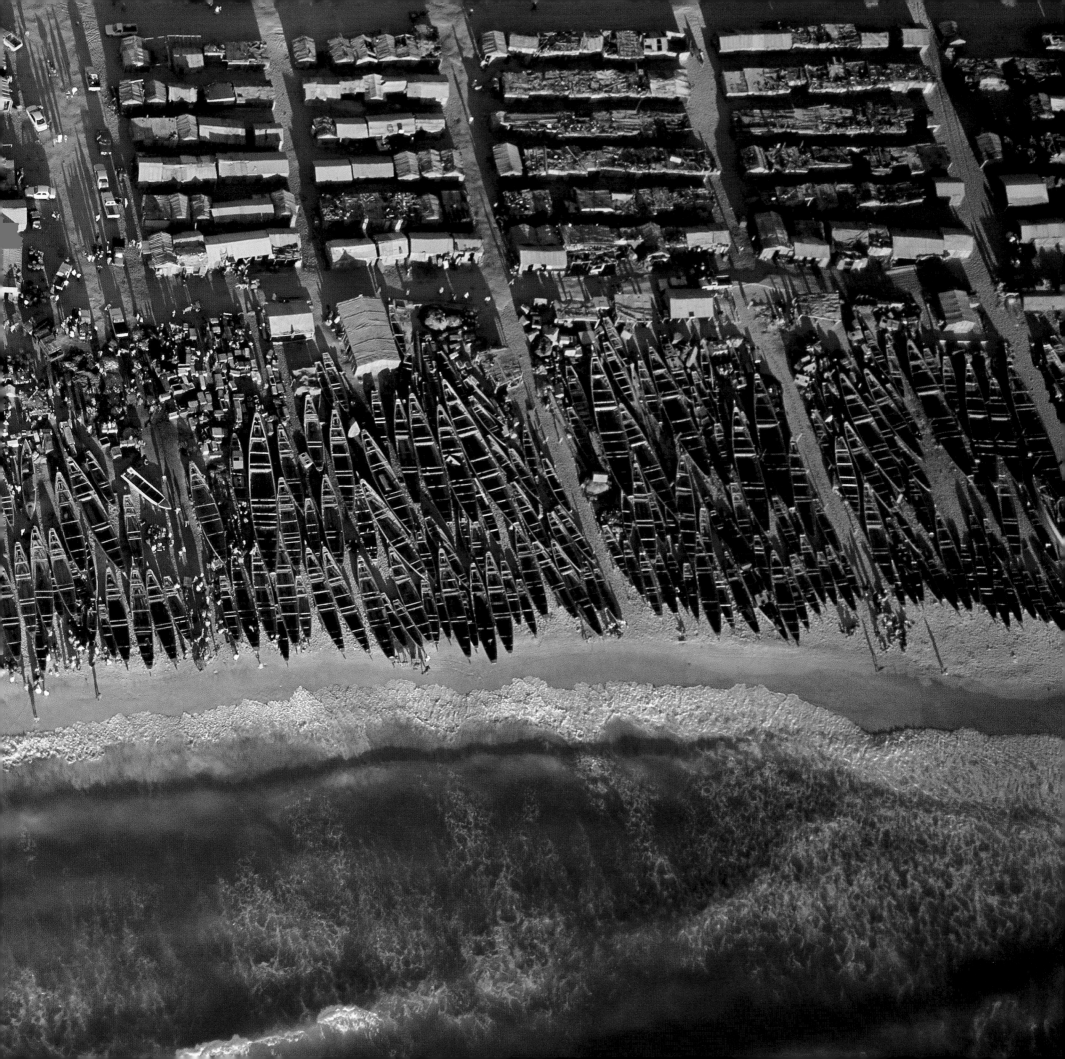

Down through the centuries, the history of humanity has been directly associated with the use of natural resources. That relationship constitutes one of the foundations on which all the great civilizations, cultures and nations have been built. In the constant struggle to improve their living standard, the peoples of the world have developed sophisticated techniques to produce foods. They have found different energy sources to meet their needs, and built numerous arteries of communication to reach the most distant communities.

Along the way, however, we have stripped nature of virtually all the fertile land on the planet. An aerial view of the footprint we have left on the earth's surface is a true eye-opener. If we continue as we have done thus far, the wilderness areas still in existence run the risk of disappearing. And along with them, the extraordinary biodiversity they still contain, threatening the sustainability of the world we live in.

On CEMEX's hundredth anniversary in business, aware of the environmental challenge we presently face, and as part of our commitment to sustainable development, our company has once again joined up with well-known organizations to tackle the issue and subject of the book, *The Human Footprint: Challenges for Wilderness and Biodiversity.* In this book, researchers with the Wildlife Conservation Society analyze humanity's rapport with the Earth, as well as the threats posed by the resulting loss of biodiversity. For this task they had the support of Agrupación Sierra Madre, Conservation International, The WILD Foundation, and the International League of Conservation Photographers. Our thanks to all of them for their valuable collaboration.

Scientific evidence points to the growing importance of protecting large wilderness areas as an indispensable means for preserving the biodiversity of our world. That is why for the last six years CEMEX has actively participated in recovering the great El Carmen-Big Bend biological megacorridor along the border between Mexico and the United States. During this time we have purchased lands and signed agreements with private individuals, conservationist groups and government agencies to protect 140 thousand hectares of forests, grasslands and deserts that form one of the last-remaining wilderness of the planet.

In the El Carmen-Big Bend megacorridor we also urged the recovery of such flagship species of native wildlife as the bighorn sheep. Working in coordination with the National Commission of Natural Protected Areas of Mexico, we managed to secure the first official designation of some twenty thousand hectares as Wilderness Area. Through such initiatives we hope that never again will the mark of the human footprint be left in this pristine territory.

Restoring areas that have been disturbed to some degree, by way of processes that can return them to their natural condition, is a commitment we have shouldered in our ongoing effort to build a better future. In celebrating the first centennial of our company, we hope the texts, pictures and maps in this book—another in the series about environmental strategies that CEMEX has been publishing for more than a decade—help identify those places where we must focus our attention and incite action to conserve our planet's extraordinary biodiversity. That is one of the greatest legacies we can leave to future generations.

CEMEX

The human footprint is one of a small handful of mental images that suggests a way to understand our role on Earth and to envision a future that protects wild nature and sustains human life at the same time. A sustainable future—not challenge, empire, or economic control—is the greatest quest of our time.

For the first time in human history, the human footprint extends to the utter domination of the Earth system. Approximately half of all the products of photosynthesis are human-managed. The unperturbed wild is a small and shrinking part of the globe, restricted mainly to inaccessible or inhospitable corners of the world. The scale and productivity of human life are on the rise, and salvation of the wild rests squarely in human hands.

Clearly, these human hands have been the source of so much loss to nature. But it is well to remember also that these are the same human hands that painted the caves of Lascaux—and many others around the world—with beautiful, timeless images of wildlife and erected great architectural monuments to nature. The fact that the wild has always been the wellspring of human culture must give us hope.

We have suffered a "nature deficit" for a long while. The world is urbanizing, people live at a distance from the wild, and the public philosophy of globalization is predicated on the conquest of nature, turning raw materials into human wealth. Deferring to the wild has been lost to modern culture, and the priorities of conservation are no longer in the users' manual of our planet.

For this reason, we must take the lessons of conservation in densely inhabited parts of the world seriously. Our future depends on getting wiser fast, learning to combine high degrees of human influence with successful wildlife and ecosystem protection. This volume helps us understand the possibilities for humans and nature and to recall that fundamental truth of human existence: We are not outside nature, but a part of it. The future of the Earth will be measured by the scale, the impact, and the artistry with which civilization places the human footprint on the global map.

STEVEN E. SANDERSON
President and Chief Executive Officer
Wildlife Conservation Society

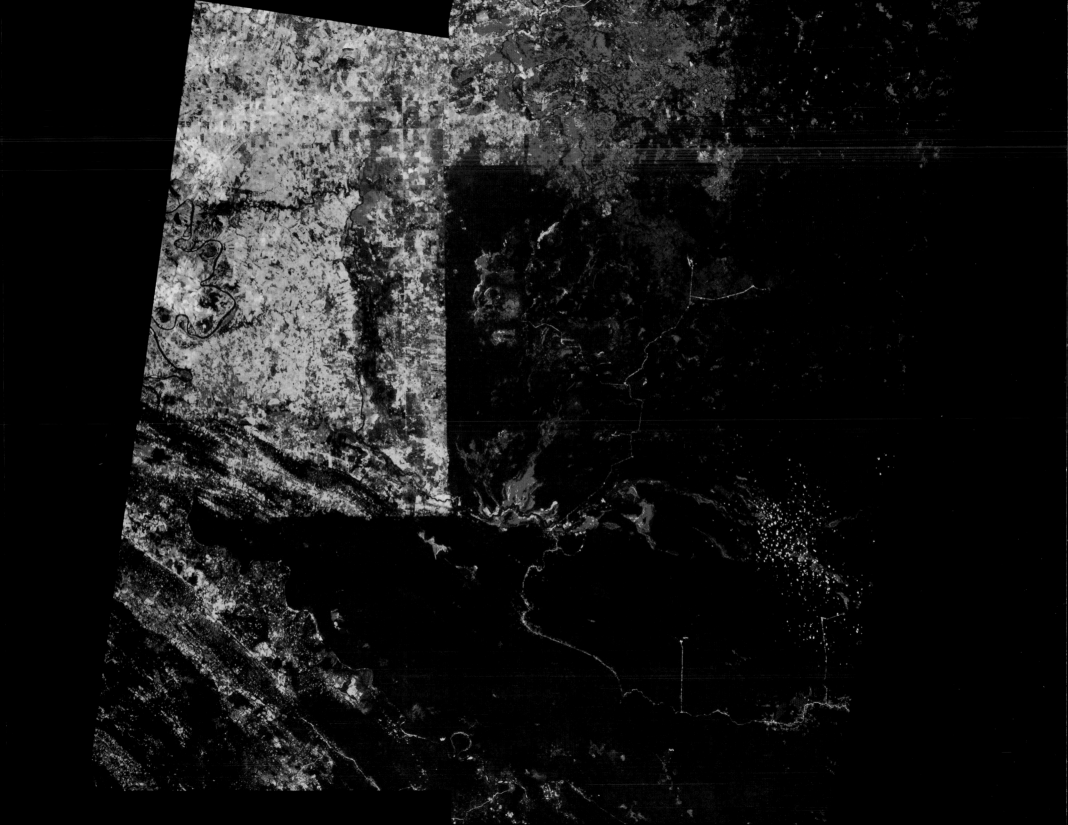

Seemingly drawn with the precision of a huge carpenter's square, the border separating Mexico and the northwest of Guatemala, with an obvious line of deforestation on one side, is easy to spot in this photograph. The clearly-defined fragmentation on the left side is visible from an altitude of several thousand meters. This marked difference is due to several factors, but chiefly the opening up of new access roads into virgin territory.

This picture was published in 1989 in the *National Geographic* magazine, causing much concern among Mexican conservationist groups because it flatly confirmed existing fears about the great loss of Mexican tropical forests. That same year saw the establishment of Agrupación Sierra Madre, whose mission has been to help protect large wilderness areas and their biodiversity.

Knowing that competition in any society to attract the public's attention is always fierce, we realized from the very beginning that if we wanted to achieve our conservationist objectives, we would have to become outstanding "sellers" of nature. So Sierra Madre took a marketing approach and focused on raising people's level of awareness as a means to encourage conservation of nature.

Observing the Earth from the air was uncommon. The perspective can be somewhat surprising. I am always hearing colleagues and friends talking excitedly of the discoveries they make when they go into the Google Earth website and find their home or their office. Contemplating our planet from the air is a unique attraction, allowing us to see above the forests and the mountains, to travel to remote places and see things from a whole new angle. The satellite picture of the Mexico-Guatemala border has never failed to confound and unsettle me. So dramatic is the impression this picture gives that we have used it several times in our communication campaigns to stress the impact we are having on the Earth.

On my last visit to Google Earth I again zoomed in on the corner between these two countries, and the scenery I found was very different from that of 17 years ago. The border was no longer as easy to pinpoint because roads had been opened in Guatemala, prompting widespread deforestation and, as a result, seriously breaking up the ecosystem, isolating patches of vegetation and wildlife populations, and jeopardizing the largest mass of tropical forest in Central and North America. These satellite pictures evidence the relentless advance of the human footprint.

In 2002 we produced for CEMEX the book *Wilderness: Earth's Last Wild Places*, in collaboration with Conservation International. The latter organization established the criteria for defining these regions: 1. Human presence of fewer than five inhabitants per square kilometer, not counting population centers; 2. An area greater than 10 000 square kilometers, and 3. Retention of 70% of the original plant covering intact. Going by these criteria, about half of the planet still retains these conditions. Also named were the five great preeminent biomasses, on account of their biodiversity, endemic species and wilderness.

Around the same time, Wildlife Conservation Society, a highly prestigious conservationist organization, published a geographical survey in which they identified the last wilderness regions, calling them the "last of the wild." The survey analyzed man's impact on the earth's surface using variables like population density greater than one inhabitant per square kilometer, means of transportation (highways, railways or navigable rivers), use of farm land and urban land, and even pollution from nighttime illumination. In this manner, combining satellite images and other sources of geographical data, they put together an extraordinary map—as interesting as it was impressive—which they called the "human footprint."

The suggestion to include this idea in CEMEX's collection of books about nature was met with great interest, both for its historic importance in the conservation of biodiversity and for its value in protecting the wilderness areas. No less interesting were the discussions on how to update and enhance the theme. Cristina Mittermeier acted as coordinator between different groups and organizations like Wildlife Conservation Society, Conservation International, The WILD Foundation, and Agrupación Sierra Madre.

For our book to come up with a worthwhile proposition, it was divided into two parts. The first deals with human activities that have left their mark on the planet over the centuries. It provides significant insight that helps to understand the challenge we are facing. The second part examines the priorities that force us to concentrate our efforts for conservation on those places where we can make the greatest difference. This second section ends with a portfolio of images of those regions that still conserve their natural wild state.

Due to the obvious impact and irrefutable truth of aerial pictures, only photographs taken in flight, from an aircraft ranging from a spacecraft to an ultra-light airplane, were selected for this book. The bird's-eye view clearly exposes the human footprint, startling us when we fly over regions considered the last of the wildlife areas. Credit goes to the important participation of the International League of Conservation Photographers, whose members not only obtain extraordinary pictures but involve themselves in efforts to support species and regions, each making it their personal business to collaborate with conservationist organizations. In this case the League's photographers are working together in a group effort alongside scientists and conservationists.

The pictures and texts convince us to seriously question our lifestyle. Our unsustainable use of resources calls for an immediate change and obliges us to seek solutions to curb man's incursion into the last wild spaces.

To this end, I think it is vital to create successful conservation models that can be replicated in different parts of the world. One such example is El Carmen-Big Bend, a bi-national region on the Mexican-United States border, where Agrupación Sierra Madre has been actively involved for 15 years in concrete conservationist measures.

For the El Carmen-Big Bend Conservationist Corridor Initiative, the two countries' government agencies in charge of protected nature reserves met this year with ranchers, national and international conservationist organizations, funds, foundations and one corporation to reach an understanding and design a joint work plan to guarantee the long-term permanence of this biological mega-corridor of 4.5 million hectares. In light of the border conflicts between these two countries, the initiative represents a great opportunity to ensure a more secure stretch along the frontier. And, more importantly, to conserve a region where we can guarantee the long-term permanence of its wild spirit and biodiversity.

In its commitment to the region, CEMEX has not only purchased several properties in Mexico and the United States, joining them under a single administration to counterattack fragmentation; the company is also "re-wilding" them by removing cattle and fences and reintroducing native species that had disappeared, like the bighorn sheep. Moreover, to show how keen CEMEX is to defend the planet's last wild sanctuaries, the company has turned over 20 000 hectares to be designated as the first wildlife region in Latin America. Actions like these definitely open new approaches and let us glimpse a future in which we can turn back the human footprint.

Many years have passed since that day when I opened *National Geographic* and saw that picture of Mexico and Guatemala. And with the passage of those years, many good intentions, disappointments, successes and failures. I recall a comment of my friend Exequiel Ezcurra during a discussion about the future of the wilderness: *Man has always tried to leave behind his footprint, sometimes spectacularly as in the case of the great pyramids, cathedrals and other structures that are a source of pride for humanity and all nations. Today we can see how the use of natural resources has left our prints practically everywhere on the planet. The challenge now is to about-face and pride ourselves in not leaving any prints at all.*

PATRICIO ROBLES GIL
President
Agrupación Sierra Madre

Take only photographs, leave only footprints is a long-serving ethic for wilderness trekkers. It evokes respect for nature untrammeled by human activity, and a synergism between humankind and the natural world. This book invites reflection on that important maxim.

Leave only footprints—which infers a light and harmless human activity and attitude—is, ironically, not the footprint to which the title of this book refers. The human footprint herein is decidedly more permanent. It is the heavy mark of our development and technological prowess, coupled with the sheer weight of human numbers, that has become more or less indelible. This footprint is not a spoor in moist soil or a mere broken twig along the track, soon to disappear as the natural elements play upon it. This footprint too often replaces rather that reinvigorates natural processes. Unfortunately, this type of footprint is the result of a misstep, and disavows one of our most essential and ultimately inescapable compacts with wild nature —simply put: As you have spawned us, so we will protect you.

Human development is as inevitable and important as it is challenging. The question is not "if" but "how", and "how" can be derived only through intense observation of the natural world, and subsequent modeling of our actions after natural systems that sustain themselves and their environment. Technology is perhaps only the easiest part of the process through which we conceive and implement life-supporting models of development. The greater part of the "how" is the practice of an essential attitude of humility and appreciation for the natural world that birthed and continues to support us. We can choose what type of footprint we leave. With the right attitude, we can't go wrong.

Take only photographs… evokes this attitude, and amply demonstrates one way to redeem the irony of the human footprint. The wonderful images within this book, of wilderness landscapes and their amazing biodiversity, only speak for themselves, but they evoke for the viewer the dedicated aspiration, skill, endurance of long hours of physical hardship and the devotion of the conservation photographer.

When we consider CEMEX, one of the world's largest cement companies, we sense both the irony and the redemption. Cement is a heavy footprint, yes. But we can see the effort of CEMEX to service human development while also trying to understand the natural systems and processes that need to be honored and protected, and act in their benefit. The examples are many: Production of this book (one of many in a long and illustrious series of such works); support of the International League of Conservation Photographers (some of the results of which are seen herein); volunteering to play a visionary and key role in the El Carmen-Big Bend Conservation Corridor Initiative, and more.

We hope this book helps you to consider anew the wilderness, your own footprint, and the increasing effect of our human stride across the planet.

VANCE G. MARTIN
President
The WILD Foundation

The next time you find yourself on an airplane, take a moment to look out of the window. If the weather is clear, you might be able to see the landscape of human influence. I must confess that I was initially uncertain about the idea of using aerial photography to illustrate this book. I was worried that the distant perspective would remove the viewer from the intimate setting provided by our very familiar and almost always comfortable planet. I now realize, however, that looking down at the features of our every day life—the city, the forest, the river, the dam—is how we can best understand our not-always-kind relationship with our planet. From this advantageous perspective, we can truly see how the impact of the human footprint has touched almost every corner of the globe and, most importantly, where the absence of a human footprint allows the last of the wild to persist.

The decision to use only aerial photography was a bold one. Explaining the plight of our planet with images that speak of the beauty and irreplaceability of Earth's ecosystems and species is a tall order. To do so, we called on some of the best photographers in the world to share their vision of the human footprint and the last of the wild as seen from the air.

What we have in this book is a fantastic collection of images that are more than mere snapshots taken from a jetliner's window; they are images captured with breathtaking photographic skill and endowed with a sense of purpose that, we hope, invites action.

With the journalistic determination of war-time reporters, conservation photographers have two duties: The first is to use their talent, their understanding of their equipment, and their sensitivities to explain the world to those who cannot see it with their own eyes. We are, by definition, witnesses and we have an obligation to allow ourselves to become a tool for the weak, for those who cannot speak for themselves; the endangered, the oppressed, those who don't realize they might be the last few of a whole species or tribe; the poor who become poorer as the environment around them degrades; those who have no choice but to harm or see their children starve; and those who do have a choice but opt to be governed by greed. We have to show it all and we have to do it in a compelling, honest, emotional way.

Our second obligation is to give our images a higher purpose. Creating the image is not enough. Stepping away from the camera to do whatever is necessary to make an image work for conservation is the trademark of a real conservation photographer. Many of the artists whose work is featured in this book form part of the International League of Conservation Photographers, an organization that aims to recognize their individual commitment and efforts towards a sustainable future for our planet.

As photographers, we understand that conservation arguments must be based on strong scientific evidence. We also know, however, that arguments need emotions to inspire people into action. Effective conservation images are seeped with a sense of purpose; they are crafted with emotion, with urgency, with tears; they are meant to show the beauty, the wildness and the incalculable value of what is being lost to those who cannot see it with their own eyes.

In this letter, I wish to recognize and salute those photographers whose work brings an accurate and honest portrait of our planet to these pages. Their dedication, skill and commitment to conservation must be recognized and valued.

As Executive Director of the International League of Conservation Photographers, it is my privilege to serve with some of the best men and women in the field of image-making. As this book travels around the world, we hope our images will make you smile, reflect, cry and, most importantly, spring into action to help turn the human footprint from a destructive force into one of hope.

The International League of Conservation Photographers is an initiative of The WILD Foundation. Its members are selected on the strength of their commitment to conservation, their ethical behavior and their mastery of art of photography.

CRISTINA GOETTSCH MITTERMEIER
Executive Director
International League of Conservation Photographers

A book whose title contains the phrases "human footprint" and "wilderness and biodiversity" runs the risk of immediately arousing two dismissive reactions. The first is to the phrase "human footprint". It is tempting to reflect that the world already holds billions of starving people; the human footprint is inevitably so big that we no longer have the option of limiting it, so why even discuss it? The other reaction is to the phrase "wilderness and biodiversity", which is often viewed as a luxury. A common one-liner tells us that we must balance the environment against the economy. We mustn't do anything for the good of biodiversity and the environment that would damage the economy. Those endangered species of lousy earthworms don't deserve attention; what we really care about is people. Such thoughts make the whole subject depressing.

To see what is wrong with these knee-jerk reactions, let's first take the subject of the human footprint. Yes, we humans are absolutely dependent on renewable biological resources: Especially on forests that give us our wood and paper; on fish that constitute the dietary protein for about two billion of the world's people, most of them poor; and on the worms, plants and microbes that maintain the texture and fertility of our soil, which we use to grow crops and raise domestic animals; and on wild places to replenish our soul and inspire the human spirit. Our footprint is growing as we deplete the world's forests, fish stocks, and soils, and as we trample on the last wild places on our planet.

But that expanding footprint and that depletion of resources are not inevitable. We could continue to extract, sustainably and perpetually, as much or even more wood and fish as we are extracting now—if we managed our forests and fisheries responsibly. The well-understood principles of how to do so boil down to minimizing waste, maintaining individuals of reproductive age and harvesting mature trees and fish only as rapidly as new trees and fish are regenerated by reproduction. Many of the world's forests and fisheries are already well-managed, including many of the forests of Sweden, Canada and Pennsylvania, and big fisheries such as those that process Alaska wild salmon, U.S. Pacific Coast halibut and Australian rock lobster. Those examples teach us how other forests and fisheries that are badly

managed at the moment could be well managed. This makes me hopeful, not depressed.

What about biodiversity? Is it, as is often said, a dispensable luxury? No, biodiversity is a matter of life and death for human societies. Mismanagement of biological resources, especially forests, was among the most common causes of collapse of great societies in the past. Famous victims included societies of the Fertile Crescent (the mother societies of civilization), the Classic Lowland Maya (the most advanced New World societies before Columbus), the Anasazi and Easter Island. That one-liner about balancing the environment against the economy has it exactly backwards: Economic considerations are the strongest reason to take good care of the environment. Environmental problems are relatively cheap to avoid, or to cure in their early stages, but they become horrendously expensive or impossible to solve when full-blown. That was a hard lesson learned by Americans last year when our stubbornness in refusing to spend a few hundred million dollars fixing the dikes protecting New Orleans ended up costing us a few hundred billion dollars in damages and the expense of rebuilding a major city, not to mention the lost economic worth of over a thousand dead Americans.

Or let's take that one-liner about caring more for some lousy earthworms than for us humans. The most important reason for caring for those lousy earthworms is that they are essential to maintaining the soil for growing the food of us humans. Pesticide-related declines in earthworms have been a major cause of China losing half of its high-quality cropland in recent years. Dismissing the importance of some species of lousy earthworms and plants is like dismissing the importance of some of those lousy rivets holding together an airplane: You can get away with letting some of those rivets fall out, but if you keep it up you are bound to lose your airplane.

Naturally, biodiversity, forests, fish and soil were not the only problems endangering human societies in the past and they are not the only problems today. Water, climate change, alien species and population growth were problems in the past and they still are. Energy and toxic chemicals are additional new problems that we now face for the first time on top of those old problems. People often ask me: What is the single most important problem on which we should focus our attention? The most common responses to that question are energy, population or climate change, and people therefore immediately jump to the conclusion that we should give priority to finding a solution for one of those major problems and forget about our other problems for the time being. But the challenge facing us today is that there are a dozen major problems any one of which could do us in, so we have find workable solutions for all of them. If we solved the problem of energy and climate change but not water, or if we took care of population and toxic chemicals but lost our soil, then water or soil problems alone would still suffice to ruin us.

What can a single individual do about those dozen major problems facing the world? Is it hopeless? It often feels that way when we consider the overwhelming forces that seem to be aligned against biodiversity and the environment, such as governments and big businesses. But the reality is that individuals make governments and big businesses, and even a lone individual can do a lot. One simple thing that you can do is vote: Some recent elections in the U.S. have been famously decided by very small numbers of votes. You can consume selectively, buying from companies whose environmental policies you admire and boycotting companies whose policies you dislike: The biggest companies in the world have been responding to consumer pressure in recent years or are in the process of responding. You can talk to other people, including your children, who, in turn, will talk to others: One of the most common causes of CEO's of big businesses suddenly waking up to environmental issues is that their children have begun asking them what their company is doing for our planet. Another thing you can do as an individual is donate selectively to environmental organizations, many of which are incredibly cost-effective.

The problems now facing biodiversity are those that we have caused ourselves. In order to promote our own interests by protecting biodiversity, all that we need is the will to stop causing those problems. Many are already convinced of this and we only need to convince more, which is why I am cautiously optimistic that we can save ourselves by stabilizing the human footprint and saving the last of the wild.

JARED DIAMOND

INTRODUCTION

In Genesis, God charges human beings to take dominion over the fish in the sea, the birds in the air, and every other living thing. We are entreated to be fruitful and multiply, to fill the earth and subdue it. The good news, and the bad news, is that we have almost succeeded.

STATE OF THE PLANET, CIRCA 2000

As humanity enters the new millennium, we have embarked on a new phase in human history and, in fact, in the history of the world. There are now more than six billion human beings on the planet and it is estimated that by mid-century there could be eight to twelve billion. Such population levels are unprecedented for a large, intelligent, tool-using animal: An animal that has developed some very remarkable tools at that. Internal combustion engines, access to fossil fuels and a profound understanding of chemistry and physics have enabled us to equip a single human being with enough power (for example, a bulldozer) to modify the environment in ways that would have required an army of men with shovels and picks in times past. Combine this technological prowess with an evolved and perfectly understandable desire on the part of all six billion—and perhaps, eventually, twelve billion—individuals on the planet to be well-fed, warm and secure, at least as much as their neighbor and preferably as much as their favorite television celebrity, and it is no wonder that the natural abundance of our blue and green Earth is under siege.

The good news is that this same technology and the quest for a better life have also brought us remarkable achievements. We live in a time of conquered diseases, reduced infant mortality and extended life expectancies (at least for those of us in the developed world). We now have a better understanding of ourselves, our planet and our universe than had ever been thought possible. And while social injustices remain much too common around the world, we have nonetheless improved human rights, reduced the number of cruel and totalitarian governments and expanded access to education, communication and opportunities for a better life. Unfortunately, even these essential benefits of being a 21st century citizen are not available to all.

The bad news, as scientists have taken pains to explain to us, is what is happening to our planet. For example, the Intergovernmental Panel on Climate Change report (IPCC 2001), the Pew Oceans report (Pew Oceans Commission 2003), the Millennium Ecosystem Assessment (MEA 2005) and similar recent studies are all thoroughly-documented, extensively-researched, hotly-debated, broadly-written scientific reports that give one consistent warning to humanity: Watch out! We are using too much too quickly. Human beings are consuming so much and polluting the rest to the extent that we are threatening the lifelines on which a moderate climate, productive oceans, functioning ecosystems and the circle of life depend.

One tragic manifestation of human over-consumption is the loss of plants and animals, biodiversity, and the wealth of living species that we share our planet with, especially as this loss is irreversible. Plants and animals take millions of years to evolve into new species and we are losing them at a pace measured in decades. Based on the fossil record, extinction rates are estimated to be running at 100 to 1 000 times faster than at any other time in geological history. Iconic wildlife species around the world—elephants, tigers, buffalo—have lost vast parts of their range. But we do not need scientists to tell us this story. At the beginning of the new millennium, it is difficult to find an adult who has not seen the natural values of the place they grew up diminished in their own lifetimes: Woodlots converted to farmlands, farms converted to suburbs, suburbs built up into cities. Think of a stream you knew as a child near where you lived. How is that stream doing today?

Surprisingly, and despite the dire warnings and everyday evidence, the message of planetary balance is not being heard. In the United States, opinion polls and recent election results indicate that the public does not view environmental protection as a critical issue in deciding how to vote in national elections. The international community has made some attempts, but has not yet mobilized sufficient resources to respond to the global environmental crisis. Although studies indicate that the costs of conserving biodiversity worldwide are manageable, especially compared to some of humanity's other problems, funding has yet to be made available on anything approaching the necessary scale to avert major losses of the world's remaining biodiversity.

There are many explanations for the lack of response. Some place their trust in innovation and expect that new technology will intervene in time to resolve the planet's environmental problems. Some believe that the cause is already lost and we are already doomed. Some feel that conservationists have been crying wolf for too long and no longer give credence to their warnings. Many, because they grew up in an already degraded environment, think the world has always been this poor. Others simply live for today and could not care less about tomorrow.

The point is that we have entered a new time in history, and for this new time we need new wisdom. Many of the ideas of the past, particularly those regarding the relative bounty of nature and the desperate plight of human beings, need to be revisited. In the past, the world was big and ferocious and needed to be tamed; because people were few and nature was resilient. Medicine was rudimentary, science non-existent and poverty massive. Now the scales have tipped the other way. People are many and nature is fragile and fraught, bending under our weight. Now the individual decisions of six billion people add up to a global phenomenon in a way unique to our time. We call this weight, these decisions, our collective impact on the surface of the planet, the "human footprint."

This book is an introduction to the human footprint in words, maps and pictures. In it, we illustrate the human footprint using some of the best tools available to conservationists and we suggest some of the answers to the pressing problems of the footprint. We combine state-of-the-art mapping from satellite imagery from the world's space agencies and photography from the world's best nature photographers with technical analyses, essays and letters from several of the world's leading conservation organizations. Together, we want you to know about not just the severity of the problem, but also what can be done—by individuals, institutions, and governments—to make the situation better. But let us begin with how we got to know the human footprint.

MAPPING THE HUMAN FOOTPRINT

In its simplest form, the human footprint is just a map. Until recently, mapping the human footprint was not possible because data on human activities at the global scale were simply unavailable. This situation changed during the 1990s due to the fortunate confluence of several factors. Rapid advances in observing the Earth using satellite technology, led by NASA and other space agencies, meant that verifiable global maps of land use and land cover were available for the first time. In addition, the end of the Cold War and calls for government efficiency in the United States meant that other sources of geographic data, for example on roads and railways, were released to the public for the first time by those great compilers of geographic information, the world's military. Improved reporting of population statistics at sub-national levels enabled geographers to create global digital maps of human population density. Finally, advances in computers and the software required to produce combined maps (called geographic information systems or GIS) provided the necessary technology to collate data on the world's people, land use, and roads and technology: No small task. Although the datasets are imperfect instruments, they do enable us to take a first look at the "human footprint" on the land surface.

Ironically perhaps, the map of the human footprint grew out of a desire to map wilderness areas. Wilderness areas have been traditionally mapped by what they are not: Not densely settled, not built up, not crisscrossed by roads, etc. There is a recent tradition of wilderness mapping in conservation: The Sierra Club and The WILD Foundation, the United Nations Environment Programme, the Wildlife Conservation Society, Conservation International and The Nature Conservancy as well as numerous academics involved in mapping and characterizing wild places. Wilderness conservation has been a powerful and often successful biodiversity conservation issue that is still, and must continue to be, of great importance in a world dominated by the human footprint; but the story also leads us in other directions.

To map the human footprint, a team of scientists from the Wildlife Conservation Society and Columbia University (Sanderson *et al.* 2002) used four types of data as proxies for human influence on nature: Population density, land transformation or use, road access, railways, major rivers, coastlines, and electrical power infrastructure as a measure of technological prowess. Nine datasets were found to represent these four data types and, remarkably, each of these datasets could be expressed at scale of one square kilometer on a global basis (see Table 1). These datasets were selected for their coverage (global),

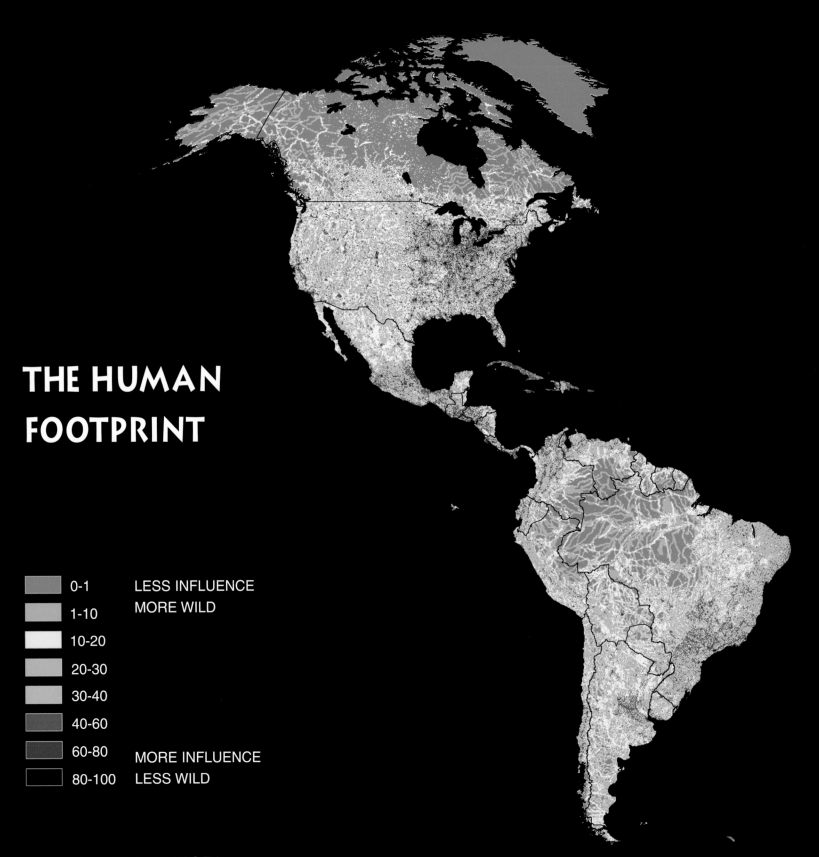

THE HUMAN
FOOTPRINT

	0-1	LESS INFLUENCE
	1-10	MORE WILD
	10-20	
	20-30	
	30-40	
	40-60	
	60-80	MORE INFLUENCE
	80-100	LESS WILD

CIESIN - COLUMBIA UNIVERSITY

WILDLIFE CONSERVATION SOCIETY

consistency (developed by a single source using consistent methods), availability (public domain and free), and relevance (from the 1990s), but are only an incomplete description of human influence on nature. We did not explicitly include climate change, ultraviolet radiation from holes in the ozone layer, pollution, soil degradation, grazing lands, or many other factors like consumption patterns as we lacked data at a comparable scale with the other dataset data. In this sense, our human footprint is a conservative view of the influence people have on the planet.

Human Population

Human population density is a fundamental driver of human interactions with the environment, where higher human densities lead to higher levels of influence on ecosystem structure and process. Human population density is frequently cited as a primary cause of declines in species and ecosystems. For example, a recent study showed that 98% of the variation in extinction rates in national parks in Ghana over a thirty-year period could be explained by the number of people living within 50 km of the park and the size of the park, with higher densities and smaller parks leading to higher extinction rates. Others have found similar results for national parks in the western United States and small reserves across Africa. In terms of hunting for subsidence in tropical forests, if human population densities much exceed one person per square kilometer, even under the most productive circumstances, wildlife numbers will decline. There are numerous other examples, but perhaps the most compelling evidence can be found by simply taking a drive from an urban area out through the suburbs into the countryside and wilder areas. Most of us agree that, as a general rule, the fewer the people, the greater the number and variety of species and wildlife encountered; however, there are important and interesting exceptions to this.

Despite this fundamental understanding, there is little guidance in conservation literature about exactly how human influence scales with human population density. The consequences of interactions between human population density and the environment depend on the nature of the interaction and the par-

Table 1. Geographic datasets used to map the human footprint

Dataset type	Dataset Name	Year(s)	Sources[a]	Reference
Population Density	Gridded Population of the World	1995	CIESIN	CIESIN 2000
Land Transformation	Land Use / Land Cover Version 2	1992-1993	USGS/UNL/JRC	Loveland et al. 2000
	Vector Map Level 0 Built-up Centers	1960s-1990s[b]	NIMA	NIMA 1997
	Vector Map Level 0 Population Settlements	1960s-1990s	NIMA	
Access	Vector Map Level 0 Roads	1960s-1990s	NIMA	
	Vector Map Level 0 Railways	1960s-1990s	NIMA	
	Vector Map Level 0 Coastline	1960s-1990s	NIMA	
	Vector Map Level 0 Rivers (major rivers defined as rivers represented by continuous polygons to the sea)	1960s-1990s	NIMA	
Electrical Power Infrastructure	Defense Meteorological Satellite Program Stable Lights Dataset	1994-1995	NOAA/NGDC	Elvidge et al. 1997a
Biome Normalization	Terrestrial Biomes	2001	WWF	Olson et al. 2001
	Terrestrial Biogeographic Realms	2001	WWF	

[a]Acronyms:
CIESIN = Center for International Earth Science Information Network, Columbia University
USGS = United States Geological Survey
UNL = University of Nebraska, Lincoln
JRC = Joint Research Centre of the European Commission
NIMA = National Imagery and Mapping Agency
NOAA = National Oceanic and Atmospheric Administration
NGDC = National Geophysical Data Center
WWF = World Wildlife Fund for Nature – United States
[b]Although the Vector Map Level 0, Edition 3, datasets were published in 1997, the datasets on which they are based derived from Defense Mapping Agency Operational Navigational Charts developed from the mid-1960s through the early 1990s.

LAST OF
THE WILD

TROPICAL AND SUBTROPICAL MOIST BROADLEAF FORESTS

TROPICAL AND SUBTROPICAL DRY BROADLEAF FORESTS

TROPICAL AND SUBTROPICAL CONIFEROUS FORESTS

TEMPERATE BROADLEAF AND MIXED FORESTS

TEMPERATE CONIFEROUS FORESTS

TROPICAL AND SUBTROPICAL GRASSLANDS, SAVANNAS AND SHRUBLANDS

TEMPERATE GRASSLANDS, SAVANNAS AND SHRUBLANDS

FLOODED GRASSLANDS

MONTANE GRASSLANDS

MEDITERRANEAN SCRUB

BOREAL FOREST AND TAIGA

TUNDRA

DESERTS AND XERIC SHRUBLANDS

MANGROVES

SNOW AND ICE

LAKES

CIESIN-COLUMBIA UNIVERSITY

WILDLIFE CONSERVATION SOCIETY

ticular species, ecosystems or processes in question, which is a good thing because if we can find ways for people and nature to live together, we can all win.

Land and Water Transformation

Land transformation has been called the single greatest threat to biological diversity, resulting in habitat loss and fragmentation of the remaining habitat. Land transformation refers to processes like logging, mining and asphalting that change a nature-dominated ecosystem into a human-dominated one. Land transformation removes habitat directly, but it also affects whatever habitat remains, subdividing it, disconnecting blocks of habitat, and eventually leading to a nasty downward spiral of biological side effects. Of course, human beings often transform land for good reasons, for example, to build settlements, grow food and produce other economic goods and, fortunately, different land uses differ in the extent to which they modify ecosystem processes and affect the quality of habitat for different species. In some cases, human actions may actually enhance some aspects of an area's biodiversity. For example, it is possible that the Amazonian forests have such high density of palms and other edible fruit because of what people did in the past. Knowing these factors and planning to minimize the negative impacts of human activity while enhancing its positive aspects is the goal of intelligent land use planning.

Land transformation also includes the direct effects of roads and railways. Not all species and ecosystems are equally affected by roads but, overall, the presence of roads is highly correlated with changes in species composition, including: Increases in the number of introduced species brought in from elsewhere; reduced wildlife populations through direct mortality (like road kills) and indirect mortality (like increased competition with the introduced species); and the modification of waterways and soil profiles that shape how ecosystems work. One study estimated that one million vertebrates are killed on roads in the United States every day. Another estimated that American roads affect a band approximately 700 meters (or yards) wide on either side of roads.

Human Access and Resource Extraction

Human access by road, major rivers and coastlines provides opportunities not only to enjoy nature and appreciate the great outdoors, but also to litter and pollute, to transform ecosystems, and to hunt and fish, whether legally or otherwise. Although in the western world market wildlife hunting is for the most part no longer a significant source of food, in most of the world wildlife hunting (e.g. elephants, gorillas, chimpanzees, monkeys, antelopes, turtles, snakes, etc.) and the associated disruption of ecosystems is of major concern, with the result that some forest ecosystems may be "emptied" by over-hunting. Resource extraction includes logging and mining, which typically require roads suitable for large trucks or large waterways for barges. Unfortunately, hunting is often combined with other kinds of resource extraction as people, such as those who live deep in the forest, often turn to local wildlife for sustenance.

Power and the Power of Energy to Transform

Many of the dramatic changes in human influence during the twentieth century have literally been driven by fossil fuel. Prior to the industrial revolution, human capacity to modify the environment was limited to human and animal muscle power. Today, one person with a bulldozer can apply the power of 300 horses to modify the environment. Electrical power provides an excellent estimate of the technological development of a local area and the use of fossil fuels. In the United States, where electrical power is available nearly everywhere, the lights visible at night from satellites provide a proxy of population distribution and have been correlated with human settlements (see Electric Power Infrastructure map on pp. 50-51). We should also remember that the power generation infrastructure has a footprint of it own. It takes heavy equipment to get oil out of the ground, including roads, pipelines, derricks and living quarters for oil workers; and as oil becomes scarcer, we have to move everything, pushing increasingly deeply into previously untrodden areas.

THE HUMAN INFLUENCE INDEX

Adding all these datasets on human population, land transformation, access and power together creates a map we call the "human influence index." The human influence index provides an absolute measure of human influence on the land surface. According to the human influence index, 83% of the land surface of the planet is influenced by human beings, and 98% of the places where it is possible to grow three major crops (rice, wheat or maize, according to FAO estimates) are influenced by people. The analysis of the highest scores reads like a list of the world's largest cities: New York, Calcutta, Beijing, Durban, London, etc. The minimum score (0) is found in large tracts of land

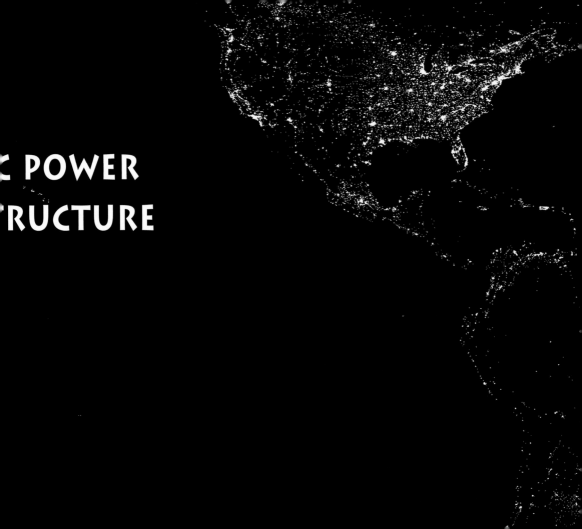

in the boreal forests of Canada and Russia, in desert regions of Africa and Central Australia, in the Arctic tundra and in the Amazon Basin. However, the majority of the world (~60%) lies along the continuum between these two extremes, in areas of moderate but variable human influence.

THE HUMAN FOOTPRINT

The human influence index (HII) makes a profound statement about the extent to which human beings have modified the world, but it also treats the planet as if it were a blank slate on which human influence is written. We know this is not the case. The distribution of major ecosystem types and the human histories of different regions weigh heavily when determining the biological outcomes of human influence. For example, an absolute score of 25 in the deciduous forests of eastern North America might have a different effect, and definitely a different biological context, than the same score in tropical rainforests in Africa. Biodiversity is different, human diversity is different, and cultural, institutional and social factors are all sufficiently different that a human influence score has a different significance from place to place.

Another way to say this is that wildness is relative. It depends on context and what you are comparing it to. Central Park in New York City is not wild if compared to the Amazon Forest, or even New York's Adirondack Mountains, but it is wild compared to midtown Manhattan! Even in our largest cities, rain falls, plants grow and wildlife persists: In other words, nature persists. All places boast some elements of nature still struggling to exist; just as no place on our planet is entirely untouched by humanity. Our challenge is to understand what a given level of human influence means for people and for the rest of nature.

This concept of relative wildness is built into the human footprint map. Because we were interested in the interaction of human influence with the natural environment, we used a scientific procedure called "normalization" to rescale human influence values within the world's ecosystems. A 25 on the human footprint scale means that that place is among the 25th% wildest (or 75th% least influenced) within that ecosystem in that part of the world. The map of ecosystems is based on a set of biomes—e.g. forests, grasslands, deserts—defined by the World Wildlife Fund for conservation purposes. We assigned a revised score of 0 to the cell with the minimum HII value in each biome in each realm and a score of 100 to the cell with the maximum value, stretching intermediate values linearly between these extremes.

The result is the human footprint (see The Human Footprint map on pp. 42-43). The human footprint expresses relative human influence as a percentage in every biome on the Earth's land surface. A score of 1 in moist tropical forests in Africa indicates that that place is among the 1% least influenced or "wildest" area in its biome, the same as a score of 1 in a North American broadleaf forest (although the absolute amount of influence in those two places may be quite different.) In fact, there is considerable variation in human influence levels between ecosystem types. The subtropical grasslands of India have the most influence in the world; North American tundra has the least, and other ecosystems have different distributions of influence. Examining the human footprint on a larger scale shows the patterns of roads, settlements, land uses and population density for an area: The geography of human influence. For example, on a map of northeastern United States, urbanization in the coastal region is clearly visible, as are major highway corridors along the shore and up the Hudson River and Connecticut River valleys. Relatively wilder areas also appear in the Catskill, Adirondack and Green Mountains.

The science of conservation biology suggests that this geography of human influence is roughly the inverse of the geography of natural processes and patterns in the region. Given what we know about the effects of the input factors on nature, we expect that where human influence is highest, ecosystems will be the most modified and species under the most pressure from human activity. Where the human footprint values are lower, we expect more intact and functioning natural communities. However, the exact consequences of human influence in any given location are complicated, depending on local history, the types of current influence and the parts of nature that concern us. We know that some aspects of nature survive and even thrive in an urban context while simultaneously, even in the wildest places, we frequently find that human influence has reduced natural values; and yet, it is in these wildest places that the greatest freedom and opportunity to conserve the full range of nature still exists.

FINDING THE LAST OF THE WILD

It follows from mapping the human footprint that it is also possible to map the relatively least influenced or "wildest" areas in each biome. This may be done in a number of different ways, but we chose to begin by finding all of the places that were in the wildest 10% of their biomes and then identifying the 10 largest contiguous areas: We call these areas the "last of the wild" (see Last of the Wild map on pp. 46-47). Bigger is better because of the well-known benefits of putting together the largest possible conservation areas. Bigger areas can support larger wildlife populations, capture more kinds of habitat, allow ecosystem processes to express themselves and, in general, provide more of what nature—and biodiversity—needs.

As a result, some of the last of the wild are very big—well over 100 000 km^2 in some biomes; in other biomes we could not find even ten areas larger than 5 km^2. The sizes and shapes of these areas depend on the biome in question and the extent of the human footprint. Frequently, roads are the dividing line, separating one wild area from another. The proportion of area represented by the last of the wild varies dramatically between different biomes, depending on the distribution of human influence. Thus, over 67% of the area in the North American tundra is included in the last of the wild, while the wildest 10% of the Eurasian tropical forests (all in China) encompasses less than 0.03% of that biome's total area.

The last of the wild offer us a guide to opportunities for conservation, identifying places where we might conserve the widest range of biodiversity with minimum conflict. Generally, conflict means higher conservation costs. Where land is already developed and needs to be restored to a more natural state, or where land is already owned and must be bought back for conservation purposes, conservation costs will be high because both purchases and restoration are expensive. It is not easy to turn a parking lot back into a forest. Wild areas are important not only because nature tends to be fuller and more functional there, but also because wild areas are cheaper to protect. They provide an investment bargain where you can save the most nature for the least amount of money.

Given the ways that human beings have developed the world and the places where we actually choose to live, some of the largest wild areas remaining are also areas with the least biodiversity: Deserts, taiga, tundra and Arctic ice. Biodiversity is unevenly distributed across the planet and some wildernesses will have more species than others, especially those in tropical forest ecosystems. It is important to remember, however, that the last of the wild are defined so as to represent all the biomes in the world. The last of the wild provides a guide to mangroves and rainforests, savannas and Mediterranean shrub lands, forests and deserts, and everything in between. The last of the wild tells us where the wildest areas are in all the biomes of the world, so by investing intelligently across them, a wide range of biodiversity can be conserved. As we make those investments, we also consider the biodiversity value of an area, the level of threat that it faces, and factors like political feasibility and impact on local peoples.

THE CHALLENGE FOR BIODIVERSITY CONSERVATION

The human footprint is a map, assembled simply from what we know about where human beings are and how we have changed the face of the planet with our presence, our use of land, our access and technology. But the human footprint also poses a question to all of us: How do we want to live on our planet now that there are so very many of us? In this sense, the human footprint challenges all of us to conserve biodiversity, wildlife and everything else we hold dear on our beautiful, green and blue, cloud-swathed planet.

Humanity has succeeded so far because of the wealth of the Earth's natural resources and our ingenuity in using them. Fortunately, these same two advantages are still available to us, although the balance is inexorably leaning toward a need for greater ingenuity in the face of diminishing resources. Now our challenge is to use our experience, our intelligence and our wisdom to find new ways of interacting with nature so that we meet the needs of our burgeoning human population without sacrificing the diversity of life and the wildest places on Earth.

We know we can meet these challenges because many of the answers are already available. Through the photographs and the chapters in this book, we hope not only to impress upon you the extent of the problem, but also to suggest positive ways that people, working individually and collectively, can make a difference. The chapters in this book are written by conservationists from a number of the world's great conservation organizations and illustrated with pictures taken by conservation photographers around the world. These pictures, maps and words lay out a vision for a better world and help chart a path to get there.

As you leaf through this book, absorbing its pictures, texts and maps, we believe you will come to recognize two broad ways of responding to the human footprint: Saving the last of the wild and transforming the human footprint.

Saving the Last of the Wild

In the not so distant past, the world was mostly "wild". Human-dominated spaces were the rare exception, while the common rule was wild landscapes, full of wildlife and supportive of biodiversity. In those times, the notion that that wilderness was something to be saved made no sense; the need was simply not there. Now, however, all that has changed.

Today, we live in a very different world; only 17% of the world is wild and 83% is dedicated to human uses. Fortunately, the idea and practice of "wild place" conservation is well advanced. We know one strategy that works: Protected areas, that is, legally-enforced limits on human uses of natural areas and the knowledge and capacity to manage them correctly in all of the world's biomes. Protecting natural resources and managing them in areas dedicated to conservation is the legacy of the world-wide national park movement. However, protected areas are not enough. Conservation also requires a willingness to forego exhausting the last portions of natural ecosystems for short-term economic gains because we know that once they are gone, they will be very difficult and expensive to bring back, if indeed they can be brought back at all. Conserving the last of the wild will require investing our talent and our financial resources to reclaim a more balanced relationship with the natural world.

As Michael Hoffmann and colleagues show in their chapter on wilderness and biodiversity, the collapse of wildernesses worldwide is threatening the preservation of a biodiversity that has taken millennia to evolve and develop. Some wildernesses have more value for biodiversity conservation than others because they have more species, many of which cannot be found anywhere else. The loss of these species, also known as endemics, is irreversible, which makes their conservation even more pressing. In other words, the "irreplaceability" of some areas is low because, in fact, there are still many options for their conservation. A few precious regions are classified as of low threat but high irreplaceability, meaning that they are still relatively wild and relatively unique (in some cases absolutely unique) and as such are a conservation bargain. These areas have been mapped as "high biodiversity wilderness areas" and include places like the Amazon Forest, the Congo Forest, the Miombo-Mopane woodlands in Africa and the deserts in North America. In these places, we have an opportunity to conserve both large areas of natural habitat as well as a very significant portion of the planet's biodiversity.

As John Pilgrim and his co-authors reveal, the loss of biodiversity is partly due to both the uneven distribution of human influence, as mapped by the human footprint, and of biodiversity itself. Recent global assessments of amphibians, mammals, birds and other species give us the first opportunity to map biodiversity loss directly. One of the criticisms of the human footprint is that it does not explicitly include biodiversity criteria, but these data provide the opportunity for us to rectify this problem and understand the direct relationship between biodiversity and human influence at the global scale.

At a more local scale, conservation will require the creation of new protected areas, and the management of existing ones, in areas dominated by human use. Conservation must stretch out of protected areas into the surrounding landscape and that landscape must be brought alive by working with people and wildlife, as emphasized in the chapter written by David Wilkie, Amy Vedder and Karl Didier. Some conservation organizations have taken to using suites of landscape species, carefully selected for their ability to represent the landscape and for their importance to people, as the basis of their efforts to save wild places.

Sadly, these wild places are more endangered than we think, as Jessica Forrest, J. Michael Fay and colleagues demonstrate in pictures and words. They have analyzed some of more than 110 000 aerial photos collected by Fay over Africa, as part of a collaboration with the National Geographic Society and the Wildlife Conservation Society to document what Africa really looks like today. The colors on the human footprint map translate into pictures of once-wild landscapes penetrated by roads, then by agriculture, then given over to suburbs and, finally, big cities. Yes, there is still wildlife in Africa, but you will probably have to go to national parks to see it.

Transforming the Human Footprint

Saving the last of the wild is critical, but it is only part of the solution if only because it excludes 83% of the land surface: The 83% where most humans live. The second major response to the human footprint is to try to transform it so that it not only supplies what people need, but also conserves, protects and honors the Earth's rich ecological heritage.

In order to create a world that will support twelve billion human beings and maintain a functional biosphere, we need to change the human footprint. We need to reshape it and reinterpret what it means. There is a middle ground between total destruction of the world's natural resources and giving up on the human race; we need to choose to moderate our influence and opt for a healthier relationship with the natural world. We need to reinterpret the colors of the human footprint so that red identifies areas where nature is most nurtured and green is where wildness thrives. And we need to let the wild places remain wild.

However, it will not be easy. As Larry Gorenflo shows in his chapter on human population trends, the current state of the world's population has been a long time in the making. Fortunately, there are clear signs that the population may level

off over the next century, which means that conservation efforts today are exactly what is required to get over this demographic hump into a world which is not necessarily less populated, but which suffers no further increases. As a result, what we learn today may set the stage for what our planet will end up looking like for centuries to come.

As the human population grows, we need to deal with resource extraction and land transformation. Elizabeth Bennett, Jefferson Hall and Kent Redford show what happens at even the most basic levels of subsidence in some of the most species-rich ecosystems in the world: Tropical forests. Timber extraction and bushmeat trade are primary threats to the preservation of biological diversity in tropical forests. In order to conserve these forests, wild areas need to be protected, laws passed and best business practices implemented, and the forests themselves need to be respected for more than just the bottom line.

Development through roads, forest conversion and the introduction of agriculture are not problems unique to tropical forests but to the entire developed world. As Michael Klemens, Katrina Brandon and Jodi Hilty write, sprawl is in our backyard too. Currently, lands are being converted for human use at rates never seen before on the planet. Fortunately, good conservation efforts that strive to maintain connectivity, influence development to work for nature and people, and minimize the negative effects of agriculture are all underway.

The final linchpin is energy. The human population needs energy to fuel its societies, but energy comes at a physical, biological and political cost that all of us who live in the early 21st century know only too well. Michael Totten, Jon Beckmann and Steve Zack take up the question of how we can build a more sustainable energy strategy to supply our needs without diminishing some of the last great places on Earth.

The Human Footprint: Next Steps

Wendell Berry wrote that there is no such thing as a wild place —it is an intellectual construct—and if it existed, no-one would want to live there in the absence of music, the arts, family love, community and ideas. By the same token, a place without nature entirely dominated by man is both a fictitious and horrendous concept: Even the most hardened urbanite needs a walk in the park now and then. We humans cannot remove ourselves from nature no matter how much we would like to; we are, after all, products of the natural world, just like every other living thing on the planet.

Most of the world is a continuum characterized by two idealized but impossible states: The wild and the not-wild. But our concern is with what lies between those extremes: Places like the Congo Forest, where elephants struggle to live in the last refuges more than twenty kilometers from a road, and places like New York City, where little bits of salt marsh hang on for dear life, tiny green havens in the gray, stone city.

The human footprint is a vast continuum in motion, moving away from the greens and yellows on the map towards the blacks and purples: More people, more roads, more cities, more agriculture, fewer wild places, fewer habitats for elephants, loons and reefs; and less of what is so lovely about our world: The font of our arts and ideas, our emotions and our courage: Our home.

The challenge of reducing this vast human footprint is a shared challenge to which we must all contribute because, in the end, it is where we live. Wherever you are, whatever nature surrounds you, it is your neighborhood. It does not matter if you live in Africa, Argentina or Arkansas, nor, all said and done, does it matter if you live on a dollar a day or a million dollars a day. Our lives are intimately interwoven into the fabric of nature; we are irrevocably dependent on each other.

All humans need to assume the role of conservationists. We all need to try to save our planet's last wild places and try to soften the color change here and there, improving the human footprint map day by day, one place at a time. As humans, we all share the love of family and home, the spirit of inventiveness and goodwill, and the quest for a better way and a better life. We must hold onto the belief that we may yet find a way to reverse the trend of the human footprint, find a new palette, clean up the mess and discover a healthier wild-not-wild place than where we are right now. To that end, we hope that this map, this book and these pictures are of help to you.

ERIC W. SANDERSON   VANCE G. MARTIN
AVECITA CHICCHON   CRISTINA G. MITTERMEIER
PATRICIO ROBLES GIL   RUSSELL A. MITTERMEIER
LARRY J. GORENFLO   KENT REDFORD
JOSHUA GINSBERG   JOHN ROBINSON
LEE HANNAH   AMY VEDDER
CYRIL F. KORMOS

POPULATION

At a meeting held for the international staff of a major conservation organization in 2000, the featured guest speaker asked an audience of a couple hundred what was the greatest challenge facing biodiversity in the 21st century. Although the vast majority of those attending the presentation were biologists and ecologists, responses were dominated by a single, decidedly non-biological answer: Human population. For the few researchers in attendance working on human population and related issues in the context of biodiversity conservation, the response made perfect sense. The total population of the world had just reached 6.0 billion and humans lived in—indeed, in many cases, *dominated*—a huge number of terrestrial ecosystems, placing heavy demands on many. For the speaker the response made sense as well; his foundation was supporting several studies that examined the impact of human population on biodiversity conservation. What was surprising was the general agreement among conservationists whose backgrounds did not include the human sciences and who focused their efforts on topics very different from human demographics. There seemed to be a shared recognition that the enormous human population inhabiting our planet, and the demands that this population placed on Earth's resources, were at the root of biodiversity loss that had reached crisis proportions.

How had human population come to threaten so much of global biodiversity? Although one can identify negative effects of people on plant and animal species in the distant past (McKee 2003), the vast majority of impacts are quite recent and appear to be associated with the huge number of human beings that now inhabit the Earth. When agriculture emerged about 10 000 years ago, millions of years of slow population growth by humans and their hominid ancestors had produced a global population of only about 5.0 million (Cohen 1995). By around 1800, the world's population reached 1.0 billion for the first time—a result of population growth over the preceding 10 millennia that, although still quite slow by modern standards, was much faster than during preagricultural times (Carnevale *et al.* 1999). Scarcely two centuries later, in early 2006, global population is approaching 6.5 billion (U.S. Bureau of the Census 2006). More than 5.0 billion people had been added in about two centuries. The millions of years once required to add a billion people to the world's population had been reduced to about a decade; the addition of 5.0 million—the global population at the onset of agriculture—now takes less than one month (see CD-Fig. 1.1).

One consequence of this enormous population has been environmental change at comparable scales to meet growing human demand. For instance, during the final two decades of the 20th century, the amount of land used for agricultural production increased globally by more than 130 000 km^2 per year (Food and Agriculture Organization 1997), much of it converted from natural habitat. In large part as a consequence of such impacts, the loss of plant and animal species is 1 000 times greater than historic rates (Pimm *et al.* 1995), placing the world amidst mass extinction of a magnitude virtually unknown in our planet's history.

The reasons for the enormous increase in global population since the emergence of agriculture are complex. They involve, among other things, the establishment of food production that provided more reliable subsistence, fixed settlements and an associated economy that allowed larger families, and technological advances that helped to reduce mortality (Cohen 1995). Demographers do not expect population growth to continue forever. But they do anticipate global population to increase until fertility and mortality come into balance, somewhere around 2050 when the world's inhabitants reach a maximum of about 9.1 billion (United Nations 2005). Much of the Earth's future rests on how humankind incorporates this additional 2.6 billion people. Part of understanding the impact of human population on biodiversity lies in understanding where people live—the footprint of population—with respect to the localities important for conserving the diversity of life.

As recently as two decades ago, precisely identifying the footprint of human population would have been difficult if not impossible. Computer mapping—notably geographic information system technology—was still in its early development, and the data necessary to define the global footprint of human population were unavailable at a resolution much below the *state* or *county* levels. Advances on both the technological and data fronts today make it possible to explore the pattern of global human habitation with considerable precision. Here we employ recently released databases showing the spatial distribution of global population and population density in 2005 and 2015 (CIESIN *et al.* 2005a, 2005b, 2005c, 2005d). The data are arranged as grids that cover the globe, with each grid cell about 5 km to a side at the equator (becoming slightly smaller towards the poles). Mapping these data with geographic information system technology enables one to propose where the footprint of human population currently occurs, and what it will look like in the near future.

One of the main challenges in mapping the footprint of human population is to define exactly what constitutes the footprint. At first blush, the most obvious response might seem to be anywhere that people live. But with a focus on conservation, we need to define a footprint where that level of human presence can have a negative impact on biodiversity. Ultimately, the impacts on plants and animals in a particular area depends in part on the number of people present in that area and in part on their *activities* (Gorenflo 2002). For example, very few people living in an area but involved in hunting or commercial logging can have a much greater impact on biodiversity than a larger number of people living in that same area but employed in small-scale manufacturing. An earlier attempt to define the human footprint based on several variables proposed 10 persons per km^2 as a density of human occupation beyond which impacts on biodiversity tend to occur (Sanderson *et al.* 2002). More recent research on a particularly fragile desert environment indicated that 10 persons per km^2 indeed is a good cut-off for human impacts, with areas more densely settled rarely associated with high biodiversity (Gorenflo 2006). In defining the footprint of human population, we follow suit in using a 10 per-

sons per km^2 threshold. To be thorough, we also consider 5 persons per km^2—providing a more conservative picture of where human presence might adversely affect biodiversity, as well as a sense of how much the Earth supports population density close to levels associated with more substantial impacts.

Defining the footprint of human population at 10 or more persons per km^2 indicates that a large amount of the earth's terrestrial surface—more than 31%—occurred within the footprint in 2005 (see CD-Fig. 1.2a). In broad terms, much of the footprint was concentrated geographically, including parts of continents (much of the eastern third of Africa, most of southern and western Europe, the Asian subcontinent, etc.) and large portions of many islands, with the footprint rarely occurring in far northern and southern latitudes. If this density of human occupation creates conditions incompatible with biodiversity, then much of the world, including a large portion of the tropics, presents a challenge for conservation. Decreasing the threshold for defining the footprint of human population to 5 persons per km^2 increases its size substantially, to more than 40% of the earth's terrestrial surface (see CD-Fig. 1.2b). The geographic impact of this slight reduction in the threshold includes both an expansion of the footprint beyond its prior boundaries and filling in areas already containing 10 or more persons per km^2. Population densities between 5 and 10 persons per km^2 are not likely to present serious challenges to biodiversity, though they may define that portion of the earth's surface approaching occupation levels that will have adverse impacts, as well as places where coordinated conservation and development can help avoid such impacts.

Demographers project that global population will increase between 2005 and 2015, reaching about 7.2 billion based on the medium projection scenario developed by the United Nations (United Nations 2005). The footprint of human population based on projections for 2015 indicates expanding settlement of 10 or more persons per km^2, the total covering nearly 33% of the Earth's surface (see CD-Fig. 1.3a). The geographic changes associated with the footprint expansion between 2005 and 2015 are subtle, once again involving a combination of geographic expansion and filling in areas not so densely populated in the earlier year. Reducing the threshold of footprint definition to 5 persons per km^2 causes the footprint to increase to nearly 41% of the Earth's terrestrial surface (see CD-Fig. 1.3b). The difference between demographic footprints defined at 5 and 10 persons

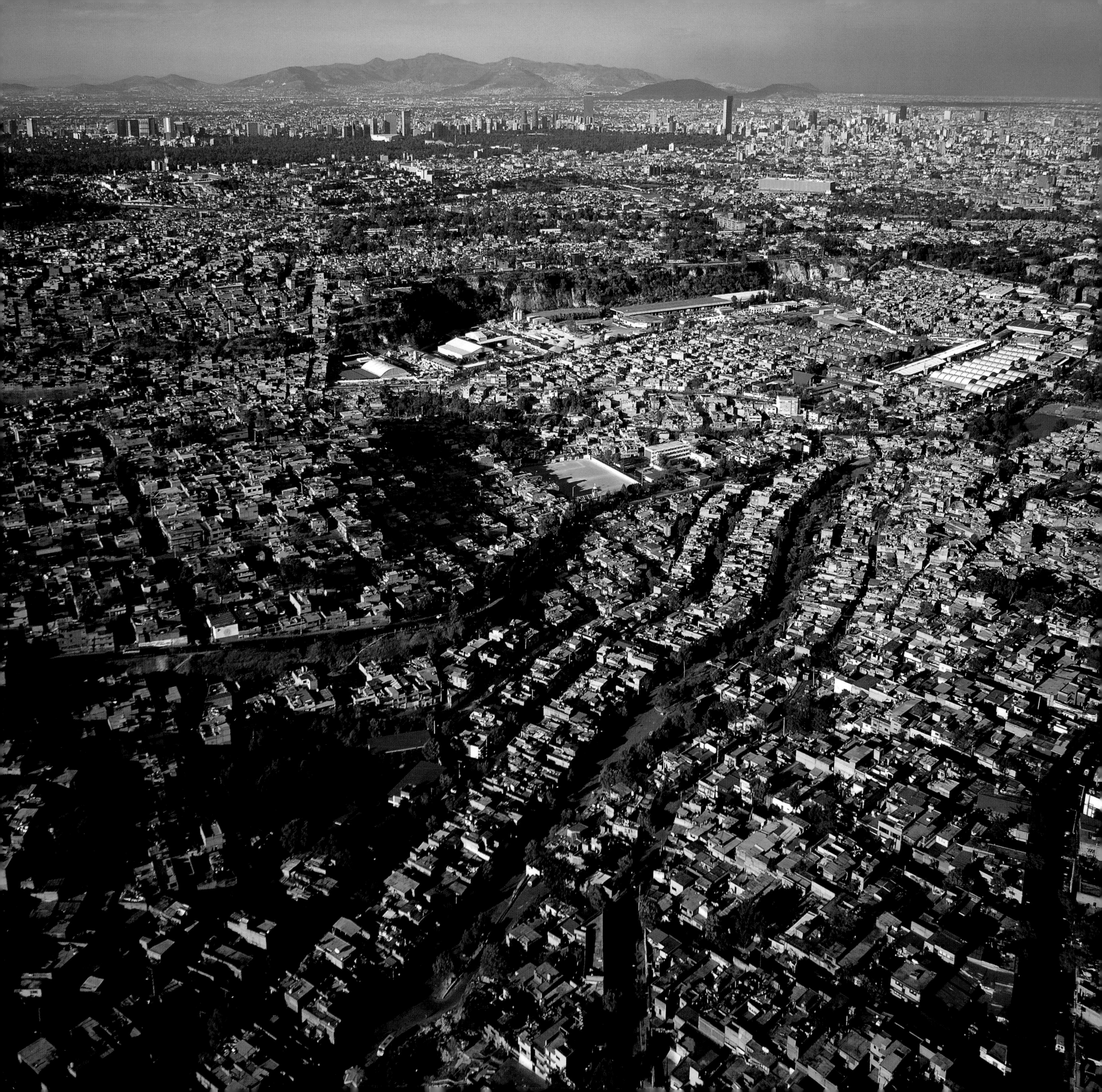

per km^2 in 2015 is similar to the difference between these footprints in 2005.

To provide a clearer sense of how the footprint of human population might affect biodiversity, we can focus our analysis on regions of particular importance to conservation—hotspots and high biodiversity wilderness areas (see CD-Fig. 1.4). Hotspots are regions that contain particularly high numbers of species found nowhere else (*endemic* species) that also have lost minimally 70% of their natural habitat to development (Myers *et al.* 2000). Recent research has defined 34 hotspots where, although their intact habitat in all covers only about 2% of the Earth's land surface, 52% of all vascular plant species and 42% of all terrestrial vertebrate species are endemic (Mittermeier *et al.* 2004). High biodiversity wilderness areas, in turn, are large regions containing high numbers of endemic species that have lost at most 30% of their natural habitat (Mittermeier *et al.* 2003). Biologists have defined five high biodiversity wilderness areas, covering about 6.1% of the Earth's surface, that contain 17% of global plant species and 8% of global terrestrial vertebrates as endemics (Mittermeier *et al.* 2003; see CD-Fig. 1.4).

The extent of the footprint of human population in hotspots and high biodiversity wilderness areas varies greatly by region. Overlaying the footprint with outlines of the biodiversity regions shows these differences graphically for 2005, for 10 and 5 persons per km^2 thresholds (see CD-Figs. 1.5a and 1.5b). Although hotspots by definition have lost minimally 70% of their natural habitat, population density in each region ranged from fewer than 4 to about 329 persons per km^2 in 2005 (see CD-Figs. 1.2a and 1.2b). The amount of each region covered by the footprint similarly varied, from less than 3% to nearly 100% in the case of the 10 persons per km^2 footprint, and from less than 5% to nearly 100% in the case of the 5 persons per km^2 footprint. Population densities in the high biodiversity wilderness areas tended to be much lower than in the hotspots, ranging from about 4 to 14 persons per km^2. The percent of high biodiversity wilderness areas covered by the footprint of human population varied, though values generally were lower than in the hotspots. The 10 persons per km^2 footprint covered between about 8% and 35% of individual wilderness areas in 2005, while the 5 persons per km^2 footprint covered between about 14% and 64% of individual wilderness areas. The tendency for high biodiversity wilderness areas to have less of their area within the population footprint than hotspots, defined by either thres-

hold, is consistent with these regions having lower human impacts than the hotspots. Nevertheless, in several hotspots the percent of their total region within the demographic footprint is lower than certain wilderness areas, an inconsistency likely explained by the economic activities and land use patterns associated with individual regions.

The coverage of hotspots and wilderness areas by the footprint of human population in 2015 was similar to that seen in 2005 (see CD-Figs. 1.6a and 1.6b). In virtually all of the regions considered, the amount of area lying within the footprint increased between 2005 and 2015. In a few instances, the percent of area within the footprint declined slightly between these two years, a consequence of rural-urban migration causing sparsely settled places to be depopulated slightly and, in some cases, to fall below one of the two footprint thresholds. However, neither increase nor decrease changed the complexion of the situation greatly, which remained similar to that seen in 2005. In the hotspots, the percent of each area covered by the two footprints ranged about as broadly as in 2005 (see CD-Figs. 1.2a and 1.2b). In wilderness areas, the percent of total area covered by the 10 persons per km^2 footprint ranged from about 9% to 49%, while the area covered by the 5 persons per km^2 footprint ranged from roughly 16% to 72%. In hotspots and high biodiversity wilderness areas, the percent of area within the footprint of human population usually changed in individual regions between these two years.

Two characteristics of the changes in population footprint between 2005 and 2015 in biodiversity regions are noteworthy. One is the continued increase in the amount of area covered by the footprint in most regions, defined under both thresholds—a continued expansion, in most cases, of human presence and the adverse impacts on biodiversity that often accompany it. The greatest increases in the footprint are projected to occur in the high biodiversity wilderness areas, as sparse human settlement expands into areas previously unsettled or occupied by very few people.

The second characteristic worth noting is the difference between the 10 and 5 persons per km^2 footprints in both 2005 and 2015. In some cases, this difference is very little. For instance, in the Guinean Forests of West Africa and the Philippines hotspots the percent of each area covered by the 10 and 5 persons per km^2 footprints are similar—indicating little area approaching the 10-person threshold (and thus facing the possible biodiversity impacts associated with it). In contrast, analyses of the Horn of Africa, Mountains of Southwest China, and (especially) New Caledonia hotspots, and all high biodiversity wilderness areas, indicate large differences between the percent area covered by the 10 and 5 persons per km^2 footprints. In cases such as New Caledonia and the wilderness areas, large amounts of territories remain outside the footprint defined by 10 persons per km^2, but established human presence provides a basis for this footprint to expand considerably with the addition of relatively few people.

As noted earlier in this paper, identifying human impacts on biodiversity solely in terms of demographics ignores the role of human activity as the ultimate measure of such impacts. Moreover, in the modern global economy the greatest impacts of population often do not occur near that population—a consequence of extracting resources and transporting them elsewhere to meet the demands of a population. As a result, focusing solely on the footprint of human population in some cases likely misses areas that have been greatly affected by people and in some cases likely identifies adversely affected areas that in fact have avoided such impacts. The analysis of hotspots and high biodiversity wilderness areas provides some examples of this. For example, in 2005 the Caribbean Islands, Philippines, and Western Ghats and Sri Lanka hotspots had large percentages of their areas within the human footprint defined by than 10 persons per km^2, while New Caledonia, Succulent Karoo, and Southwest Australia had small percentages within that footprint the same year, yet all have lost 70% or more of their natural habitat. The New Zealand hotspot and North American Deserts wilderness area both have similar percentages of their geographic extent within the 10 persons per km^2 footprint in 2005, but the former has lost most of its natural habitat while the latter has maintained most of its habitat. The footprint of human population ultimately provides a rough sense of the potential for human impact, as well as a sense of the impacts *on humans* of conservation actions in such areas. Its greatest benefits come in the relatively wide availability of population data, and in the ability to project future demographic footprints with reasonable confidence and accuracy.

Examining the footprint of human population reveals the enormous geographic extent of human settlement in our world, helping to explain the geographic breadth of biodiversity loss. But its implications for conservation are not all negative. For instance, a recent analysis of places where key species occur outside the existing network of protected areas (such as national parks) revealed that nearly three-quarters of the locations identified contained contiguous tracts of land 10 000 ha or larger with population densities less than 10 persons per km^2 (Gorenflo and Brandon 2006). Moreover, more than 61% of these locations contained large tracts of habitat compatible with conservation (that is, with no indication of major conversion from its natural state) with population densities of 10 persons per km^2 or less. Such results suggest that many of the most important conservation opportunities occur outside the footprint of human population, at least as defined by 10 persons per km^2. Capitalizing on these opportunities by implementing some sort of conservation action can contribute greatly to the conservation of global biodiversity. Because they lie outside the footprint of human population, conserving these areas should have minimal adverse impact on local populations while avoiding major effects generated by local peoples. In the coming decades, the footprint of human population is certain to expand. Knowing where and how it will expand will enable steps to be taken that help conserve remaining biodiversity amidst a growing human presence.

LARRY J. GORENFLO

HUMAN ACCESS

Humans have always relied on the natural world for subsistence and, in more recent times, to raise cash. Access to natural resources and between human settlements necessitates paths and watercrafts and, when commercial levels of market access are required, roads, with long distance transport enhanced through trains, aircraft and large ocean-going vessels. Roads are also considered essential to development, bringing people closer to schools, potential jobs, and markets. The human footprint shows that, except in the most inhospitable and unproductive parts of the planet, roads are ubiquitous.

Humans who exploit resources on a largely subsistence basis tend to occur at low population densities, and have little access to markets or have it limited to few, very high value items. Under these conditions, the impacts of most human settlements on the natural world are relatively minor and localized, except for those few highly valued items such as incense, rhino horn, macaw feathers or ivory, which merit long, potentially difficult journeys by foot or river to distant markets. With more extensive commercial access, as areas are opened to larger urban markets, sometimes international in nature, the impact on the natural world is immediate, and often severe. At the highest levels of access, as characterized by the developed world, densities of roads are higher, market connection is complete, and the natural world is often largely overwritten by a human-dominated world. Under these conditions, good habitat and resource management and even restoration can occur (though it does not always), so that roads and high levels of biodiversity, with optimal management, might coexist. In many national parks in the United States, for example, large, spectacular animals can be seen from roads and, in the east of the country, white-tailed deer and even bears are abundant in areas with dense road networks.

In this chapter, we focus on the role that roads have played, and continue to play, in increasing human access and driving the increase in the human footprint. In particular, we focus on access associated with increasing commercial activity, since impacts when roads are first driven into a previously roadless area are often dramatic. They change the entire local socioeconomic climate, giving people access to markets and allowing them to become more tightly enmeshed in a cash economy. New roads usually result in extensive land clearance, and often in major extraction of resources which were previously inaccessible, or for which access to markets was uneconomic. This situation is of major concern to conservation today. This is especially true in tropical forests, in which the spread of roads in the past 50 years or less has led to dramatic and alarming losses of wildlife and plants, causing local extinctions and threatening global extinctions.

Many factors have led to the rapid spread of roads in tropical forest countries, including concerns for rural development and national security. By far the greatest increase has been due to the spread of commercial extractive industries, with vast and extensive networks of roads spreading rapidly through the most remote forests in the rush to extract timber and other resources. An estimated 50 000 to 59 000 km^2 of tropical forest is opened up to logging for the first time every year (Johns 1997), and up to 80% of the remaining forests in some tropical countries are under timber license. With timber and mining licenses come roads, to allow the resources to be extracted and taken to markets, both near and far.

Increased road access leads immediately to increased extraction of forest resources. First is the trees themselves—indeed, timber extraction is often the primary reason for the roads, although government policies encouraging the opening up of the land for economic development, integration, and national security contributes to the spread of logging in some cases, so cause and effect are intertwined. No matter what the primary reason for a road, the underlying drivers of opening access are almost always accompanied by a set of secondary drivers that have an impact on the natural world, including through the unsustainable extraction of many types of organisms. One of the most dramatic of the ancillary impacts is hunting, causing rapid losses of wildlife, thereby having severe consequences for conservation, and also for the livelihoods of local communities who depend on the resource (Robinson *et al.* 1999).

DIRECT EFFECTS OF TIMBER EXTRACTION

Where national road building policies aim to open up remote areas to settlers, facilitating clearing land for settlements, agriculture or pastureland, trees on the road frontier are felled primarily to clear land. If this is part of a well-planned land use policy, with natural areas for conservation and for sustainable natural resource extraction, and intensive use areas as part of a sustainable landscape (Robinson 1994), then the balance between human and conservation needs can be attained. If not, then construction of the roads means that forests and their multiple benefits are irreparably lost.

If a primary aim of the roads is extraction of timber *per se*, a well developed road network, including major highways for long distance transport to mills and ports, secondary roads for access to camps, and third order roads connected to skidder trails, is essential for industrial timber extraction. Rivers, railroads and even helicopters can form part of the timber transportation network, but in many areas roads are the core of the system.

The pattern of timber extraction from those roads varies between tropical continents, as a result of the differing tree species composition and the density of highly valuable timber species. In Asian tropical forests, many tree species from the same plant family, the Dipterocarpaceae, are felled for "medium-light" meranti timber, and the different species are used interchangeably. Up to 60% of the basal area can comprise dipterocarps, so timber extraction volumes are high. In addition, many of the forests currently being logged are on steep slopes, so that incidental damage from building roads is immense, with wide bare screes on slopes on both sides of the roads scarring the landscape.

In Central and South America as well as West and Central Africa, a large price gap exists between high value species such as the mahoganies and other species known to international timber markets. Typically, forests are initially logged for only a few extremely valuable species. With the most valuable trees gone, timber companies often withdraw from the area, leaving behind a road network for immigrants, outsiders extracting resources, and local communities with only limited previous experience with highly competitive cash economies. Typically, abandoned concessions are taken over by companies looking to take advantage of an established transportation network and

mill infrastructure as forests are invariably well stocked in other, albeit less valuable, timber species. The result is a sequential exploitation of species of decreasing commercial value, which is generally incompatible with long-term forest management. Repeatedly entering the forest to extract species by order of value leads to long-term forest degradation.

INDIRECT EFFECTS OF TIMBER EXTRACTION

Even though timber species and densities differ between continents, in all regions a disturbing path often leads from selective logging to forest conversion. Where timber is extracted for maximum profit with little attention to regeneration, forests become impoverished and degraded. Whether it is okumé forests in Gabon, where the canopy is dominated by a single timber species, highly diverse Asian forests where many species have similar uses and are often harvested in a single felling cycle, or American and African forests where selective harvests successively eliminate timber species, there comes an economic "tipping point" where the most valuable short-term land use is conversion to agriculture. Thus, seemingly remote forests in Southeast Asia are replaced by oil palm and West African forests are replaced by cacao. Industrial banana and coffee plantations replace large areas of Central American forest. Logging roads are often the first sign of this often all-too-predictable sequence of events.

Even before this has occurred, the penetration of roads into formerly remote tropical forests generates a cascade of social and economic changes in areas previously only accessible to forest-dwelling inhabitants, the most notable of which is the dramatic increase in hunting. Roads allow outside hunters, colonizers and traders access to forests so that the number of hunters increases dramatically, whether they are hunting for sport, their own food or for commercial trade. If the roads are built by timber companies, their presence is usually associated with immigration into the forest by logging company workers and their families. Such people often hunt for their own subsistence, sport or trade, or buy wildlife from local hunters for their own consumption. They are usually outsiders, living only temporarily in the area, so have little knowledge or regard for local hunting traditions, and no incentives to conserve the resource. In the Malaysian state of Sarawak, a transit camp of 500 people hunted some 1 150 animals or 29 tonnes of wild meat annually (Bennett and Gumal 2001). In a single logging camp in northern Congo, the annual harvest was 8 251 animals, or 124 tonnes of wild meat (Auzel and Wilkie 2000)

In addition, the advent of roads causes enormous social and

economic change amongst forest communities. They enter a cash economy, and generally obtain cash by selling forest produce, including wildlife. The roads allow them to obtain modern hunting technologies, from shotgun cartridges and snare wire to flashlights and batteries, all of which make hunting more efficient. Often the only means of obtaining the cash to buy hunting technologies is by selling wildlife, so an escalating cycle of hunting occurs. The incentive for local people to conserve their own resources vanishes if they see outsiders over-hunting. The result is greatly increased rates of hunting by local communities as roads enter their areas. Per capita hunting rates in local communities adjacent to logging roads in Congo were three to six times higher than in communities away from such roads, with up to 75% of the meat by weight being sold (Auzel and Wilkie 2000).

The productivity of tropical forests for wildlife is extremely low, an order of magnitude lower than more open habitats. As roads push into forests much of the mammalian biomass comprises primates and other slow-breeding, often large-bodied, species. Maximum sustainable production of wild meat from tropical forests is only about 152 kg per km^2 per year, or enough to support only one person per km^2 if they depend entirely on wild meat for their protein (Robinson and Bennett 2000). Typically, this means that the rapid increase in commercial hunting as roads enter an area for the first time follows a "boom and bust" pattern, with rapidly increased harvests followed by population crashes of exploited species. This wave of exploitation and crashing wildlife populations spreads across the landscape as the road networks expand. In Congo, wildlife densities, as reflected by hunting return rates, decreased by more than 25% within a single three-week period after logging roads opened in an area (Wilkie *et al*. 2001). In Sarawak, no primates or ungulates remained in areas of forest which had been accessible for at least a year (Chin 2002). And in Bolivia, hunting in accessible areas in logging concessions has reduced wildlife populations to levels that, according to workers, "it was not worth the effort to hunt" (Rumiz *et al*. 2001). Almost all species are hunted, and if roads through tropical forests spread unchecked, hunting and massive loss of wildlife down the roads to distant markets results in whole forests are being defaunated of animals larger than about 1 kg and sometimes even smaller.

Loss of wildlife as a result of roads also has deleterious consequences for local people who depend on the resource. Between 1975 and 1985, as their area became more opened up by roads and outside pressures, the proportion of successful hunts of the Agta people in the Philippines declined from 63% to 16%,

and the number of kills per hunt declined from 1.15 to 0.16 animals. The Agta went from being hunters of abundant wildlife in primary forests to being struggling foragers with inadequate wildlife resources (Griffin and Griffin 2000). The hunting success, measured as weight of wild meat hunted per unit time, of a Penan community living close to a logging road in Sarawak was only 15% of that in a nearby community 6.5 km from the logging road (Griffin and Griffin 2000). And the protein intake of the Yuquí Indians in Bolivia declined from 88g to 44g of protein per person per day after their lands were opened up to outsiders (Stearman 2000) People newly entering a cash economy as the road front hits them often have few alternative sources of cash and income and frequently lack the education or cultural context to take advantage of potential new jobs being created, so can be driven further into poverty as their natural resource base disappears.

CONCLUSIONS AND SOLUTIONS

Humans have extended their reach to all parts of the globe and few areas remain largely free the impact of the human footprint. As the recently-completed Millennium Assessment states, in the aggregate, changes to ecosystems have contributed to substantial gains in human well-being over the past centuries with people better nourished, living longer and healthier lives, rising incomes, and more participatory political institutions. However, they note that these gains have been achieved at growing costs including degradation of many ecosystems, increasing risks of nonlinear changes, and the growing poverty of some groups (MEA 2005). And clearly, these gains have been made at the expense of wild nature, with many species and ecosystems extinct or threatened and many other components and attributes of biodiversity seriously degraded.

Both the gains in human welfare and the threats to wild nature have come about largely because of increased access to previously less-accessible areas and the activities made possible by this access. Roads in particular have been the primary vehicle bringing about access to the terrestrial regions of the globe. Thus, roads are both a blessing and a curse. On the one hand, they bring development with its increased access to markets, education, and health care. On the other hand, they can bring disease, market pressures, competing land claims, loss of cultural and environmental services and resource overexploitation.

It is clear that any vision of a sustainable future must require a careful strategy for the management of roads, to ensure that their benefits are not outweighed by the costs, especially to biodiversity conservation, and to rural peoples by loss of resources driving them even further into poverty.

For roads considered essential to national development, careful placement with due consideration of the impacts of the roads is crucial. They should be part of an holistic land use planning program, which is rigorously implemented to ensure that roads do not result in unplanned degradation and ultimate loss of forests.

In addition, roads should be kept as far from boundaries of protected areas as possible, and all efforts should be made to ensure that they never run through protected areas. Some "no go" areas for roads are essential in the case of high value conservation areas, especially if the capacity to control access along them is low.

If there is no option but for roads to run close to protected areas or other areas of high conservation importance, a suite of mitigating measures is critical to ensure that they do not result in degradation of natural resources. They include permanently-manned gates and checkpoints at key places (e.g., bridges, forest entry/exit points, major junctions). For timber, they also include a professional management system so that only designated timber trees can be extracted, and a chain-of-custody system is in place between the concession and the markets to prevent unauthorized timber leaking into the system. For wildlife, strict control of transport and sales is essential.

Commercial forestry has directly and indirectly created the conditions for unsustainable extraction of trees and wildlife, and in many tropical forests throughout the world, the timber companies represent the only significant institutional presence, and are in the best position to address the problems. Hence, key regulatory mechanisms should focus on timber companies and forest concessionaires. National legislation has begun the process of involving logging companies in the management of wildlife populations. In Sarawak, Malaysia, a recent law bans all commercial sales of wildlife. Government agencies can enforce the trade ban in urban areas, but logging companies have been instructed to enforce the trade ban in their own concessions. They are not to allow their vehicles to carry wild meat or their staff to hunt. In addition, the companies have to ensure that domestic animal protein is brought into logging camps for the workers. Similar legislation for logging companies has been enacted in Bolivia and Congo. Increasingly, international agreements are also trying to promote such management. For example, in 2003, the World Bank "Forest Law Enforcement and Governance" initiative resulted in an inter-ministerial declaration of African ministers which recognizes that all aspects of management must be improved to address unsustainable timber extraction and wildlife hunting and trade in forests across the continent.

Although national legislation and international agreements can provide both negative and positive incentives, ultimately the move towards control of resource loss through logging roads must depend on a cultural shift within the logging industry. Some companies are moving this way, assisted by the positive incentives provided by "green labeling" and independent third-party certification. In Congo, for example, collaboration between a logging company (Congolaise Industrielle des Bois), a conservation organization (Wildlife Conservation Society) and the Congolese Government has resulted in a multifaceted management program, including: Incorporation of wildlife management into company regulations; education programs; bans on the use of snares, and of hunting protected species; strict controls of wildlife movements within the concession and a ban on all wildlife leaving the it, enforced by permanently-manned checkpoints; and provision of alternative sources of protein. The result is that abundant wildlife populations occur in an active logging concession with its extensive road networks (Elkan *et al*. in press). Similar programs are being initiated in other parts of Central Africa and Southeast Asia.

These programs focus primarily on over-exploitation of wildlife. Further steps are essential to include other non-timber forest products, and also to prevent over-exploitation of timber species, to prevent the sequential extirpation of the most valuable species, and the sequential loss of habitat to agriculture. Finally, systems to capture rent for ecosystem services should be explored more fully than at present, to offset the perceived costs of good management.

Although this piece has concentrated on the problems associated with road access to tropical forest, the general pattern can be extended to non-forested ecosystems. Road access to savannahs, grasslands and deserts, as well as to lakes and rivers, can bring about the same types of damage, not only to the target resource, but to many other parts of the ecosystem.

Ultimately, the only way in which the benefits of roads are not to be counteracted by vastly damaging unsustainable resource extraction will be a change in mindset amongst key decision makers in governments and development agencies, to recognize that roads are not an unambiguous silver bullet to the problems of development, and to plan their programs accordingly.

ELIZABETH L. BENNETT
JEFFERSON HALL
KENT H. REDFORD

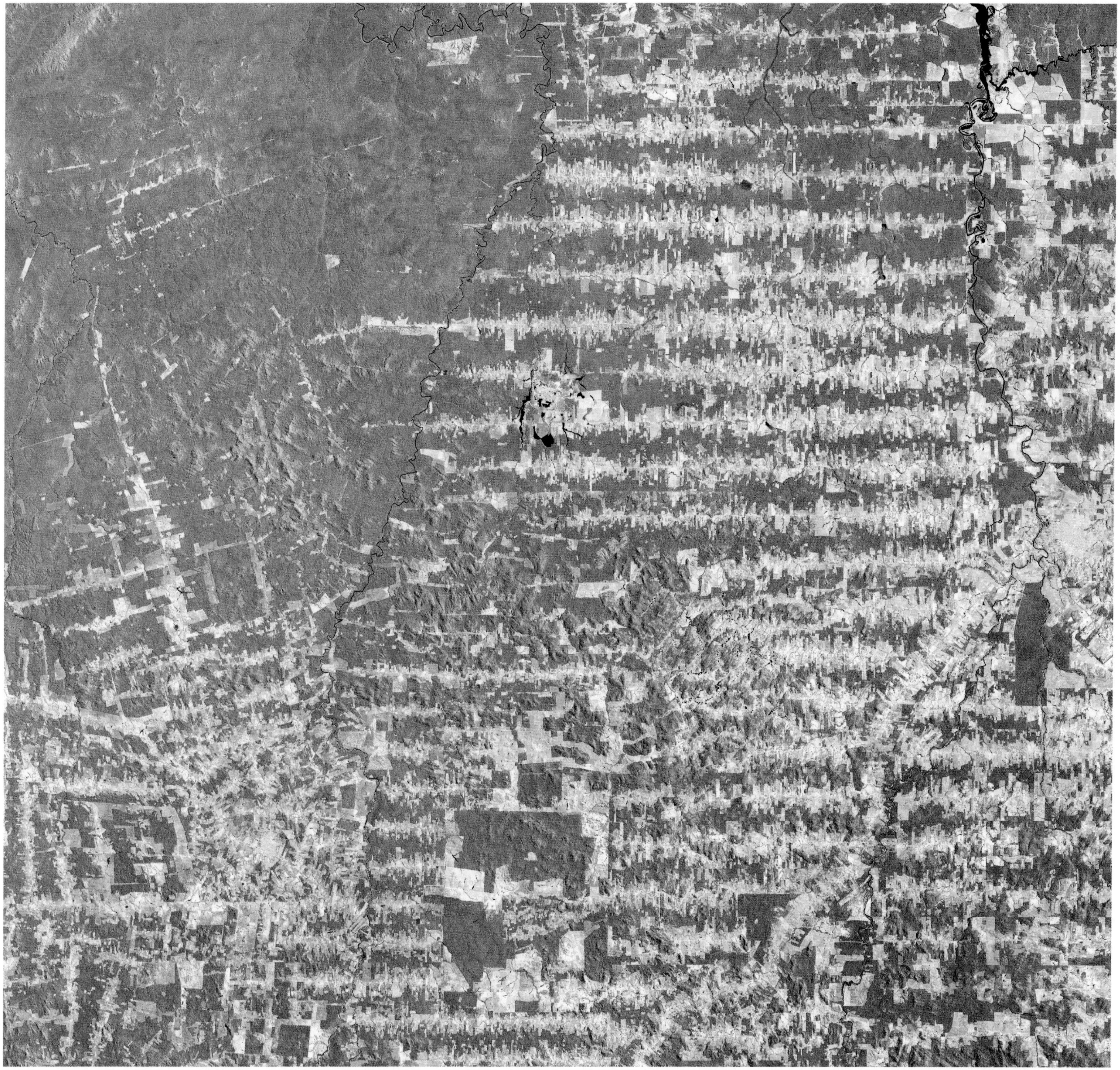

LAND USE

Humanity's footprint is causing land-use change more rapidly in recent history than at any other time. The demand for a wide variety of resources is increasing. Millions of hectares of habitat have already been converted to meet global demands for petroleum, timber, minerals, paper, soybeans, palm oil and other commodities. Resource consumption in developed countries outpaces the rest of the world. The world's richest 20% consume about 16 times more than the poorest 20%. Global demands for resources are growing with increasing human population and economic expectations. Such is the case in China and Brazil, where new demands on resources will have global consequences. Expanding Asian economies are providing the infrastructure (e.g. roads, ports and railroads) to facilitate trade and exploit natural resources.

The immediate impacts of this global transformation are habitat loss and fragmentation. Highly disturbed ecosystems often have reduced resilience, and less capacity to withstand stressors and maintain their functions (Folke *et al.* 2004). Habitat transformation contributes to species loss, reduced population sizes and truncated distributions. These, in turn, alter ecosystem processes, energy flow, and even physical characteristics. Often, non-native or adaptable native species may appear or increase, especially as the system's resilience is reduced, a phenomenon that on a global scale contributes to homogenization of species and systems through reduced biodiversity (Hilty *et al.* 2006).

URBANIZATION AND EXURBAN SPRAWL

For the first time in history, more humans live in urban than rural areas. By 2030, 60% of the world's population is likely to live in cities; some with over ten million people (UN-Habitat 2001). United Nations Secretary General, Kofi Annan, declared that, "Sustainable urban development is one of the most pressing challenges facing the global community in the 21st century" (UN-Habitat 2001). This is a major change and separates us ever further from the natural world upon which we ultimately depend for our survival. This poorly planned suburban and exurban sprawl has occurred mostly over the second half of the twentieth century. In the United States, the combination of prosperity, a network of highways, and the perception that cities had more pollution and crime facilitated the leapfrogging of suburban development into rural areas. In cities, this increased the gulf between the wealthy and the poor. Dispersed development patterns, coupled with limited public transportation created communities dependent upon automobiles that, in turn, depend upon a cheap and plentiful supply of gasoline and an ever-expanding road infrastructure.

Today, the fastest growing land-use change in the United States is exurbanization, a low-density form of residential development. This increasingly global phenomenon is exploding across China, Canada, France, Denmark, Russia, Australia, and other countries (Hilty *et al.* 2006). Burgeoning exurban developments are among the most land-consumptive of modern day human activities (Johnson and Klemens 2005) and exurbanization has increased five-fold since the 1950s (Hansen *et al.* 2005). In developing countries, sprawl is often pushed by poverty, with the rural poor migrating to cities and constructing housing on any available lands. These are often the worst places that are "left over"—steep hillsides that collapse or gullies that flood during rainstorms—destroying the shanties and few possessions the poor may have.

The fragmented habitats created as a byproduct of sprawl are dominated by edge tolerant species, inhabited by many weedy and invasive species, and vulnerable to stochastic events because these areas are essentially islands in a sea of asphalt and concrete. These remaining fragments are both drier and warmer than the continuous forest that they are carved out of. Urban areas are markedly warmer than the surrounding countryside, shifting the flora and fauna to those that can tolerate this 'urban heat island effect'. Other ecosystem services such as pollination and soil decomposition are compromised in more urbanized areas, changing soil profiles and the pollination cycles of flowering plants (Johnson and Klemens 2005).

INFRASTRUCTURE

Roads have had a more devastating impact on biodiversity than any other form of infrastructure, with the possible exception of nineteenth-century railroad development. The transformative impacts of roads include alterations of hydrological regimes, erosion and sedimentation, disturbed edges for the migration of invasive plants and animals, and road mortality of wildlife. Impacts to wildlife populations extend up to a mile or more from a large road. Many animals will not move out of forested areas to the open areas associated with the road. Light spillage from roadways, both from vehicles and from stationary illumination, disorients wildlife and disrupts cycles of plants. Chemicals placed on roadways to maintain safe travel conditions, such as road salt used in icy areas, enter the surface water supply and compromise aquatic systems (Forman *et al.* 2003).

FRESHWATER WETLANDS AND WATERSHEDS

Less than half a percent of the earth's surface is composed of freshwater ecosystems, yet they contain astounding amounts of economically important species, and provide a myriad of ecological services including water supply and flood control. Human actions that transform freshwater sources imperil not only biodiversity, but also livelihoods and human health. Yet while we use a huge amount of water, supply and demand often don't occur in the same place, and water is often diverted to meet demands in distant areas. About one-third of the world's population lives in countries with moderate to high water stress. Given present trends, water scarcity will affect 66% of the world's population by 2025. Water quality is declining globally as well, increasing the incidence of disease and infant mortality.

Watershed destruction is tremendously significant and leads to losses of biodiversity and diminished water quality and availability. Upper watersheds are often critically important for biodiversity conservation since the ecological gradients often have high biodiversity. They also harbor high numbers of endemic freshwater species. Although a global assessment of the status of freshwater biodiversity has not been completed, The World Conservation Union (IUCN) estimates at least 20% of aquatic species or more than 10 000 species are threatened with extinction worldwide.

Wetlands are also transformed directly or through changes to watersheds or sources. Open ponds and lakes, which are more desirable to humans, are often created from structurally complex and biologically diverse forested wetlands. Large, sub-terranean aquifers under many wetlands are affected by many factors, influencing wetland water levels. Subtle changes in water temperature, quality, the amount and the timing of water flow impact wetlands. Groundwater-fed wetlands are depleted when water is withdrawn for human use or for activities such as gravel mining.

Wetlands are transformed by pollution from many sources—agricultural run-off with fertilizers and pesticides, heavy metals from industry, and eroded soils as a result of poor land-use practices. Alligators living in pesticide-contaminated lakes in Florida, USA, were found to possess altered plasma hormone concentrations that ultimately caused the feminization of male alligators and reproductive declines. Many of the medicines that humans ingest pass unaltered through sewage treatment plants into rivers and streams. Wetlands are also transformed by thermal pollution as a result of water evaporating from heated road surfaces or water from factories running off into wetlands. Therefore, the input of water into the wetlands is often altered, both in quality, quantity and temperature, in turn transforming the wetlands.

AGRICULTURE

Nearly forty percent of the earth's surface has been directly transformed for agriculture and pasture. Land used for crop production during this period increased roughly 130 000 km^2 per year between 1980 and 2000, mostly by converting natural forests. Much of this transformation serves short-term low-intensity agriculture and contributes comparatively small quantities of food. Much of the natural habitat that has been transformed is too fragile to support agriculture in the long-term, leading to serious land degradation and the subsequent conversion of forests to agricultural use. The tremendous increases in agricultural productivity, doubling global food production since 1960, are attributable to intensification. Intensification is usually associated with higher levels of inputs, including labor, agrochemicals and water use—the latter two having serious negative environmental impacts.

While estimates vary, up to 40% of agricultural land is degraded, which leads to declining productivity. This, in turn, typically leads to higher use of agrochemicals. This unsustainable agricultural system threatens remaining intact habitats and biodiversity, jeopardizes ecosystem services, long-term agricultural productivity, human livelihoods and health. Especially hard hit by this unsustainable pattern are people who directly depend on the products of healthy ecosystems.

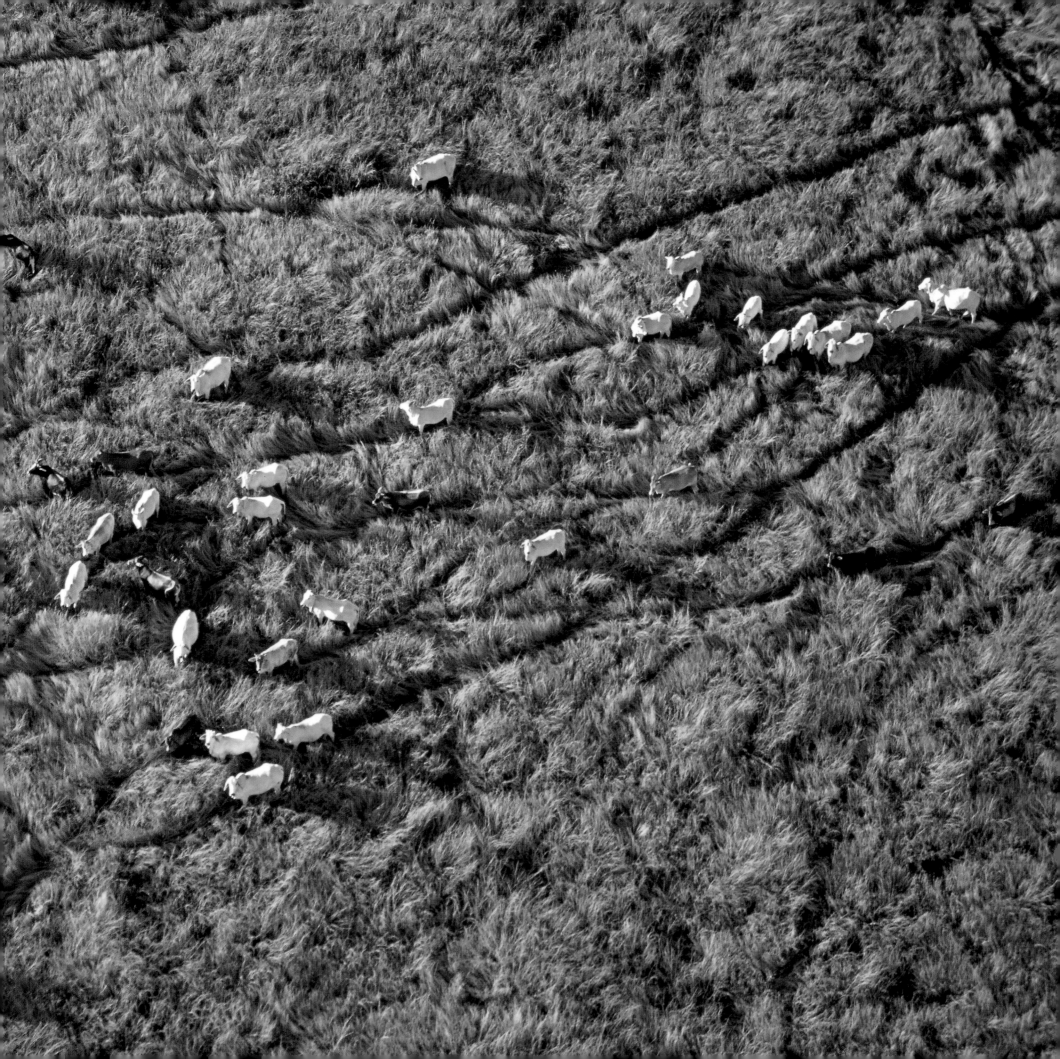

Approximately half of the world's total labor force, or nearly one-quarter of the global population (*ca.* 1.5 billion people), are employed in agriculture, or their livelihoods are directly linked to it. As natural ecosystems are compromised, they provide fewer ecosystem services and direct benefits (bushmeat, medicinal plants, fiber, fish), increasing the vulnerability of people who may already live at the margin. Existing problems of biodiversity loss, agrochemical use and soil degradation, compounded with climate change and the projected doubling of demand for food in the next fifty years, suggest that agricultural activities will have escalating adverse impacts on biodiversity.

CLIMATE CHANGE

Synergistic effects between land transformation and global climate warming can compound the effects of habitat loss of biodiversity. Most models of human-induced climate change show that there will be impacts associated with the increasing frequency and severity of extreme weather events. These events are beginning, changing the temperature, rainfall patterns and the growing season for plants as well as altering the breeding cycles of amphibians.

From a landscape transformation perspective, the current global pattern of landscape fragmentation has created islands of habitat isolated from one another by insurmountable barriers including development, roads, impoundments, agricultural fields and managed timberlands. This directly affects the ecological resiliency of plants and animals as well as ecosystems, all of which will have to alter their present distribution on the earth's surface to accommodate the changes that climate change will bring. Anticipated impacts will be the inability of coastal wetlands to move inland due to the rising sea level because coastal city infrastructures are blocking access to the hinterlands. Cold-dependent species will have difficulty adjusting their ranges northward or up the sides of mountains to escape warmer temperatures because their dispersal pathways will be blocked by roads and exurban development.

MANAGING TRANSFORMATION

Ten percent of the land on Earth is designated as protected; however, these protected area networks cannot sustain global biodiversity. One recent study mapped the ranges of 11 000 vertebrate species (birds, amphibians and mammals) and identified 1 400 sites lying outside protected areas. These 1 400 sites required conservation action so as to protect species that were not found within protected areas (Rodrigues *et al.* 2004). Creation of new protected areas is vital, but so is the management of existing ones. Most parks are not large enough to maintain adequate populations of rare or far-ranging species or to maintain ecosystem-level processes that sustain biodiversity (e.g., natural fire regimes). Most of the world's protected areas (80%) are smaller than 10 000 hectares. Such small parks may have significant local importance, but are too small to slow down long-term species loss. In many places where it is still possible, new large protected areas can serve as "intact" places providing vital ecosystem services that extend outward. These can be especially important when they are managed as one component of a broader landscape (corridors, biosphere reserves) based on zoning for intensive activities (e.g., urban use, intensive agriculture or industry).

MAINTAINING CONNECTIVITY

Beyond maintaining large wild areas, we can ensure wildlife and habitat conservation in the face of land and water transformation by habitat restoration and maintaining corridors. Restoration is important where specific regions are identified as critical for the survival of a species or the ecological community. For example, South Africa's Working for Water Program is enhancing water security, improving ecological integrity by eliminating invasive species, restoring degraded lands and promoting sustainable use of natural resources. The program invested in South Africa's most marginalized sectors, employing over 42 000 people in less than four years. Passive techniques, such as limiting access to areas to reduce fishing or grazing pressure, have also been shown to be very effective under the right circumstances (Hilty *et al.* 2006).

Corridors are critical to enabling certain species and even entire communities to survive in an ever-fragmenting landscape. In some cases, corridors may need to be restored to be useful in maintaining species or population integrity. Corridors are useful at many scales, from highway underpasses to regional linkages such as the Yellowstone to Yukon and Paseo Pantera multi-country corridors (Hilty *et al.* 2006). The state of Amapá in Brazil is establishing a biodiversity corridor spanning 10 million acre that comprises the largest tropical forest protected area (3 867 000 hectares) in the world: The Tumucumaque Mountains National Park.

Freshwater wetlands do not exist in isolation from surrounding upland areas or from one another. Yet, changing the conventional thinking about wetlands requires incorporating biological information on wetlands and wetland-dependent wildlife to create a suite of best development practices. One such approach, pioneered by Calhoun and Klemens (2002), provides development templates for upland areas surrounding and between wetlands based on their biological carrying capacity.

COUNTERACTING SPRAWL

With sprawl becoming a global phenomenon, a number of tools are needed to ensure the conservation of biodiversity. In developed countries, there are movements in some areas trying to re-establish village life and human community as an alternative to suburban sprawl. Typically, these communities concentrate people into higher densities with commercial services nearby, and include a diversity of housing costs and sizes to encourage diversity among resident configurations. Concentrating people reduces the built footprint (when compared to the number of people housed), and reduces the acreage of landscape transformation associated with exurban development. Transforming the way development occurs requires diverse stakeholders to work together and to invest in the slow process of changes in local governance and policy. For example, the Wildlife Conservation Society's Metropolitan Conservation Alliance (WCS/MCA) includes stakeholders from conservation biology, local governance and sound land-use planning thereby getting commitments from communities to retain open space and corridors and to take active measures to conserve biodiversity in their localities (Johnson and Klemens 2005). Integrating conservation biology into planning can bring positive benefits to new developments as well as improving the ecological footprint of existing communities.

Increasing attention is focused on mitigating road infrastructure impacts. Systems that alert drivers of animals on the roads and wildlife crossing structures are increasingly common. Underpasses and even wildlife overpasses are being installed in some countries. However, this type of mitigation is a poor substitute for thoughtful planning that avoids constructing roads in ecologically sensitive areas.

LAND TRANSFORMATION

Poor policies and inequitable subsidies are often the drivers of habitat transformation. Reform is needed in pricing agricultural commodities, fuels and wood. Transportation and national integration policies that include road building, subsidies for cattle ranching, and land-tenure policies that encourage colonization of frontier areas are all incentives for land transformation, rewarding short-term monetary gains as opposed to long-term sustainability. Eliminating these subsidies would both directly improve environmental management and eliminate many of the underlying drivers of habitat transformation and rural poverty.

Better landscape planning is needed to utilize lands to their best agricultural capacity. Intensifying agricultural production on prime lands can make major contributions to reducing poverty while staying the conversion of lands unsuitable for agriculture. On lands of lower agricultural productivity, especially areas that are important wildlife corridors or near protected areas, sustainable eco-agricultural production is needed. Agro-forestry will be critical in many areas because it can help to restore degraded lands while meeting human needs, and offers a better option for biodiversity conservation than plantation monocultures.

Investments in protection are small compared to the expected return; economists estimate that for every dollar spent on conserving the world's remaining intact natural habitats, society will get at least a hundred-fold return in ecosystem services. Addressing issues at the ecoregional scale may mean that conservationists will have to become advocates for newly planned, denser communities, for making existing urban areas "greener," or for "growth pole" areas that are close enough to parks for cities to act as magnets, yet far enough away to assure that resources are not depleted for urban markets. In some areas, it may mean large regional projects designed to attract the poor away from border areas and promote intensive agricultural development. In other areas, where the potential for agricultural intensification or rural industrialization is poor, it may mean creating alternatives to provide secure livelihoods. Ecoregional problem-solving requires broader conceptual thinking, building alliances between a broad array of interests and a diversity of stakeholders and integrating ecological understanding into all phases of public policy. Finally, it will require the understanding that the environment is not a competing interest to be balanced against other human endeavors but rather it is the foundation upon which all human interests rest.

Michael W. Klemens
Katrina Brandon
Jodi Hilty

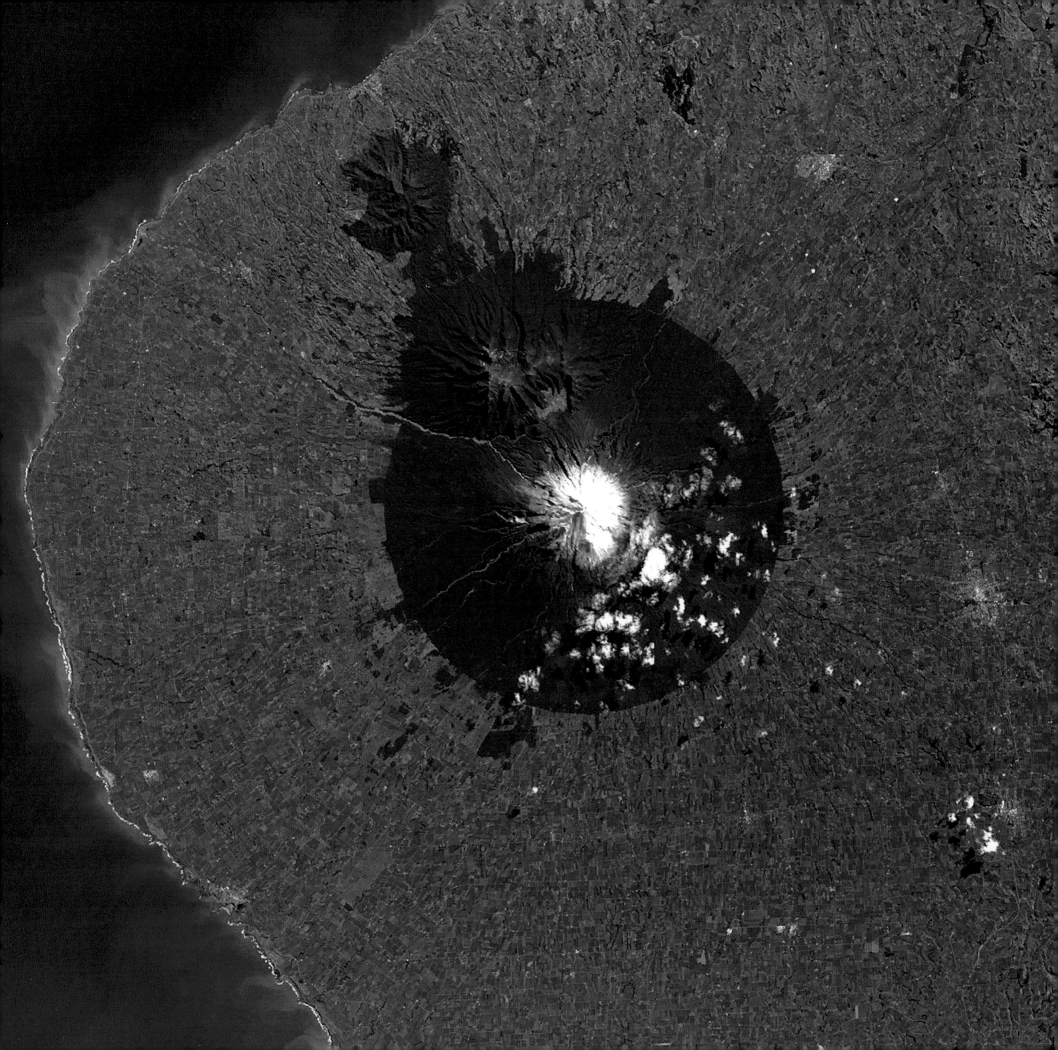

ENERGY

The human footprint exploded when fire was first harnessed as a way of transforming our environment. Since then, rising energy flows have enabled societies to emerge, expand and flourish to grand scales. Since 1800, global primary energy has increased nearly three orders of magnitude and in the 21st century, the scale of energy extraction, shipment, conversion, consumption (and waste and pollution) to accommodate the demands of an anticipated 10 billion people will result in biosphere impacts of unprecedented global and historical magnitude.

The projected amount of CO_2 released by humans each year will likely result in rapid and unparalleled climate changes that among other impacts will cause glaciers to melt, increase frequency of floods and droughts, increase the incidence of wild fires, warm the oceans, and lower the pH chemistry of seawater, with serious and long-lasting consequences for humans and wildlife worldwide.

Luckily, planetary energy resources are immense relative to current and future projections of global energy consumption, and more than a quarter century of applied research, scientific gains, technological innovations, empirical experience, and accumulated insights strongly suggest that there are abundant resources and methods for delivering the vast level of energy services humankind may require this century while dramatically reducing the size of civilization's ecological footprint and biosphere impacts.

OUR ENERGY OPTIONS:
THREATS, CHALLENGES, AND OPPORTUNITIES

Fossil Fuels

Over the past century, almost 250 billion tons of coal, 125 billion tons of oil and more than 60 trillion cubic meters of natural gas were combusted worldwide. We know that coal reserves will last several more centuries, but when it comes to the ultimately recoverable resources of oil and natural gas, opinions vary widely, ranging from shortages occurring within several decades to sufficient supplies well into the next century.

The United States, Russia, China, Australia and Germany possess 70% of all the good quality coal reserves, while two-thirds of oil reservoirs are found in Saudi Arabia, Iraq, United Arab Emirates, Kuwait and Iran, and two-thirds of natural gas reserves are concentrated in Russia and the Middle East region. In addition, substantial levels of fossil fuel reserves are located in biodiversity rich habitats throughout a number of nations, including Venezuela, Colombia, Brazil, Ecuador, Mexico, Republic of Congo, Equatorial Guinea, Nigeria, Indonesia, Malaysia, Vietnam and Thailand.

Although the actual footprint of a well-run crude oil or natural gas operation is relatively tiny compared to agricultural operations, a major concern for biodiversity experts is the habitat conversion and fragmentation occurring in the wake of access roads for exploratory drilling, as well as clearings for pipeline corridors and operations inside conservation priority sites and legally established protected areas. One dramatic example is the current rapid development of natural gas reserves inside the Greater Yellowstone Ecosystem in the United States.

The debate between national energy policy and biological conservation has mostly been played out in the western part of the country over the past 20 years, and particularly in the Arctic National Wildlife Refuge in Alaska (ANWR). Recent and alarmingly rapid development of natural gas fields in the Intermountain West has brought new attention to resource management policies on public lands in the lower 48 states. Stretching from the Canadian border all the way to Mexico, many of these deposits lay beneath some of the most rugged and beautiful areas of the west, which coincidentally also harbor important populations of some of the last large, charismatic species left in North America, as is the case of the Greater Yellowstone Ecosystem.

Human activities, like road construction associated with oil and gas development and exurban expansion, are increasingly taking place in the peripheral lands of this highly vulnerable ecosystem and will likely isolate the core areas of the Greater Yellowstone Ecosystem from other northern Rockies systems in the next few decades. As a consequence, populations of large carnivore species, such as grizzly bears and wolves, may become unviable over the next 25 years (Noss *et al.* 2002).

Over 8 500 wells have already been drilled in the Upper Green River Basin at the southern end of the Greater Yellowstone Ecosystem in western Wyoming, with another 10–15 000 approved by the Bureau of Land Management. The conundrum between resource extraction and conservation is especially apparent where energy reserves overlap areas of abundant wildlife that are still unprotected. Because the natural gas reserves in this area are directly beneath the critical wintering range for most pronghorn and mule deer in the region, there is great concern over the amount of habitat loss and fragmentation from such intense resource extraction. While linking development and protection is possible under highly specialized conditions, case studies show great costs to both society and wildlife. Compensations may occur at local levels including enhanced tax revenues, school construction, libraries, and employment. Nevertheless, such boom and bust economies often lead to long-term social and environmental ills that render landscapes unattractive to both humans and wildlife (Berger 2004).

Oil and gas development are happening too fast to allow for the timely collection of data on the impacts of large-scale development on local wildlife populations. Federal requirements to expedite reviews for approval of energy development projects have accelerated energy production to an unprecedented level. Although several oil and gas companies sponsor wildlife research, most of that research has a lag time before completion and is likely never used by federal resource management agencies or by the companies that sponsor the research. Thus, development practices are seldom adjusted to be more commensurate with long-term survival of wildlife populations in many areas.

On the arctic front, the Prudhoe Bay oilfields of arctic Alaska, which sprawl across some 1 000 square miles and are visible from space, are yet to expand dramatically. Considered one of the most evident elements of the human footprint, this region is the setting for one of the longest and most contentious environmental debates in the United States. At issue is whether the arctic coastal plain of the Arctic National Wildlife Refuge is to become part of the web of oil extraction infrastructure that feeds into Prudhoe Bay.

For biodiversity, the planned expansion of oil development will have a very dramatic effect. Compounding the fragility of arctic environs, their wildlife, and how the oil infrastructure affects them are the dramatic changes caused by global warming, which are more pronounced here than anywhere else on the planet.

The geological accident of accessible oil reserves in arctic Alaska collides with one of the last, great spectacles of wildlife on earth. The immense landscape of this region's flat coastal plain dotted with thousands of thaw lakes is a critical nursery for migratory birds from all over the world and for several large herds of caribou. The most diverse and abundant aggregations occur in the once-remote National Petroleum Reserve, Alaska, where they come to rear young during the brief, but productive arctic summer.

The appeal of the harsh arctic coastal plain to migratory birds, most of which are ground-laying shorebirds and waterfowl, is owed partly to its remoteness from nest predators. Conversely, the limiting factor for resident arctic predators is their ability to survive in the bitter and dark winter. It is the infrastructural development of the oil fields that has tipped the delicate predator-prey relationships in the arctic (NAS 2003). Landfills and dumpsters provide year-round food, and man-made structures provide perches, dens and surveillance posts that give undue advantages to the increasing numbers of predatory species.

Caribou response to oil field infrastructure is complicated and nuanced. Although the Central Arctic Herd has grown overall during the time of oil field development around Prudhoe Bay, pregnant and calving cows avoid developed areas, including former prime calving and foraging habitat. This issue is of major concern for the declining Porcupine Herd calving in the narrow coastal plain of the Arctic National Wildlife Refuge, as any further displacement by new oil development would likely leave cow caribou with little options of movement and have potential long-term consequences to caribou populations (Cameron *et al.* 2005).

Oil development is not confined to land and neither are the effects on wildlife. Bowhead whales are displaced by oil drilling

sounds, and as offshore drilling leases get underway in the Beaufort Sea, the issue will surely be magnified. The displacement of bowhead whales, the main subsistence of Inupiat natives, and of caribou, the main subsistence of Gwich-in natives, points to the important cultural effects of oil development in arctic Alaska.

A PORTFOLIO OF ALTERNATIVES
TO FOSSIL FUELS: PROS AND CONS

Hydropower

Recent concerns over climate change are accelerating hydro-dam construction worldwide. The myriad consequences of damming large rivers are well documented and include disruption of the distribution and timing of water flow, changes in productivity of riverine and riparian plant life -especially in downstream habitats, large scale flooding that often eliminates entire biodiversity assemblages, and ironically, increases in greenhouse gas emissions as sunken biomass decays. Actual measurements of emissions from catchment basins indicate hydropower dams account for roughly 7% of total global greenhouse gas emissions and this could increase to 15% given projected dam growth, yet such emissions are not fully accounted for in the greenhouse gas inventories relied upon for the Kyoto Treaty (St. Louis *et al.* 2000).

Historically, hydroelectric project planners have not addressed or adequately dealt with environmental impacts. World Bank assessments show that 58% of all dams are planned and built without any consideration to downstream impacts, including coastal erosion, pollution, and other problems. In addition, estimates indicate that at least 20% of all aquatic species, more than 10 000 species in total, are threatened with extinction worldwide, and although disruption and fragmentation of aquatic habitats due to dams has already contributed to serious species loss from riparian and aquatic habitats (Rockström *et al.* 1999), current plans call for more dams to be built this century than last century, mostly in wilderness regions and biodiversity hotspots in developing countries.

Several countries have begun recognizing the value of using mitigation measures, like allowing some minimal flow, building fish passes to allow migration, and allowing artificial floods to regenerate the resource base of downstream floodplains for local livelihoods, as is the case in the Pongolapoort dam in South Africa. Other countries are committing to the restoration of eco-

system functions and native fish through the decommissioning of dams. Additional recommendations on best practices are outlined in the World Commission on Dams "Dams and Development Report" (WCD 2000).

Bioenergy

Ten percent of total world energy consumption, especially in developing countries, is currently derived by harvesting biomass from standing forests and farm wastes, most of it unsustainably and with high pollution levels. In addition, there is an expansion of dedicated plantations for growing bioenergy feedstocks for electricity generation and mobile fuels, with sugar cane and fast-growing tree species in Brazil and corn in the USA being the largest ones.

The downside is that under a medium-growth, renewable-intensive energy scenario we would need an additional 800 million hectares of land to support the projected biomass requirements for this century. These space demands, along with the chemical inputs used to increase crop productivity, may cause considerable impacts on ecosystems and biodiversity. Furthermore, when forests are cleared to grow bioenergy crops, most of the carbon previously stored in the intact ecosystem is released into the atmosphere (UNDP 2000). One potentially promising ethanol option with a number of ancillary benefits is the perennially grown prairie tall grasses like Switchgrass (*Panicum virgatum*).

Currently, the USA devotes 74 million acres to production of soybeans used primarily for animal feed. With protein recovery processing technologies nearing commercial readiness, production of perennial grass could potentially produce the same amount of feed protein while also producing a significant amount of cellulose feedstock for hydrolysis into ethanol production (Lynd 2004).

Production of this substantial quantity of fuel would require allocation of no new land to feedstock production. The perennial forage crops utilized for both feed and fuel production could cost-effectively provide 25% of current U.S. gasoline consumption while still producing the amount of animal feed protein currently generated by this land now. Perennial grasses also require substantially less pesticides and herbicides than corn or soybeans and reduce soil erosion losses by 99%.

In conclusion, an aggressive plan to develop cellulosic biofuels between now and 2015 could enable America to produce the equivalent of roughly 8 million barrels of oil per day (122 billion gallons per year) by 2025. This is more than current

domestic oil extraction, as well as equal to half of current total U.S. oil use in the transportation sector.

Solar

Our single largest sustainable energy source is the 125 000 Terawatts (TW) of sunlight continuously landing on the planet. In comparison, we use only 10 TW a year, of which solar currently provides only a fraction of 1%. Research indicates it is feasible that solar photovoltaic power systems could supply these levels of energy services with a small ecological footprint relative to all other energy supply options (Zweibel 2005). Unfortunately, public and private research, development, demonstration and commercialization activities as well as public policies, regulations and incentives at all levels of government are inadequate to even remotely achieve this extraordinary solar vision.

For example, the total current electricity demand for the USA could be supplied by modestly efficient (10%) commercial solar photovoltaic systems covering only 0.4% of the nation in a high-sunlight area such as the desert Southwest—an area about 29 000 km^2 (2.9 million hectares). For comparison, there are two million ha in U.S. farm set-aside programs, another two million ha of domestic U.S. military bases, and 55 million ha of suburban/urban real estate.

Nearly 60% of U.S. electricity could be satisfied through "Building-Integrated Photovoltaic" solar systems, which not only supply electricity but also serve as façade and cladding materials of the building, displacing costs for polished stone or aluminum panels. One key to achieving competitive photovoltaic systems is to use a similar cluster production model used so successfully in achieving breakthrough cost reductions and extraordinary productivity gains in Liquid Crystal Display (LCD) manufacturing (Keshner and Arya 2004). The result would make photovoltaic systems a highly competitive electricity choice.

Wind

Some of the energy coming from the sun is converted into wind energy. Even if only 20% of this power could be captured, it could satisfy 100% of the world's energy demand for all purposes and over seven times the world's electricity needs. There are, however, several practical barriers that need to be resolved to fully realize this potential (Archer and Jacobson 2005).

Wind power is now competitive in cost with new coal, natural gas or nuclear power plants in the USA and Europe. Ongoing innovations will further reduce the cost of wind-generated electricity. To the extent that remote wind farms are concentrated in farming and ranching regions (e.g., 95% of U.S. winds are located on the Great Plains), the income from wind farm royalties would be a major supplement to farming/ranching income (Williams 2001).

Better yet is that a wind farm only takes up 5% of the land area, and roads for installing and maintaining the farm another few percent, so that more than 90% of the land is still available for farming and ranching. With the wind royalty fee providing the rural landowners with a sustainable income source, they could entertain adopting a more resilient, ecologically sustainable type of farming and ranching, including restoration of deep-rooting, carbon storing grasslands.

The major environmental issue confronting wind power has been the possibility of avian and bat collision mortality. It is worth noting, however, that recent research on these issues, show that avian mortality is low at most potential wind energy sites, approximately 1-2 birds per turbine per year or less, while in comparison, in the U.S. and Europe vehicles kill 60 million to 80 million birds and bats every year and collisions with buildings and windows kill another 100 million to 1 billion birds. The small number of birds killed in collisions with wind turbines is far outweighed by wind's role in preserving habitat and reducing greenhouse and air pollutant emissions. It is imperative though that wind resource-rich nations implement rigorous protocols for site selection, construction and monitoring to minimize hazards to birds and bats.

Three countries with some of the world's largest hydro resources—Brazil, India, and China—have far greater wind resources that are likely to cause only a fraction of the ecological impacts resulting from hydro development. China's 2 000 GW of wind resources are four times larger than its massive hydro resources and five times larger than all of China's current electricity generation. China's goal is to construct 3 GW by 2010 and 30 GW by 2020. In September 2005, renewable energy and conservation advocates launched "Wind Force 12 – China," concluding, that with market-based incentives and regulatory policies China can harness 40 GW by 2020, 100 GW by 2030 and 400 GW by 2050.

Nuclear Power

Nuclear power now generates 16% of global electricity, with reactors located in 29 countries. The tragic accident at the Russian

Chernobyl reactor in 1986 that released 190 tons of toxic materials into the atmosphere during a radioactive fire that burned for 10 days had a decisive role in nuclear power growth. The health consequences in the region have been tragic, and will persist for several generations (CCPI 2005, UN/SADC 2005). A number of bullish nuclear power assessments have been published in recent years putting forward the case for electricity, hydrogen fuels and desalination generated from new nuclear reactor designs. These new designs are claimed to be not only economically attractive, but clean, inherently safe, and even proliferation resistant.

Despite the often cited claim that one ton of uranium can displace 20 000 tons of coal, uranium-generated electricity carries some intrinsic downsides that are inherently intractable (Feiveson 2001, Allison 2004, Ferguson and Potter 2004, and Lovins and Lovins 1981), including diversion of uranium fuel for military or terrorist use in fabricating atomic bombs, proliferation of weapons-grade material, ever-present target of nuclear facilities for military or terrorist attack, contaminant fuel wastes that remain radioactive for millennia; and, as happened in Chernobyl, generating systems that can fail catastrophically with disastrous human health and ecological consequences lasting for generations and economic impacts lasting for centuries (Bund and Weir 2005).

Even under the most favorable conditions, nuclear could only play a modest role in providing global electricity. For example, in order for nuclear to displace all projected coal use worldwide by 2100 would require constructing a 100 MW nuclear reactor *every 10 hours* for the entire century. The high nuclear fuel demand would require reprocessing weapons-grade plutonium for use in breeder reactors by 2050. This would result in some 5 million kilograms of plutonium, the equivalent of 500 000 atomic bombs, annually circulating in global commerce (Williams 2001).

Efficiency and Sufficiency

Energy efficiency is the largest pool of cheap, clean, safe, reliable and 'renewable' energy services available to humankind. It is derived from that greatest of human assets, knowledge. Finding ways to intelligently deliver heating, cooling, lighting, refrigeration, mobility and shaft power, resulting in less use of natural resources, less generation of wastes and pollution, and direct and indirect monetary savings and ancillary benefits is the ultimate energy source (Lovins 2005).

For the sake of humanity and biodiversity now and for generations to come, it is critically important to achieve a world five to ten times more efficient than conventional energy markets and current government rules, subsidies and regulations will allow. Capturing the immense pool of efficiency gains is core to stabilizing the Earth's climate, ending massively widespread, crushing poverty and preventing one of the largest species extinctions in planetary history.

Developing countries present the largest potential savings, given the fact that 80% of all new energy consuming products and services will be purchased in these nations over the next several decades. There are myriad other savings and earnings as well; avoiding the health and environmental externalities of pollution emissions is equivalent to many hundred of billions of dollars per year in health benefits.

China stands out as one of the most impressive efficiency stories of the past quarter century. The nation's energy intensity has fallen fourfold since 1980, declining by an average annual rate of 5.3%. The efficiency gains between 1990 and 2000 eliminated the combustion of 3 billion tons of carbon. However, China can do much better—from 1990 to 2001, the EU produced three times the GDP of China with a net increase in CO_2 of only one-eighth that of China's. China's energy intensity per unit of GNP still requires 50% more energy than the global average. The country's revved economy is projected to quadruple by 2020, barring unforeseen setbacks. It has been estimated China spends 12 times more on expanding energy supplies than on efficiency. However, in August 2005, President Hu Jintao and Premier Wen Jiabao, stated China's 11th five-year plan (2006-2010) would put energy, resource and water efficiency ahead of expanding supplies—the first time ever.

Per unit of output, China uses five times more energy than the USA and up to 10 times more than Japan. Only one in every 20 Chinese buildings is energy efficient and over 80% of new housing are energy guzzlers, according to Vice-Minister of Construction Qiu Baoxing. Residential buildings in Beijing require three times the energy used in a similar one in northern Germany, though both climates are similar. Even worse, the 510 biggest government buildings and office blocks in Beijing use as much electricity as all the residential buildings in the capital combined.

The construction market in China is the largest in the world with over two billion square meters per year of development. Premier Wen Jiabao issued an order in 2005 requiring all new buildings to be at least 50% more energy-efficient than existing

ones, and 65% better in Beijing. The newly completed 8-story Ministry of Science and Technology building in Beijing appears no different than most of the inefficient government towers. However, by using readily available technology and 'green' construction materials, the 1300 m^2 building was made 70% more energy-efficient.

Antiquated Regulations and Subsidies

Perverse subsidies, failure to internalize externalities, and skewed public policies and archaic regulatory rules concentrate investment in resource options with overly large ecological footprints, as well as incurring higher costs and risks than necessary.

Globally, 568 billion dollars *per year* will be *invested* through 2030 to expand large power plants (mainly coal and natural gas fueled, and hydrodams), transmission lines, remote foreign oil exploration, extraction, pipelines, global shipping, refinement and delivery. Worldwide, meeting projected demand will entail cumulative investment of some 16 trillion dollars from 2003 to 2030, or 568 billion dollars per year. The electricity sector will absorb the majority of this investment. This expansion is backed by significant government subsidies exceeding several hundred billion dollars per year (Van Beers and de Moor 2001).

In addition to these direct and subsidized energy investments, there are also significant externalized costs not included in energy prices. These include adverse health impacts, economic losses, and environmental damage caused by air pollutants, acid rain emissions, greenhouse gases, land and water contamination, radioactive wastes, dammed and channeled rivers, aquatic species extinction, etc. Economic estimates of these externalities, where possible, vary widely, but certainly comprise many hundreds of billions to trillions of dollars per year.

A significant amount of the ecological impacts associated with society's energy footprint could be prevented, reduced and moderated relative to business-as-usual. By adopting the current best demonstrated policies, regulations and incentives proven effective over the past several decades, combined with promising new ones that continue to emerge through feedback of what works best, society can foster an ecologically sustainable, low-footprint energy system worldwide.

MICHAEL TOTTEN
JON P. BECKMANN
STEVE ZACK

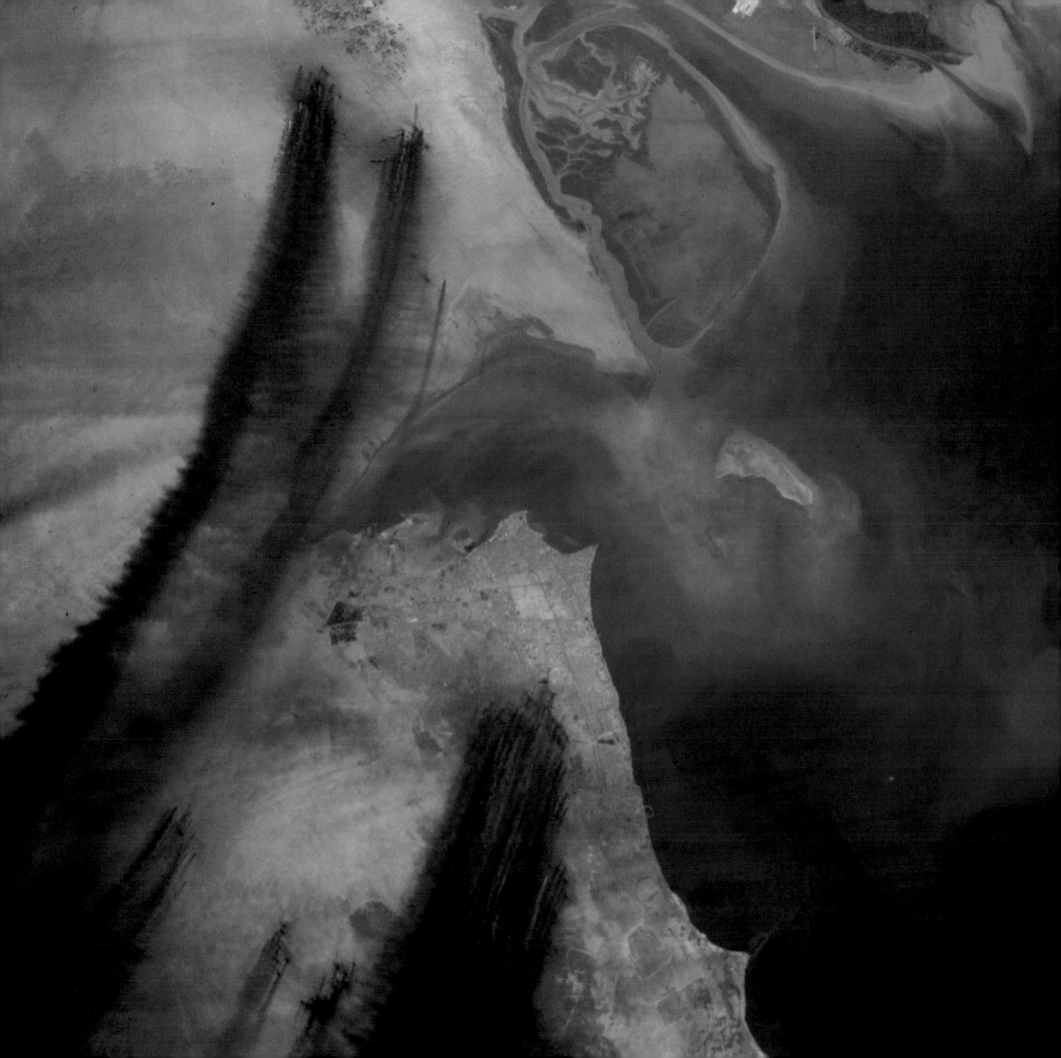

REDUCING THE HUMAN FOOTPRINT

THREATENED BIODIVERSITY

THE HUMAN FOOTPRINT
AS A MEASURE OF VULNERABILITY

Humans have caused a biodiversity crisis, with species extinction rates up to 1 000 times higher than background rates. The wider ramifications of this are only now being taken seriously, as environmental systems crucial to human life start to break down—from global carbon sequestration and climate regulation to local supply of clean water and air. In the face of this overwhelming extinction crisis, it is important to remember that all biodiversity is important and worth conserving, but also essential to know where and what to conserve first. Conservation prioritisation is a method that seeks to identify which elements of biodiversity need action first, rather than—as is sometimes believed—which elements deserve action and which do not. Prioritisation is necessary to ensure efficient allocation of scarce conservation resources and to maximise persistence of all biodiversity in the face of a crisis of unprecedented proportions.

Prioritisation is based on the recognition that elements of biodiversity differ in the number of places they occur, and thus can be conserved (their 'irreplaceability'), and in their likelihood of being lost in the future (their 'vulnerability') (Margules and Pressey 2000). Global conservation prioritisation approaches such as the biodiversity hotspots are based on this combination of irreplaceability and vulnerability. The human footprint (Sanderson *et al.* 2002; Introduction of this same volume) is one of a number of global measures (see chapter 6 of this same volume) of vulnerability, and this chapter explores and compares a rather different measure: Threatened species.

Wilson *et al.* (2005) separate vulnerability into three dimensions: Exposure (the probability of threatening processes affecting an area); intensity (the magnitude, frequency, and duration of threatening processes); and impact (the actual effect of threatening processes on biodiversity). Although The Human Footprint map (see pp. 42-43 of this same volume) is dramatic, and has many potential applications, it is not able to measure the impact of threatening human processes on biodiversity di-

rectly. This is primarily due to the fact that all of the broad-scale variables used to produce the index were measures of the potential (roads and railways, coastline, rivers) or actual exposure (current land use), or potential intensity (overall population density, distribution of night-time lights) of threatening human processes, rather than measures of the consequent impact on biodiversity. Only three measured impact (built-up centres, population settlements, plus roads and railways again), and this at a small-scale.

A negative process of the same intensity and exposure will have a different impact on global biodiversity when affecting different areas among and within biomes—for example, such a process may threaten more species of higher irreplaceability (i.e. those with fewer spatial options for their conservation) in tropical moist broadleaf forest than in boreal forest, or in temperate broadleaf forest in southwest China than in the same biome in England. Likewise, as acknowledged by Sanderson *et al.* (2002), the intensity, exposure and impact of each of the chosen variables vary substantially across the world, a factor only partially corrected for by normalising by biome. For example, the distance that people travel from roads and rivers (and thus affect natural habitats) varies greatly in temperate versus tropical regions, and the use and impact of minor roads differ significantly between the eastern United States and the Congo. This is likely to be a particular problem when trying to convert the human footprint from terrestrial to aquatic realms. In addition, the index attempts to measure only negative human processes, rather than positive ones such as policies that reduce hunting or increase the suitability of farmed habitats for biodiversity. All of these factors are further complicated by the fact that biodiversity is distributed unevenly across the planet.

Ideally, the best way to measure human impact on biodiversity would be to measure the changing state of biodiversity itself. Although proximate threats to biodiversity are wide-ranging and include habitat loss, exploitation, invasive species, climate change and changes in native species dynamics, nearly all are ultimately anthropogenic. The few exceptions are relat-

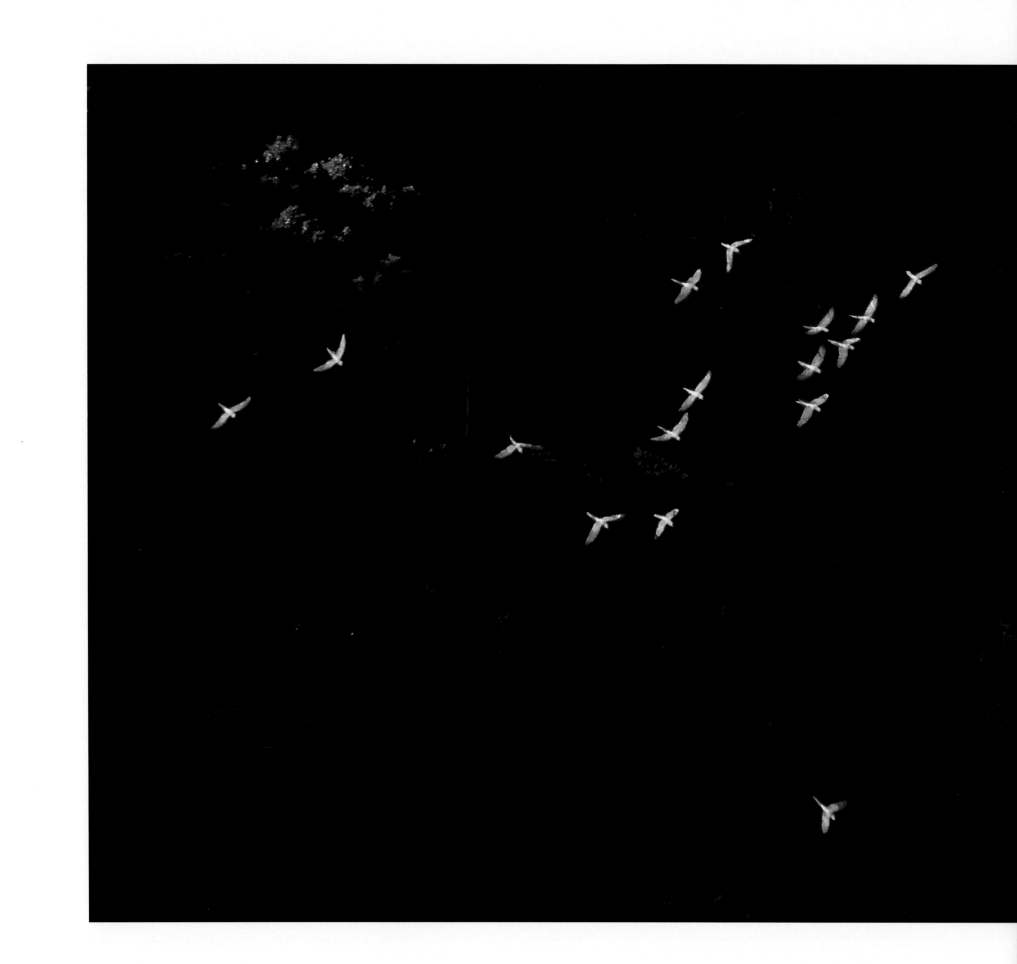

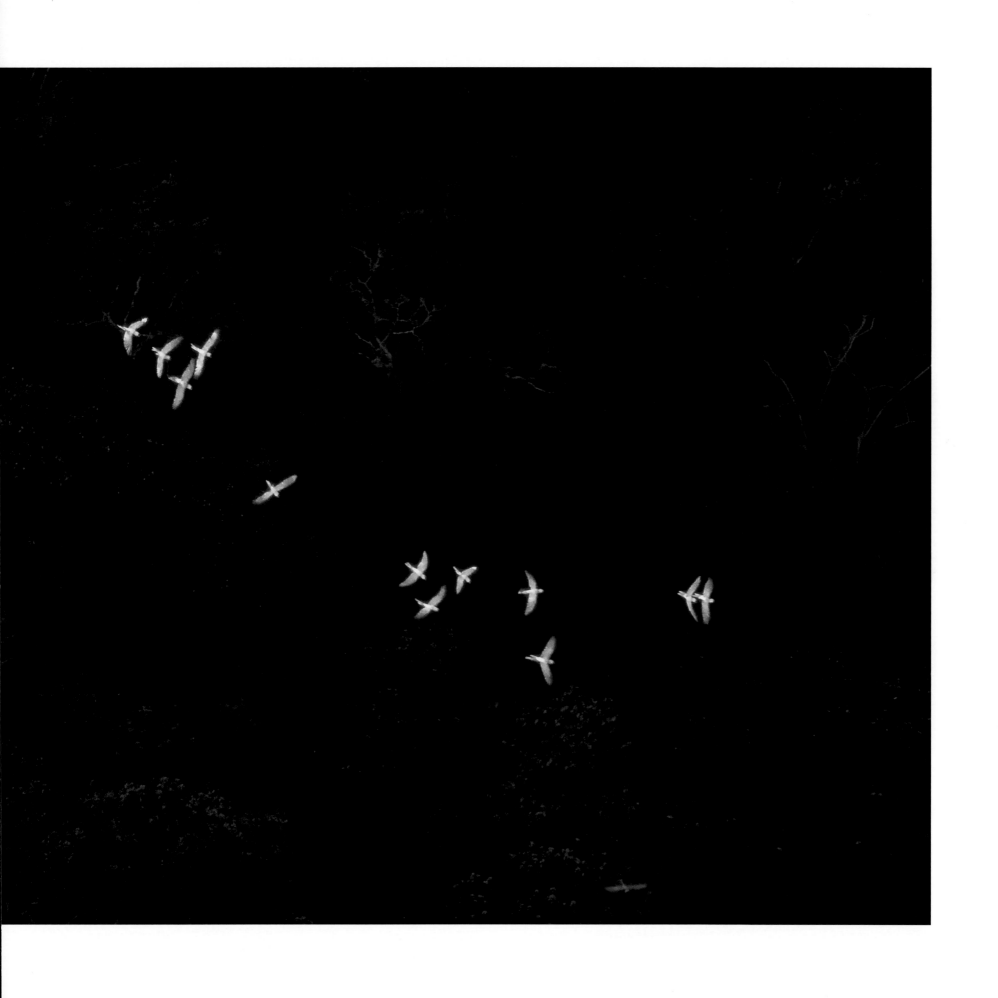

ed to natural disasters and some of the few incidences of disease. Given this, the changing state of biodiversity is almost entirely a reflection of human impact, and thus would be the most accurate measure of the current human footprint, or 'vulnerability'. Measuring the vulnerability of biodiversity in a comparable way to the human footprint of Sanderson *et al.* (2002) would require spatial data on the distribution of biodiversity, data on the status of individual species, and—if conservation implications are to be drawn—data on which human processes are causing any changes in a species' status.

THE UNEVEN DISTRIBUTION OF BIODIVERSITY

Not surprisingly, human society has invested a much greater effort in mapping the distribution of humans and their infrastructure than the distribution of other species. Thus, a greater quantity and resolution of data has been available for measures of human land use, as used by Sanderson *et al.* (2002), than for measures of the magnitude of impact in any given area on species. Nonetheless, this situation is changing, with baseline maps of 'extent of occurrence' (limits of distribution) now completed for many major groups of species, largely through the efforts of initiatives linked to IUCN (The World Conservation Union). These include all bird (www.birdlife.org), terrestrial mammal (Global Mammal Assessment: www.iucn.org/themes/ssc/programs/-gma/index.htm), and amphibian species (Global Amphibian Assessment: www.globalamphibians.org). Among other vertebrate species, maps have already been completed for all terrestrial/freshwater turtles (http://emys.geo.orst.edu/) and global assessments of reptiles and freshwater fishes are underway (Baillie *et al.* 2004). While a Global Plant Assessment will take a long time (Baillie *et al.* 2004), various smaller initiatives are underway. In the marine realm, several efforts have focused on mapping the distribution of fish (particularly under the FAO Species Identification and Data Programme www.fao.org) and other vertebrate species. A forthcoming Global Marine Species Assessment will do much to improve availability of marine species' distribution data (Baillie *et al.* 2004). The largest remaining gap overall is for non-vertebrate taxa. Distribution data for the megadiverse invertebrates have largely been restricted to very small groups of commercially important species such as cephalopods, but this situation is changing due to efforts of collaborations such as the Ocean Biogeographic Information System (www.iobis.org).

Density maps of species richness, as shown in CD-Figs. 5.1, 5.2, and 5.3, illustrate dramatically the uneven distribution of biodiversity across the world, with the most obvious bias being towards high species richness in the tropics – a relationship that holds true even when one takes account of varying land areas at different latitudes (Baillie *et al.* 2004). In general there are also broad relationships among taxa, with peaks and troughs of species richness in similar geographic locations for mammals, birds, amphibians, and turtles. However, these relationships are not exact, due to general biological differences between taxa, such as the enhanced ability of flying birds to disperse over water or of birds and mammals to cope with hot arid regions that are hostile to amphibians.

Although most species have small range sizes (Gaston 1996), richness maps are primarily driven by the ranges of widespread, common species (Lennon *et al.* 2004) that are often less likely to suffer impact from threatening human processes. Thus, species richness maps are useful for demonstrating the uneven distribution of biodiversity, but are still a long way from measuring potential human impact. The cumulative distributions of centres of endemism (with at least two 'restricted-range' species that have extents of occurrence less than 50 000 km^2) are shown in CD-Fig. 5.4. Restricted-range species are even more unevenly distributed than species more generally (see CD-Figs. 5.1, 5.2, and 5.3). Restricted-range species generally occur in topographically variable or isolated areas, such as mountains, peninsulas, and islands, particularly in the tropics. These species, due to their limited distributions, generally have fewer options for conservation and thus the areas they inhabit have higher irreplaceability. All else being equal, similar human pressure in such areas of higher irreplaceability is likely to have a greater global impact on biodiversity.

MEASURING THE STATUS OF SPECIES ACROSS THE WORLD

Species' range size and extinction risk are often correlated, but other factors are also involved. Thus, a consistent methodology is needed to measure species' extinction risk. A number of methods have been suggested, but the IUCN Red List of Threatened Species (www.iucnredlist.org) is the global standard (Rodrigues *et al.* 2006). The Red List, as it is commonly known, is the most comprehensive assessment of the global conservation status of plants and animals. It uses a set of quantitative and objective criteria, based on factors that include range size, but also population size, fragmentation and rates of population and range decline to assign species to categories related to their extinction risk. These factors are largely based on current or previous threat, but also include estimated predictions of future declines. From humble beginnings in the early 1960s, the Red List is rapidly

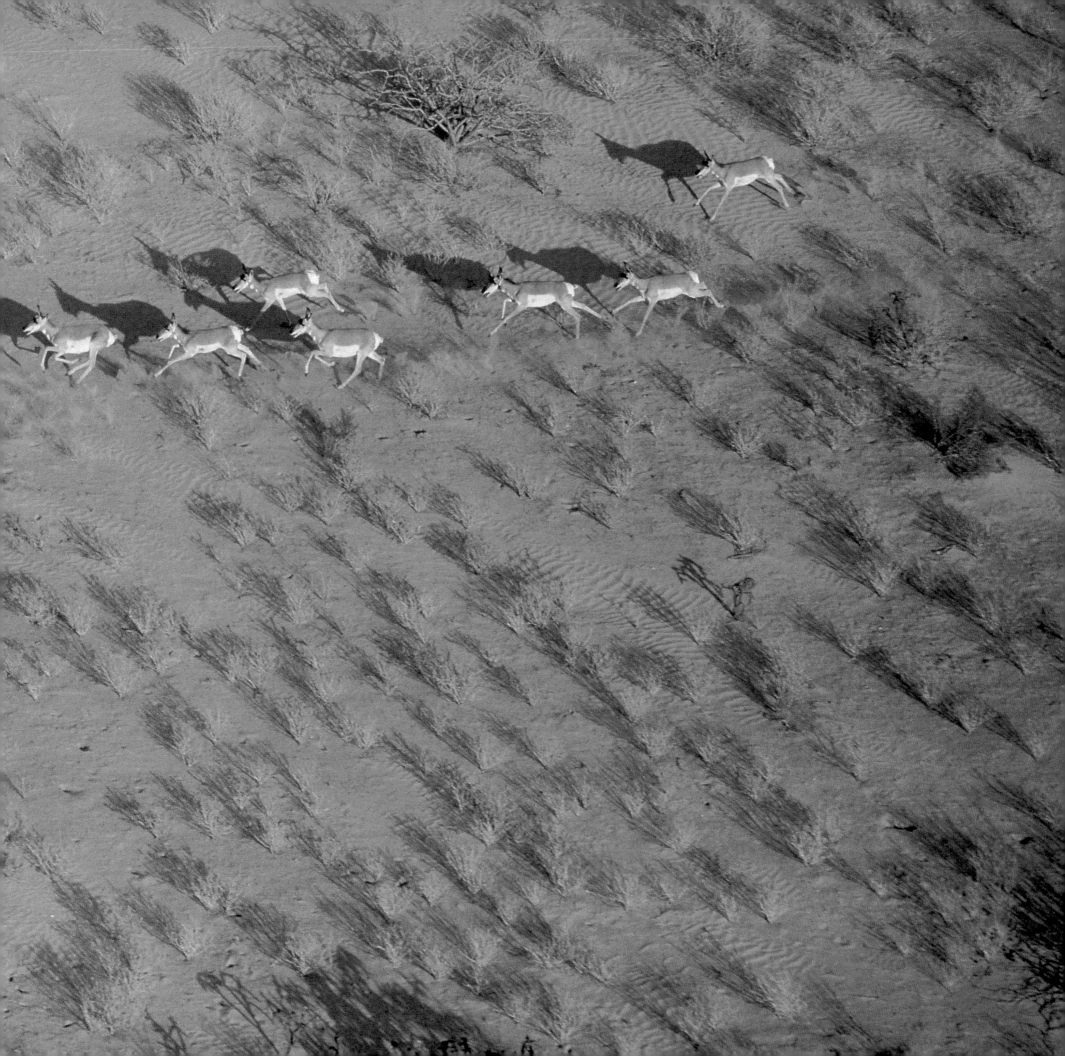

growing to incorporate comprehensive assessments of taxa (i.e., all species within major classes), including many more species (the number of species assessed nearly doubling between 2000 and 2004), increasingly supported by a wealth of data that are also published online. Since its global standardisation enables consistent estimation of extinction risk among taxa and regions, the IUCN Red List provides an excellent tool for understanding the geographic and taxonomic spread of species threatened with extinction by humans. Transparent collection of supporting data for the Red List enables analysis of which threatening human processes are causing declines.

The richness of threatened species of mammals, birds, amphibians, and turtles on the 2004 IUCN Red List is illustrated in CD-Figs. 5.5, 5.6, and 5.7. Comparable maps can be produced for other realms (e.g., CD-Fig. 5.13), in contrast to the measures of Sanderson *et al.* (2002) that cannot be directly compared between biomes. The maps in CD-Figs. 5.5, 5.6, and 5.7, at first appear strikingly different—most notably due to the relative lack of threatened amphibians in most of the world compared with the other groups, although threatened amphibians are generally more geographically concentrated (up to 44 species per half degree grid square, compared with 24 for both mammals and birds). The maps also do highlight differences—such as the low number of threatened birds and mammals in Mesoamerica compared with amphibians, which are suffering substantial threats there due to the synergystic effects of a pathenogenic chytrid fungus and climate change. Nonetheless, the maps—in many ways reflecting congruent patterns of endemism—show many similarities, with the northern Andes, Atlantic Forest, West Africa, Madagascar, IndoChina, and insular South-east Asia consistently highlighted as areas of high threatened species richness. These maps of threatened species richness bear some resemblance to the human footprint map of Sanderson *et al.* (2002), highlighting areas that not only have a high degree of exposure to intense human pressures, but also contain species that are being impacted by these pressures. Thus, much of India is highlighted on the human footprint map of Sanderson *et al.* (2002), but in CD-Figs. 5.5, 5.6, and 5.7 only the Western Ghats and Himalayas stand out prominently, since these are the areas with higher numbers of species—many with restricted ranges—that are being impacted.

Inclusion of extinct species (see CD-Fig. 5.8) in these maps would help to reflect the historic human footprint. For example, the Caribbean holds many threatened birds and amphibians, but not such a large concentration of mammals in CD-Figs. 5.5, 5.6, and 5.7—this is likely to be due to historical mammal extinctions.

A more accurate depiction of the vulnerability of biodiversity is given when threatened species richness maps are normalised to account for the overall species richness in any given area. Although this makes species-poor regions such as those at high latitudes very sensitive to small changes (since just one species out of four makes a change of 25%, while one species out of 100 only makes a change of 1%), it more accurately reflects human impact on biodiversity. For example, a few threatened birds in a high latitude biome (e.g., three threatened birds out of 50; 6%) are more likely to reflect a high impact from human processes than twice as many in a richer biome (e.g., six out of 300; 2%). CD-Figs. 5.9, 5.10, and 5.11 accounts for varying species richness around the world, and is thus a much more accurate depiction of vulnerability of biodiversity per se than CD-Figs. 5.5, 5.6, and 5.7.

CHALLENGES TO THE USE OF THREATENED SPECIES AS A MEASURE OF THE HUMAN FOOTPRINT

If all species were already assessed for the Red List, it would provide a powerful measure of the human footprint, as these extinction risk assessments integrate information on exposure, intensity, and impact of threatening human processes. However, three main challenges currently limit the use of the Red List as a direct measure of the human footprint: Lack of comprehensive assessments; data availability and resolution; and uneven geographic threat to species. Weighting of extinction risk is also an issue that requires careful consideration.

Until all species within a given taxon are comprehensively assessed on the Red List, they do not provide globally comparable data useful for analyses of impact. As described above, this situation is improving rapidly through the efforts of IUCN-linked initiatives such as the Global Amphibian Assessment, but there is still a long way to go.

Availability and resolution of data are factors, as acknowledged by Sanderson *et al.* (2002), that will affect any attempt to produce a globally consistent assessment of the human footprint that is also useful for finer scale conservation planning. While the Red List is thus not alone in facing this issue, it has historically suffered in particular from a deficit of spatial data on species' distributions. Data resolution is a more complicated issue to address since extent of occurrence maps give many errors of commission—areas within the overall range of a species, but which it does not regularly occupy. Some efforts are attempting to refine such extents of occurrence with maps of available suitable habitat derived from remote sensing data (e.g., Rondinini *et al.* 2005). The resulting maps are a little closer to representing a species' area of occupancy, and are useful for improving estimates of

habitat loss that affect a species, and thus refining Red List assessments. Other efforts are tackling issues of resolution from a different angle by compilation and synthesis of point locality data for species from the wealth of data in museums, herbaria and similar sources (Bisby *et al.* 2000). Such high quality fine-scale data obviously necessitate considerably more effort to obtain and synthesise and so efforts to date have generally prioritised the most threatened species within globally assessed taxa for which larger quantities of point data are available.

One of the few—but perhaps the most important—such global datasets is of the most threatened (Critically Endangered or Endangered on the IUCN Red List) species that are confined to single sites, compiled through the Alliance for Zero Extinction (Ricketts *et al.* 2005). CD-Fig. 5.12 shows all sites that hold the last remaining populations of such mammal, bird, amphibian, and conifer species, as well as reptiles that have been globally assessed to date. This map thus depicts sites that have the highest irreplaceability and highest vulnerability. It bears many similarities to CD-Figs. 5.5, 5.6, and 5.7, once again highlighting the Andes, Atlantic Forest, West Africa, Madagascar, IndoChina, and insular Southeast Asia. In CD-Fig. 5.12, however, greater emphasis is given to the most irreplaceable sites, thus more strongly highlighting some areas with smaller numbers of threatened species overall, but with greater threat, while giving less emphasis to areas where larger numbers of more widespread species overlap. In this way, greater emphasis is given to the Caribbean, Hawaiian Islands and Western Ghats of India, but less to the Himalayas.

Efforts are also underway to map known localities of threatened species more generally. The most advanced of these is the BirdLife International Important Bird Area (IBA) program to identify globally important sites for birds, with one of the major criteria for identification of IBAs being the presence of significant populations of threatened species. IBA identification is underway globally, and initial inventories have already been completed in over 160 countries, including across Africa, Asia, Europe, the Middle East and the Tropical Andes, with over 3 000 sites now identified for threatened species worldwide (all mapped and searchable online at www.birdlife.org/datazone). Expansion of the IBA methodology beyond birds—towards the 'Key Biodiversity Areas' approach (Eken *et al.* 2004)—is more severely hindered by data availability, particularly in the aquatic realms, but is gaining momentum through a series of regional assessments.

While issues of data availability and resolution are gradually being overcome, uneven geographic threat to species is an inherent issue that must be understood and taken into account. Issues particularly emerge with a subset of widespread species, such as the Black Crowned-crane *Balearica pavonina*, that suffer significantly greater threats in some parts of their range than others. Simple mapping of the range of a threatened species across its range will not take account of varying levels of species' vulnerability within its range and thus may give a distorted impression of the human footprint. In the case of globally threatened species, range maps will suggest that vulnerability is equal across the range even if the species is less threatened in parts of the range. Conversely, some species not globally threatened may still suffer high vulnerability in parts of their range. This issue is thus most likely to be problematic in areas that have low numbers of threatened species, including some species that are widespread and under uneven geographic threat (such as in high latitude areas), or when data are viewed at increasingly fine scales (where greater importance is inevitably given to more minor differences that may actually be artefacts).

One promising way to address this issue is through looking at species' range contraction. Habitat loss, depletion of food, and persecution of some animal species has transformed the landscapes of continents and led to massive contraction of geographic ranges of some species that once were widespread across many continents. For example, over the last 100 years, the Gray Wolf *Canis lupus* and the Brown Bear *Ursus arctos*, though both globally Least Concern (www.iucnredlist.org), lost respectively 53% and 42% of their historic range. For many wide-ranging species, from tigers to elephants, from lions to bison, their level of threat is measured in part by their loss of range. Indeed, this is an intrinsic criterion on the IUCN Red List. Recently, investigations have compared patterns of changes in the distribution of species at risk in North America with the levels of human influence that affect those patterns. To test the relationship between these, current and historical ranges of selected wide-ranging species were compared to the human footprint (e.g., American Black Bear *Ursus americanus* [Least Concern]: CD-Fig. 5.4). Although responses varied, patterns of range collapse in most species examined were related to the human footprint. The bad news is that these species seem to be retreating before the human footprint. The good news is that studies like this help develop thresholds that relate human influence to species survival. These thresholds help policymakers to understand how much development might be compatible with a species' presence. These same relationships, between species distributions and the human footprint, could also be used to map uneven geographic threat to species. For example, studies in Cambodia showed that Tigers *Panthera tigris* (Endangered) were found to occur more frequently away from areas of human influence.

Wilson *et al.* (2005) stress the importance of careful consideration when weighting extinction risk during assessments of vulnerability. Such weighting can highlight the greater impact being suffered by the most threatened species. Fundamentally, weighting systems increase the resolution of results to highlight particular areas of interest, or add emphasis to biodiversity elements considered of value. For example, while calculating the 'Red List Index' (an indicator showing trends in extinction risk for suites of species), Butchart *et al.* (2004) examined the two main ways of weighting the categories of threatened species on the Red List. They used an 'equal-steps' approach in broad-scale analyses, and an 'extinction-risk' weighting to examine trends in the most threatened species. In the equal-steps approach the weights were 0 for Least Concern, 1 for Near Threatened, 2 for Vulnerable, 3 for Endangered, 4 for Critically Endangered and 5 for Extinct, Extinct in the Wild and Possibly Extinct; reflecting the ordinal ranks of the IUCN Red List categories. The extinction-risk approach instead based weights on the relative extinction-risk associated with each category, ranging from 0.0005 for Near Threatened and 0.005 for Vulnerable to 1.0 for Extinct. This approach thus gives much greater weight to the species in the highest categories of extinction risk and therefore may give a more useful impression of impact than 'equal-steps weighting', which does little to modify the overall picture given by threatened birds in CD-Figs. 5.5, 5.6, and 5.7.

Although helpful in many respects, such weighting necessitates very clear interpretation of resulting scores or maps. For example, an area with many moderately threatened species might have an overall score similar to that of an area containing a few species at imminent risk of extinction (Gaston *et al.* 2002). Unfortunately, this issue is inherent in any system attempting to combine multiple factors, and having to weight some against others. It will thus remain a problem with any attempt to measure the human footprint. It may best be tackled by ensuring that combination and weighting of different factors is as simple and transparent as possible.

CONCLUSIONS

In summary, threatened species are a more direct measure of biodiversity and thus have high potential to incorporate all aspects of vulnerability, thus most closely approaching an ideal measure of the human footprint that can function across all realms and—crucially—incorporating the element of impact lacking in earlier methodology. Maps of threatened species richness (e.g., CD-Figs. 5.5, 5.6, and 5.7, and 5.9, 5.10, and 5.11) help

to clarify the human footprint map of Sanderson *et al.* (2002), highlighting areas that not only have a high degree of exposure to intense human pressures, but also contain species that are being impacted by these pressures. However, threatened species data are limited by their availability and resolution, and by uneven geographic threat to species. Until such factors are resolved, measurement of the human footprint would best place threatened species in a central role, supported by existing complementary measures of exposure to, and intensity of, threatening human processes. Ultimately, however, such a human footprint measure can only reflect "human influence on the land surface" rather than 'human influence on biodiversity' because biodiversity—and thus site irreplaceability—is spread so unevenly across the world. Human influence on biodiversity as a whole can only be measured by combining measures of vulnerability with measures of irreplaceability.

Improved measures of the human influence on biodiversity will help better direct conservation efforts. Such efforts most urgently need to prevent imminent extinctions and safeguard the most irreplaceable sites. More proactively they need to identify and conserve those large biodiversity-rich landscapes and seascapes that are currently least impacted by human pressure (see chapter 6 of this same volume). In regions where such intact landscapes are already gone, restoration of species' populations will be necessary, through tactics such as re-connection of fragmented habitat by dispersal corridors that will allow animals to move across the landscape. Such restoration efforts must be accompanied by changes in policy and human attitude to be successful. Hopefully people will recognise the role of wildlife in maintaining the ecological integrity upon which their livelihood ultimately depends. Even highly influenced areas can be made more suitable for wildlife by encouraging policies that eliminate poaching and lessen conflicts between people and wildlife. Even big fierce animals might be able to coexist with people at higher human pressures than currently, as long as there are favourable political, economic and cultural conditions.

JOHN D. PILGRIM

THOMAS M. BROOKS

GOSIA BRYJA

STUART H.M. BUTCHART

NAAMAL DE SILVA

GUSTAVO A.B. DA FONSECA

MATT FOSTER

MICHAEL HOFFMANN

DAVID H. KNOX

PENNY F. LANGHAMMER

RUSSELL A. MITTERMEIER

ERIC W. SANDERSON

WES SECHREST

SIMON N. STUART

THE GLOBAL IMPERATIVE OF WILDERNESS

A HUMAN-DOMINATED PLANET AND THE BIODIVERSITY CRISIS

During the course of the 20th century, the global human population increased from 1.65 billion to 6 billion people. In April 2005, the United Nations launched the results of the Millennium Ecosystem Assessment (www.maweb.org), a four-year effort involving 1 360 scientists from 95 countries aiming to assess more precisely how this burgeoning human population is impacting the planet's biodiversity and ecosystem services and, conversely, how those changes are affecting human well-being. The key finding to come out of the Millennium Ecosystem Assessment is that, over the past 50 years, humans have changed the planet's ecosystems more rapidly and more extensively than in any other comparable period of time in human history, largely to meet rapidly growing demands for food, fresh water, timber, fiber, and fuel. The most important direct drivers of change in ecosystems are habitat change, overexploitation, invasive alien species, pollution and climate change (Millennium Ecosystem Assessment 2005).

The evidence for this dramatic finding is made eminently clear in the pages of the Millennium Ecosystem Assessment. More land was converted to cropland in the 30 years after 1950 than in the 150 years between 1700 and 1850. Cultivated systems (areas where at least 30% of the landscape is in croplands, shifting cultivation, confined livestock production, or freshwater aquaculture) now cover one-quarter of Earth's terrestrial surface. In the last 20 years, some regions have experienced very high rates of forest loss, particularly in the tropics: In Central America, Amazonia, the Congo Basin, the forests of eastern Madagascar, and south-east Asia (mainly in lowland regions), and it is projected that a further 10-20% of grassland and forest-land will be converted between 2000 and 2050 (primarily to agriculture). More than two-thirds of the area of two of the world's 14 major terrestrial biomes and more than half of the area of four other biomes had been converted by 1990, primarily to agriculture. On the other hand, particularly low rates of forest loss were experienced, and are predicated to occur, in boreal forests and tundra (Millennium Ecosystem Assessment 2005).

From a human welfare perspective, such dramatic changes are of primary importance because of the direct linkages between ecosystems and the essential services that they provide to humanity, including provisioning services (e.g., food, fresh water, fuel), regulating services (e.g., climate regulation, flood regulation, disease regulation) and cultural services (e.g., spiritual, recreational, educational). That such changes already are having a dramatic effect on human society is undeniable. We already know, for example, that the impacts of the massive Tsunami that struck Aceh province in Indonesia on December 26, 2004, could have been significantly less were it not for the loss of coastal mangroves and offshore coral reef systems (e.g., Marris 2005). Similarly, the aftermath of Hurricane Katrina, which devastated the Gulf Coast, and in particular the city of New Orleans, may rekindle interest in bolstering the wetlands south of New Orleans to provide more of a barrier to future hurricanes (Travis 2005).

The important connection here is that these aforementioned drivers of change are *firstly* leading to a significant, irreversible loss of Earth's biodiversity—the very foundation upon which these ecosystem services are built. Scientists have shown that current species extinction rates are 100-1 000 times higher than the normal rate of extinction (Baillie *et al.* 2004). At least in the last 500 years alone, nearly 800 documented extinctions have

occurred, which is clearly an underestimate since this figure is based only on those species actually known to have gone extinct within this time frame (Baillie *et al.* 2004). More worryingly, at least one recent study suggests that we could lose at least *three times* this number of species within just a few decades (Ricketts *et al.* 2005).

The best indication of the deteriorating status of biodiversity can be found in the output of the IUCN Red List (www.iucn-redlist.org), the global standard for the threat status of species worldwide, which reveals the startling fact that one in eight birds, one in four mammals, and one in three amphibians is at risk of extinction in the near future (Baillie *et al.* 2004). As with extinct species, these numbers are clearly underestimates, since there are still many species for which we have insufficient information available to make a reliable assessment of a species' threat status. For example, some 23% of amphibians are considered as data deficient, and many of these species are likely to be threatened. Nonetheless, these rates of threat should give us particular cause for concern. Amphibians, for instance, are excellent indicators of ecosystem health, so the precarious nature of many populations should serve as a warning about the state of our environment (Stuart *et al.* 2004). This is reinforced by more recent studies that show a synergistic relationship between some of these declines and global climate change (Pounds *et al.* 2006).

BIODIVERSITY CONSERVATION AND WHERE TO REACT FIRST

With biodiversity under siege and intact ecosystems crumbling as a result, the challenge facing conservationists looms large: How to curtail and significantly slow the current and future loss of biodiversity? All biodiversity is important, and we fundamentally cannot accept giving up on any biodiversity as being a lost cause. But with limited time and resources available, we must be strategic about where we act first for the benefit of biodiversity. As such, over the last two decades, considerable attention has been paid to the issue of setting global priorities for biodiversity conservation.

We already know that biodiversity in general is concentrated in the tropics, with decreasing species richness as one moves towards the poles (Baillie *et al.* 2004, Millennium Ecosystem

Assessment 2005). Similarly, threat is not evenly distributed across the face of the planet; rather, it tends to be concentrated in particular regions, and not necessarily those where the human population is highest. There are various ways to estimate patterns of distribution of threat, including, for example, stable lights (lights at night), human population density, and maps of net forest loss. In one recent study (and as described in the introduction), Sanderson *et al.* (2002) used four types of data (in nine different datasets) as proxies for human influence: Population density, land transformation, accessibility and electrical power infrastructure. The resulting product, the "human footprint", reveals that around 83% of earth's land surface is currently impacted by human beings. The top 10% of the highest scoring areas looks like a list of the world's largest cities: New York, Mexico City, Calcutta, Beijing, Durban, São Paulo, London, and so on. The minimum score (0) is found in large tracts of land in the boreal forests of Canada and Russia, in the desert regions of Africa and Central Australia, in the Arctic tundra, and in the Amazon Basin. However, the majority of the world (about 60%) lies along the continuum between these two extremes in areas of moderate but variable human influence (Sanderson *et al.* 2002).

This uneven distribution of both biodiversity and threat creates a dilemma for those of us concerned about the conservation of biodiversity. That is, if we are concerned about slowing biodiversity loss, then precisely how do we identify those regions or places *where* we have the least amount of time available in which to act to prevent massive losses of biodiversity from taking place?

The answer lies in the field of systematic conservation planning, the fundamentals of which hinge on two primary concepts (Margules and Pressey 2000): Irreplaceability, which is a measure of our spatial options available; and vulnerability, which is a measure of temporal options, in other words, how much time we have in which to act. In their simplest forms, for example, a region having a species confined entirely to within its borders is highly irreplaceable—if it is lost, there are no other options available where that species can be conserved; likewise, we have less time to act to save biodiversity in a region of higher threat than in a region of lower threat. These two tenets of conservation planning combine in complex ways that enable conservation planners to identify regions and sites of high priority,

with places of high irreplaceability and high threat corresponding to the most urgent priorities.

Perhaps the most influential geographic expression of this is the biodiversity hotspots (Myers *et al.* 2000), those regions characterized by having exceptional endemism (as measured by numbers of endemic plants; 1 500 native vascular plant species) but also under exceptional threat (as measured by percentage habitat loss; at least 70% original native vegetation lost). Currently, some 34 such regions are recognized (Mittermeier *et al.* 2004; see CD-Fig. 6.1). They once covered nearly 16% of earth's terrestrial surface, but their remaining habitat currently only covers some 2.3% of earth's land surface, as a result of the extensive habitat loss that has taken place within these regions. Nonetheless, even within the habitat that remains, some 50% of all plants and 42% of all terrestrial vertebrates are found only in these regions. More importantly, and as concrete evidence of their urgency, around three-quarters of the world's most threatened terrestrial vertebrates are found only in the hotspots of biodiversity. Coincidentally, around one-third of the total human population is found in the hotspots (Mittermeier *et al.* 2004).

Another example of an approach that combines these principles of irreplaceability and vulnerability on a global scale is that of Rodrigues *et al.* (2004a) who used five global datasets to determine the current effectiveness of the world's protected areas network, and identified a number of urgent sites where threatened species currently have no protection whatsoever. These regions show remarkable congruence with the biodiversity hotspots, with priority sites concentrated in Central America, the Caribbean, the Tropical Andes, Atlantic Forest, Afromontane regions of Africa, Upper Guinea forests, Madagascar, Western Ghats and Sri Lanka, the Himalaya, and parts of Southeast Asia. Global studies such as these are useful for informing where conservation investment is most urgently required to effect biodiversity conservation, albeit only on a global scale.

WILDERNESS PRESERVATION
AND THE CONSERVATIONIST'S DILEMMA

However, the problem with conservation action in such super-urgent regions is that it typically is not cheap: Places of high threat tend to be expensive places in which to invest. So what

about areas characterized by lower threat? Areas of low threat and that generally are more intact usually are cheaper to invest in. But herein lies the paradox: Areas of lower threat generally also are depauperate in biodiversity. Consider again that these regions, such as the boreal forest and tundra, have undergone the lowest rates of habitat conversion (and, as mentioned earlier, are predicted to undergo low rates of change in future), and that they also tend to be poorest in terms of biodiversity.

On the other hand, such large intact areas, which many term 'wilderness', also have immense value because of the ecosystem services that they provide—hydrological control, carbon sequestration, nitrogen fixation and so on. They also have great recreational and scenic value, and they serve as strongholds for many of the world's languages (the island wilds of New Guinea has more than 900 native languages). Such regions offer excellent opportunities for pre-emptive action at low cost. But, given the uneven spread of biodiversity, how would the goals of such wilderness preservation compare with those of biodiversity conservation? Would investing in wilderness regions result in the distraction of scarce and valuable resources away from the regions we already know are most in need of conservation action? Or, would it be possible to invest these same resources in areas where they could serve the dual purpose of preserving large tracts of wilderness, while at the same time benefiting biodiversity?

One way that we can investigate this question is by comparing different approaches to identifying areas of low threat and relative intactness and seeing where and how they differ or overlap, and where and how they compare with regions already known to represent urgent priorities for biodiversity conservation.

The first attempt to map wilderness was generated by McCloskey and Spalding (1989) and launched at the 4th World Wilderness Congress. This survey relied on jet navigation charts to identify areas over 400 000 acres (161 943 ha) with no permanent infrastructure. The conclusion was that approximately one-third of the planet consisted of wilderness. Building on this study, Hannah *et al.* (1994) produced a GIS map of global human disturbance in natural systems. The study produced a Habitat Index, with three categories of areas: Undisturbed, partially-disturbed, and human-dominated. Undisturbed areas were those that retained primary vegetation and had population densities lower than 10 people per square kilometer (and under 1 person per square kilometer for arid, semi-arid, and tundra communities). Partially-disturbed areas had secondary but naturally regenerating vegetation with some agricultural development. Finally, human-dominated areas were urban or agricultural areas. The minimum units mapped were 40 000 ha (98 000 acres). Mixed units were mapped using the dominant land-cover, and aggregated into 100 000-ha units (247 000 acres). The resulting findings were that 52% of the planet was undisturbed, 24% was partially-disturbed, and 24% was human-dominated.

More recently, Dirk Bryant and colleagues at the World Resources Institute focused only on forests to identify those regions that meet the following criteria (among others): They are primarily forested; they are large enough to support viable populations of all native species, including wide-ranging species (and large enough to do so even in the face of natural disasters); they are dominated by native tree species; and their structure and composition are determined mainly by natural events. The results of this study found that only 22% of the planet's original forest remains as undisturbed "frontier forests" (Bryant *et al.* 1997).

A fourth study, by Eric Sanderson and colleagues at the Wildlife Conservation Society, is an offshoot of the Human Footprint project that identifies the "Last of the Wild": The ten largest contiguous areas in the 10% of wildest areas in each biome in each biogeographic realm. Overall, 568 such last-of-the-wild areas were identified (Sanderson *et al.* 2002). The proportion of area represented by the last of the wild varies rather dramatically among biomes with, for example, over 67% of the area in the North American tundra captured, while the 10% of wildest area of the Palearctic tropical and subtropical moist broadleaf forests (which is all in China) encompasses less than 0.03% of that biome (Sanderson *et al.* 2002).

Finally, Russell Mittermeier and co-workers at Conservation International incorporated a biodiversity component to the assessment of wilderness, quantitatively defining wilderness regions as those retaining at least 70% of their original habitat (the converse of biodiversity hotspots) and holding human population densities of less than five people per square kilometer (Mittermeier *et al.* 2003). This analysis identified 24 wilderness regions and found that while 44% of Earth's land can still be considered wilderness, only five of these regions (covering just 6.1% of land) are 'high-biodiversity wilderness areas' holding as they do more than 1 500 plant species each as endemics. Together, these five 'high-biodiversity wilderness areas' hold 17% of the planet's plants and 8% of terrestrial vertebrates as endemics.

By mapping the overlay of the regions identified as 'wilderness' in each of the latter three approaches (since these are the only approaches for which spatial data exist for the purpose of analysis, and they also are the only approaches that have been promoted by conservation organizations), we can examine how the geography of the regions seen as important for wilderness preservation might differ (see CD-Fig. 6.2) relative to highly threatened and highly biodiverse regions such as the biodiversity hotspots (see CD-Fig. 6.1). Importantly, we can also consider how the regions of agreed priority for wilderness preservation themselves differ based on biodiversity value.

We use the global biodiversity conservation priority template of Mittermeier *et al.* (2003) as a filter for biodiversity value to investigate the overlap of approaches within areas of low irreplaceability (see CD-Fig. 6.3a) and high irreplaceability (see CD-Fig. 6.3b). In the former, the major areas of agreement among the three methodologies are the tundra regions, as well as the Magellanic Forests of Chile, and very small areas in the forests of Tasmania and the Pantanal. This result is not surprising given the relatively low rates of habitat conversion that have been experienced in these regions. Of course, such an overlay is heavily dependent on the forests-only "frontier forests" analysis; discounting the latter, there is an obvious agreement on the wildness of desert regions, particularly the Sahara, Kalahari, Namib, Arabian, Central Asian and Australian Deserts.

In areas of high irreplaceability for biodiversity, the three approaches are unanimous in the importance of Amazonia, the Congo Basin, and New Guinea. Relative to devastated regions such as the biodiversity hotspots, such areas are still relatively intact. However, as the results of the Millennium Ecosystem Assessment attest, these same regions are experiencing, or have experienced recently, very high rates of net forest loss. These regions, therefore, are not only important priorities because of their biodiversity value, but also because they are facing higher threat, and our failure to act now could result in such regions rapidly becoming the biodiversity hotspots of the future.

In answer to our question about how the goals of wilderness preservation compare with those of biodiversity conservation, it is immediately apparent that the spatial disparities that exist between these regions mean that the goals of wilderness preservation, although significantly overlapping, do not necessarily align exactly with those for biodiversity conservation (Sarkar 1999). Nonetheless, at the very least, the investment of resources in the high-biodiversity regions of the Amazon and Congo Basins, and in New Guinea, would serve a dual purpose of both preserving large, yet threatened, intact tracts of wilderness, but which also are known to be highly irreplaceable in terms of their biodiversity.

Further, fine-scale targets of wilderness preservation and biodiversity conservation may differ even more: Specifically, while protection of 'any' wild area may suffice for the former, in the case of the latter this absolutely and fundamentally will not do. Such *ad hoc* interventions have already resulted in the incomplete nature of the existing protected areas network; for example, an analysis of protected area coverage in the Himalaya shows that on average 11 % of the protected area system consists of rock and ice, which is of low value for biodiversity conservation (Allnutt *et al.* 2002). Instead, for the purpose of biodiversity conservation, it is essential for conservation planners to determine strategically where, based on quantitative criteria, important sites are that should be conserved because of their biodiversity attributes (see chapter 5 of this same volume).

CONCLUSIONS

In conclusion, all biodiversity is important and the value of wilderness is unquestionable.

The latter has great value to humanity for the essential ecosystem services that it provides and its benefits, in turn, for human well-being. However, wilderness preservation alone cannot serve as a surrogate for biodiversity conservation because of the pattern of distribution of biodiversity, threat and human influence. If our aim, as conservationists, is the persistence of global biodiversity, then our sights must remain firmly targeted firstly on those regions characterized by high threat and high biodiversity value (e.g., Madagascar, Atlantic Forest, Philippines, etc.) because to do otherwise, quite simply and

undeniably, will result in the irreversible loss of large swathes of global biodiversity. Such a strategy, however, should be complemented by proactive interventions first in those wilderness regions that also are known to be important for biodiversity conservation (in particular, Amazonia, New Guinea, and Congo), given that these represent obvious regions where investment of resources will deliver dividends meeting the goals of both biodiversity conservationists and wilderness preservationists.

MICHAEL HOFFMANN
CYRIL F. KORMOS
RUSSELL A. MITTERMEIER
VANCE G. MARTIN
JOHN D. PILGRIM

LIVING LANDSCAPES

CONSERVING LIVING LANDSCAPES
FOR WILDLIFE AND PEOPLE

For well over 100 years, a major approach to wildlife conservation has been to set aside areas protected from human exploitation (Kramer *et al.* 1997, Dudley *et al.* 2004). These parks and reserves play a crucial role in saving the planet's plants and animals, because it is in these landscapes alone that biodiversity conservation is the primary land-use objective. Unfortunately, for wide-ranging or naturally scarce wildlife species, strict protected areas have rarely been large enough to meet their ecological needs. Consequently, focusing our efforts solely on national parks or reserves risks the progressive loss of these species and a failure to meet the underlying purpose of parks: Conservation of healthy, functioning populations of the full array of flora and fauna representative of these areas.

When few people lived in adjacent areas and our footprint was relatively light, the inadequacy of protected areas for some species mattered little, as animals like elephants, tigers, lappet-faced vultures and white-lipped peccaries moved freely in and out of surrounding areas in search of needed resources, and the needs of people and of wildlife seldom clashed. For the most part, that reality no longer exists. Our human footprint on the planet is a clearly visible result of a perennial and largely unplanned transformation of land and water (Sanderson *et al.* 2002a). Vast forests and seas of grass have been converted to farms and settlements or carved into pieces by expanding networks of roads and railroads connecting growing towns and linking people and products to markets. Overfishing and pollution similarly have degraded seascapes. The increasing ecological and institutional fragmentation of natural landscapes and seascapes and the increasing intensity of human use of much of the planet is driving wildlife out of preferred habitats and hardening land-use boundaries, blocking access to important

sources of food and shelter and limiting movements necessary for healthy reproduction, adaptation to climatic variation or establishing new populations (Terborgh 1999). This progressively larger and heavier human footprint forces wildlife into competition or conflict with people for space and resources, and often places people in 'uncomfortable' proximity to wildlife. In the United States and across the planet, as people continue to expand into wild areas and as our conservation efforts successfully conserve and restore healthy wildlife populations, the needs of people and the needs of wildlife will increasingly clash. Such conflicts will continue unless we find new approaches that help people and wildlife share these same valued landscapes.

So how do we conserve wildlife species such as lions, tigers and bears (...and loons, whales, chimpanzees and sharks...), whose ecological requirements cause them to venture outside of protected areas? How do we conserve species that live in areas where economic development and not wildlife conservation is the primary goal? We need to think at a larger scale, and see functional connections (Redford *et al.* 2003). We need to plan for change and the unexpected. And we need to leave room for 'margins of error'—typically our own. Of course, we need to think explicitly about our own human interests. But also, we need to look at the same world through the eyes of wildlife. In other words, we need to create living landscapes and seascapes that address multiple, changing needs and concerns as wildlife and people continue to spill over and across ecological and political borders. Not all human activities conflict with all wildlife in all locations, and not all wildlife are perceived as a threat to people in all places at all times. The challenge then is understanding where, when and why the requirements of wildlife and the interests of people sometimes clash, and building a community committed to adopting management practices that help avoid or minimize these conflicts. The Living Landscapes

Program of the Wildlife Conservation Society is working with field conservationists to develop and implement innovative ways to conserve landscapes that are of a size and arrangement that meet the needs of both wildlife and of people.

THE PRACTICE OF
CONSERVATION IN LIVING LANDSCAPES

How can we create living landscapes that are large enough, that contain all the ecological and land-use elements needed to meet the needs of wildlife and of people, and that are configured to minimize wildlife-human conflict? First, we must believe that it is possible to create a living landscape that can generate desired economic, biodiversity and intrinsic values. Second, we must have a keen understanding of how and why people use the landscape, and be able to map where over-use of natural resources risks the depletion of wildlife and the degradation or loss of their habitat. Third, we need to view the landscape through the eyes of wildlife so that we can understand and plan to meet their resource needs in space and time. Lastly, we need to establish the most appropriate mix and arrangement of actors and institutions to effect conservation across these complex living landscapes, and to adapt to change over time.

Understanding the Human Footprint:
Now and in the Future

A first step to designing strategies to reduce or halt clashes between people and wildlife is to understand clearly where human activities occur and document how they influence the productivity and diversity of ecological systems. The Living Landscapes Program takes two broad approaches to evaluate the impact of people on living landscapes. We rely on the knowledge of local people to map human activities in landscapes and seascapes, and we combine historical and contemporary information to predict from the past what our future impacts will likely be on the planet.

Using Local Knowledge to Map
the Human Footprint Within a Landscape or Seascape

To provide a detailed map of the distribution and impact of human activities within both terrestrial landscapes and marine seascapes, the Living Landscapes Program has developed a simple one-day process that reaps the benefits of local knowledge. That said, nothing can ever replace the profound local knowledge garnered by WCS field staff as they live, work and study in an area. Presence on the ground is vital for understanding the ecology of a landscape and the nuance of local social, economic and political systems. This knowledge is an essential first step before beginning a conservation project and an important barometer of change over time.

Our Assessment of Human Activities Workshops (Wildlife Conservation Society 2004) bring together a wide range of local, national and international stakeholders to map and prioritize those human activities that most seriously jeopardize the productivity and diversity of a particular landscape or seascape. These workshops are often the first time that these different actors have sat around the table together, and they provide a safe forum for openly airing views and getting to understand the needs and concerns of each party. Results of these workshops have helped refocus priorities and bring in new partners for more effective management of the Glover's Reef Atholl in Belize. They have convinced conservation managers in Rwanda, Uganda and the Democratic Republic of Congo that they must work together if they are to preserve not only the biodiversity but also the local livelihoods of the Albertine Rift landscape in Central Africa. And they allowed government officials and local pastoralists in the Eastern Steppe of Mongolia to see where they can stand on common ground.

These workshops are an efficient method for mapping the human footprint within a landscape and showing the location and severity of key human impacts on ecological systems. Of equal or greater importance, they often launch a process through which trusting communities committed to sustainable resource management and conservation are built.

Looking Into the Past to Glimpse the Future

Common sense tells us that human activities and the human footprint are not static but change over time in response to resource availability, economic policies and practices, demographic shifts, conflicts and natural disasters. Many human activities are manifest as visible changes in land-use, vegetation cover, river flow regimes and sediment loads, and loss or degradation of wildlife habitat. To assess these changes we have available a set of powerful tools that are built around the collection and analysis of satellite imagery and aerial photographs.

Our remote sensing analysts and geographic information system specialists in the Living Landscapes Program are skilled at interpreting the differences between satellite images from different years to map the distribution and extent of forest loss over decades in the Bolivian Amazon, document the annual intensity and spread of fires burning forests in northwestern Guatemala, and track the monthly conversion of the Great Ruaha River in Tanzania to a waterless sand river.

Our work with the WCS-Indonesia program showed with startling clarity that if current deforestation trends in the Bukit Barisan National Park continue, only 30% of the original area of the park will remain, erasing 80% of tiger habitat and an appalling 95.5% of elephant habitat. Such projections have helped decision makers in Indonesia grasp the severity of threat to the wildlife and have galvanized them into taking the necessary conservation actions.

The power of divining and making tangible the future from the past has encouraged the Living Landscapes Program to begin investing more of our staff time in developing a range of techniques to model and visualize future scenarios that can help us and others clearly grasp the likely impacts of "business-as-usual" policies and practices and encourage us to make the best possible natural resource management and wildlife conservation decisions.

Using Focal Species to See Through the Complexity of Living Landscapes

For conservation investments to be strategic and effective we need to have a clear and unambiguous understanding of what we intend to conserve (Groves *et al.* 2002). Without identifying the specific biological elements of a landscape that we want to conserve, it is almost impossible to decide what actions are priorities for minimizing human-wildlife conflicts, and we certainly cannot expect to measure whether or not we have been successful. Moreover, unless the targets of our conservation efforts are explicit neither we nor our supporters can understand what we intend to achieve and how we will measure and demonstrate our conservation impact.

In the past, too many conservation organizations have either focused their conservation actions on single species or declared simply that they were conserving biodiversity. The problem with the first approach is that single species make poor umbrellas and their effective conservation may not help conserve all

plants and animals within living landscapes. The latter is problematic because it is impossible to define what exactly is being conserved as we are unlikely ever to enumerate all biodiversity in a landscape, let alone understand the ecological requirements and interactions of all species. If we are to conserve wildlife whose resource needs are not met solely from resources found within strict protected areas, our conservation targets needs to reflect their ecological attributes (Sanderson *et al.* 2002b). If we are to ensure that parks fulfill their mission of conserving functional populations of the full complement of flora and fauna representative of an area, we need to pick a suite of conservation targets with complementary habitat needs and that, collectively, are adversely affected by the full range of human activities that are threats to biodiversity within a landscape (Wildlife Conservation Society 2001).

By selecting a suite of wildlife species that, in combination, depend on the full range of major habitat types within a wild area, we provide the basis for a strong, focused, scientifically-based approach to biological conservation at a landscape level (Sanderson *et al.* 2002b). Moreover, by evaluating the complementary needs of these landscape species, we can explicitly assess threats to their long-term persistence and set priorities for conservation actions to avoid or mitigate key conflicts with people (Wildlife Conservation Society 2002). Focusing our conservation efforts on a complementary suite of landscape species creates a comprehensive and effective canopy for conservation that helps us protect critical habitat and reduce or remove key threats across the landscape. Moreover, it allows us to be explicit about what we expect to achieve and provides clear targets for measuring our conservation success. Most importantly, by conserving a suite of landscape species we not only protect these unique icons of wild landscapes, we can save all the flora and fauna that are sheltered under their conservation canopy (Sanderson *et al.* 2001).

CREATING LIVING LANDSCAPES

Deciding How Many Animals is Enough

Knowing how many animals we want to protect in a landscape is important because it explicitly conveys our objectives to others, makes us assess how large an area we need to protect, and sets the bar for measuring our success. It is not a trivial question to ask. How many elephants are needed in the Ndoki-Likouala

Landscape in the Republic of Congo so that there is, say, a 90% chance that the population will survive for 200 years, at a density at which they can fulfill their ecological roles? Though population viability analysis can help us to estimate extinction probabilities, estimating function densities of wildlife is a challenge as it assumes that we know a great deal about how the species contributes to structure and function of the landscape. The Living Landscapes Program is working with our field sites to develop a scientifically defensible process for setting measurable objectives for wildlife numbers that reconciles ecological and cultural estimates of carrying capacity. This process of setting explicit numbers of a wildlife species that we want to conserve has pushed our field staff in Madidi National Park in Bolivia to look well beyond the park and country borders and to work with their Peruvian counterparts to ensure the protection of sufficient contiguous habitat for the long-term survival of jaguar and Andean condor.

See Living Landscapes Through the Eyes of Wildlife

After deciding how large each population of landscape species must be, the next step is to create habitat preference maps. These maps constitute the biological landscape as seen through the eyes of each landscape species. In practical terms they represent potential carrying capacity in the absence of threats that can practically be avoided or mitigated, and reflect the present and future quality of habitat across the landscape. We then create a threats landscape derived from the human footprint. This represents the expected reduction in carrying capacity associated with the different types and severities of threat across the landscape. By combining the biological landscape for each species with the threats landscape through the wonders of optimization software such as Marxan or C-plan, we can configure living landscapes that depict the highest priority areas for conservation.

Reducing the Human Footprint

With the information we glean from the biological, threats and conservation maps we can more easily identify the key local, governmental and private sector actors that use natural resources within the landscape and that do or should define and enforce resource use policies and practices. Engaging this mix of actors in discussions to reconcile the needs of people with the needs of wildlife will help characterize those areas focused on economic development, those areas where wildlife conservation is the primary objective, and those areas where land-use policies and practices allow wildlife and people shared use of natural resources over the long-term. In this way, we can help establish the most appropriate mix and arrangement of actors and institutions to effect conservation and promote human welfare within each living landscape.

LIVING LANDSCAPES AS A MODEL FOR EFFECTIVE CONSERVATION

Regional planning is not a new idea. Neither is the use of zoning to attempt to capture a full range of economic, ecological and intrinsic values from different areas within the same region. What is different about the living landscapes approach to land management is that it explicitly takes into account the ecological needs of wildlife and the human activities that are direct or indirect threats to their long-term persistence. This counter-balances a history of land management that almost exclusively focused on meeting human needs for space and resources and provides, for the first time, a clear and rigorous assessment of how we might lessen the human footprint so that both people and wildlife can share the same living landscapes.

DAVID WILKIE
AMY VEDDER
KARL DIDIER

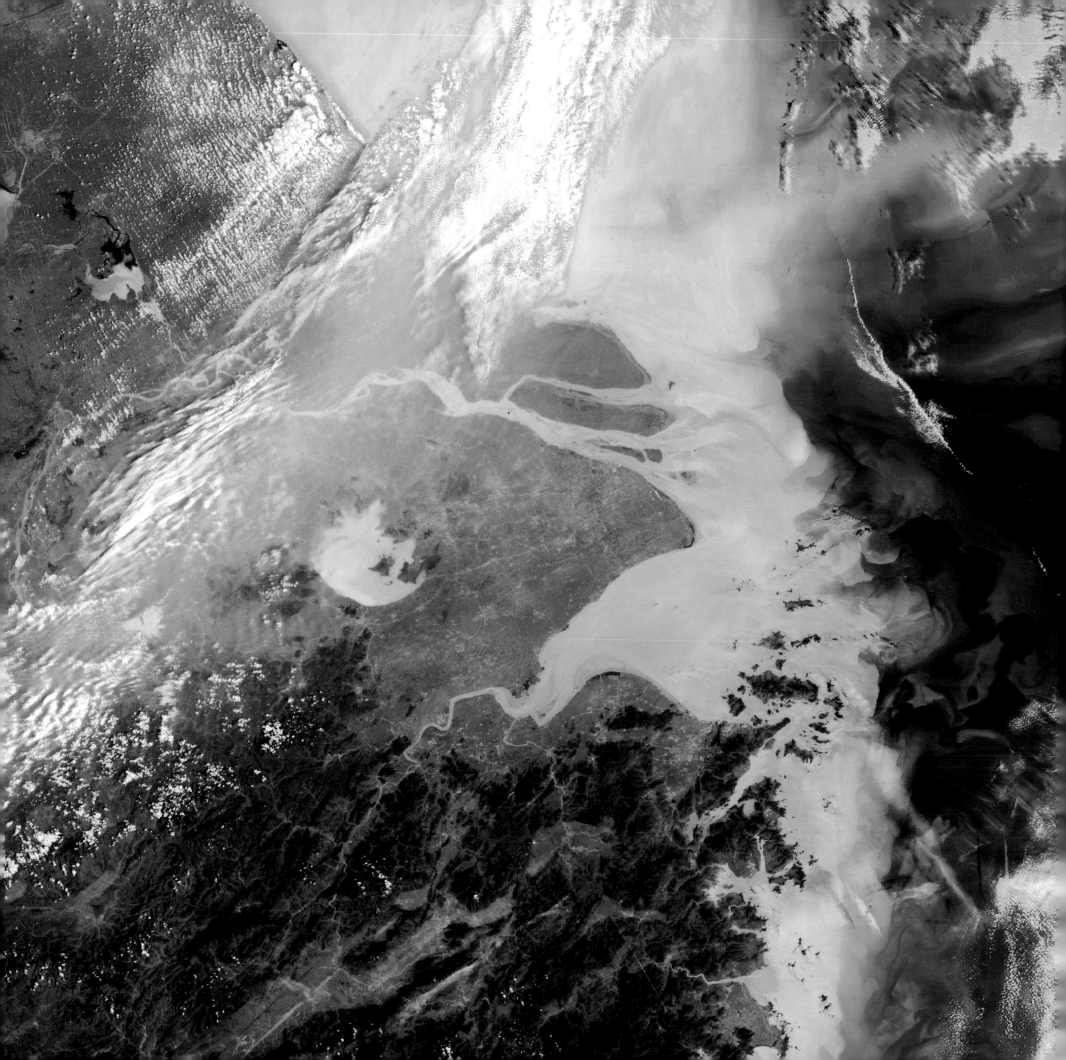

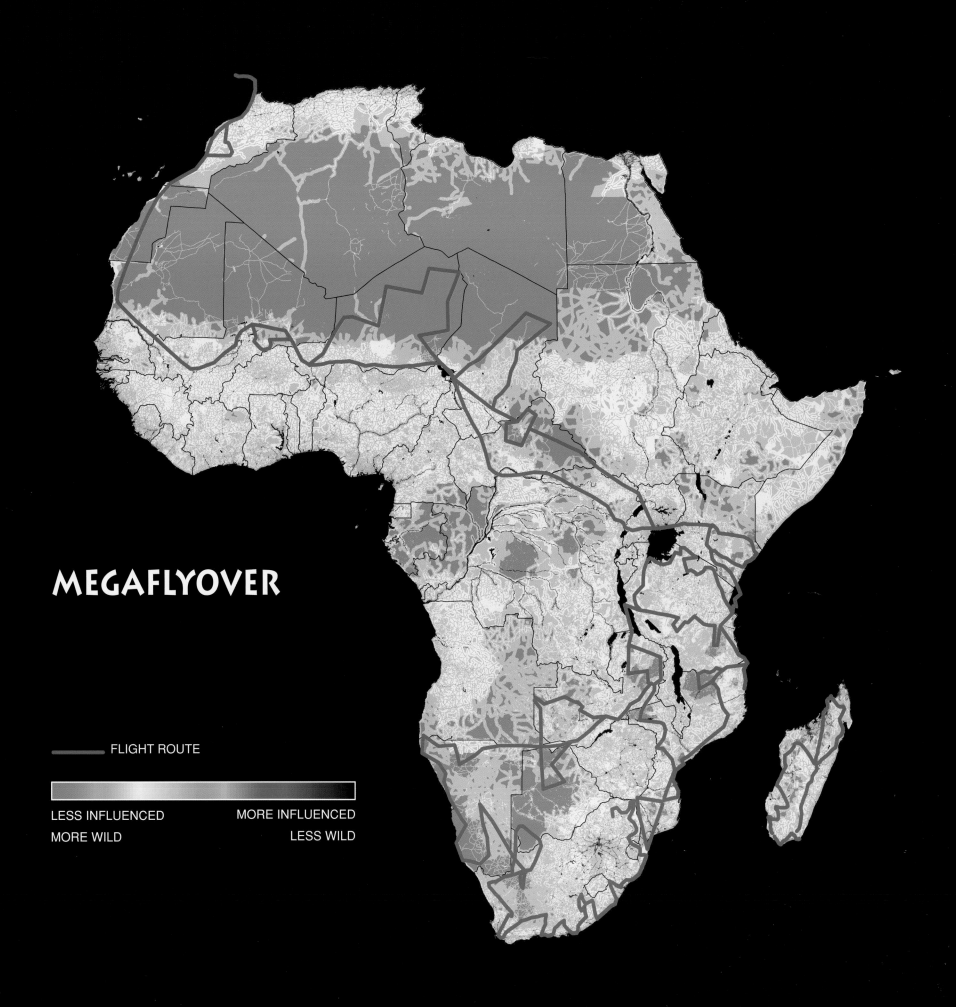

MEGAFLYOVER

FLIGHT ROUTE

LESS INFLUENCED   MORE INFLUENCED

MORE WILD   LESS WILD

AFRICA MEGAFLYOVER

When early European traders and explorers like David Living-stone and Richard Francis Burton visited Africa for the first time in the 19th century, they wrote home to a captive audience describing a mystical wild place of forests, lakes, rivers, and an abundance of animals—creating a vision of Africa as an ideal wilderness that appealed to the European imagination. The mental images they created formed the basis of perceptions about the continent that have perpetuated to some extent to this day (Adams and McShane 1992). When ecologist J. Michael Fay set out in his small Cessna plane in June 2004 from Cape Town, South Africa for a series of grueling flights that would take him across the continent, he sought to add a degree of clarity to the image of what the continent of Africa, in all its variations, cultures, and ecosystems, is today. By attaching a camera to the bottom of the plane, he was able to systematically document his seven-month journey from South Africa to Morocco, by snapping a photo every 20 seconds while en-route.

The purpose of the journey, dubbed Megaflyover, expressed at its core questions about the status of the natural world and human relationship to it. With support from the National Geographic and Wildlife Conservation Societies, Fay flew to the wildest place in each of Africa's ecosystems to better understand the nature of these wild places, assess the overall condition of each ecosystem, and document the status of wildlife throughout the continent. Using the human footprint as a guide to find the wildest places, we asked in particular what different levels of the human footprint mean for people and for wildlife, and whether the human footprint is indeed an accurate measure of human impact and ecosystem status.

At a time of unprecedented global environmental change, an assessment of what "wild" really means in today's world of the early 21st century, as opposed to the world of 50 or 100 years ago, is particularly compelling. In the past 60 years, the continent of Africa has experienced great change. The region's human population has increased exponentially, from 200 mil-

lion in 1950 to 900 million in 2005, reflecting global population growth (UN Population Division 2005). Globally, increasing human population has resulted in increasing pressure on the natural resource base, leading to the degradation or unsustainable use of fifteen ecosystem services, including water supply and purification, capture fisheries, and regulation of erosion (MA 2005). Such global changes are causing increasing hardship for many people (WRI 2005), while producing increasing conflict with wildlife for many of the same resources (Ceballos and Erlich 2002, Sitati et al. 2003, Van Dyke et al. 1986).

In Africa, many people continue to depend on the resources directly around them. This is in contrast to continents such as North America where resources used, while several times higher per capita than most places in Africa, is often displaced by hundreds or thousands of miles from the consumer (Wackernagel et al. 1997). For these reasons, developing an understanding of what "wild" and "not wild" are really like with reference to the human footprint dataset, which expresses local effects of human population and infrastructure on the surrounding landscape, is particularly interesting for this region.

PLANNING THE ROUTE AND COLLECTING INFORMATION

In the months leading up to the flight, the Megaflyover route was planned to include two major types of destinations: Wildest Place and Protected Area. Wildest Place destinations, or the wildest place in each of Africa's more than 100 ecoregions, were identified in a geographic information systems database (GIS) using the human influence index (Sanderson et al. 2002) in combination with the WWF ecoregions map (Olson et al. 2001). The human influence index assigns every square kilometer on earth to a particular human impact score on a scale of 0-60, and is composed of input layers that include land use, presence of power infrastructure, and distance to roads, population centers, railways, rivers, and coastlines. The planned route also identified more than 100 Protected Area destinations at the center of the largest protected area in each ecoregion.

To document his route, Fay attached a digital camera to a hole in the plane's floor and programmed it to snap a photo approximately every 20 seconds throughout the journey. By attaching his GPS to a laptop while en-route, Fay used GIS software to see his location in real-time with respect to the human footprint, the ecoregions, and his destinations. The result of the journey: Over 100 000 aerial photos documented with location, date, and time, taken in each of the continent's biomes and at every level of the human footprint.

OBSERVATIONS ABOUT
THE HUMAN FOOTPRINT IN AFRICA

Between June and December 2004, the small but tough Cessna aircraft enlisted for the journey carried Dr. Fay and his small crew to 25 countries, 74 ecoregions in 8 biomes, more than 200 protected areas, and across the full gradient of human influence, affording new insights about the continent never before possible. This allowed an objective comparison of different levels of the human footprint to actual features on the ground for all regions of Africa.

Consistent with expectations, the Megaflyover photos reveal a strong relationship between human influence features seen on the ground and human footprint value. For example, as human footprint scores increase, so do evidence of roads, buildings, and power infrastructure revealed by the photos. At the same time, a landscape that is largely "natural," or lacking visible human land uses, at the lowest human footprint scores shows a gradual shift to larger percentages agriculture at intermediate levels of the human footprint, to predominantly urban areas at the highest human footprint levels. These patterns vary between biomes, based on an ecosystem's capacity to support agriculture or other human land uses.

Although actual signs of human impact are more likely to be seen at higher levels of the human footprint, it is important to note that even "natural" areas are visible at these same levels. We interpret this to mean that maintenance and restoration of habitat for wildlife and ecosystem services for people are still possible even at moderate to high levels of the human footprint. At the lowest level of the human footprint, however, the photos reveal an area that is predominantly without infrastructure or intensive land use, confirming the utility of the human footprint for identifying the world's wildest places.

While the Megaflyover photos revealed some expected rela-

tionships with the human footprint, other findings were more surprising. One of the most intriguing findings is that the "wildest places" as depicted by the human footprint do not necessarily harbor the largest numbers of "wildlife." In Africa, many of the wildest places remain so because they are uninhabitable to both humans and wildlife due to unfavorable climate, soil, or disease. The Sahara Desert, for example, which is the largest wild area in Africa, has soil and climactic conditions unfavorable for agriculture; however, these same conditions unfavorable for humans are also unfavorable for most wildlife. The result of this phenomenon is that wildlife and people tend to compete for land at intermediate levels of the human footprint.

While some areas in Africa remain wild because of uninhabitable conditions, other areas remain wild because of war. These war-torn wildlands, however, do not necessarily harbor large numbers of wildlife. Such is the case in northeast Central African Republic, Africa's green heart, where tropical forests and climate could naturally support thousands of elephants. In actuality, however, rampant poaching has created a virtual desert for wildlife. Northeast Zambia, by contrast, has a much higher human footprint score but also much more wildlife. These observations suggest that even in areas with high human footprint scores, it is possible to manage resources and have policies that favor wildlife. Indeed, cultural attitudes and political climate may be even more important for predicting wildlife presence than overall levels of human impact as measured by the human footprint.

The Megaflyover study found very little total area continent-wide to have visible wildlife, in contrast to the virtual Eden described by early explorers (Adams and McShane 1992). Indeed, when the full set of Megaflyover images were randomly sampled for wildlife, only 1.4% of the images had wildlife. Noticeably, all of the images with wildlife were located in protected areas, although Fay only flew over protected areas 25% of the time. This result suggests that protected areas tend to be better predictors of wildlife presence, regardless of human footprint score, than human footprint score alone. It is not clear from this observation why this phenomenon occurs: Whether because protected areas are placed in areas already favored by wildlife, in areas of low human population, whether properly managed protected areas simply work, or for all of these reasons. An exception to this finding is in war-torn areas where protected area boundaries have little meaning, and where wildlife management is not feasible despite potentially low levels of human infrastructure and population. Regardless of these variations, we can still conclude from this result that protected areas are

good predictors of wildlife across the gradient of human influence.

While the photos gathered during Megaflyover were crucial for assessing the status of places still capable of supporting wildlife, the photos have a parallel value to assess the quality of ecosystems for continuing to support people's livelihoods. In many parts of Africa, natural resource use is at its maximum and some ecosystems are starting to collapse, affecting both humans and wildlife. Such is the case in the Usangu watershed in Tanzania, where the Ruaha river provides a source of water and food for cattle populations, rice farming, wildlife in Ruaha National Park and associated tourism income, and electrical power for the country. In recent years, water mismanagement, wetland degradation and desertification, and drought have left the Ruaha river dry throughout much of the year, ultimately affecting the power source for two-thirds of the country located at the downstream reservoir (Coppolillo *et al.* 2006). These and other examples demonstrate the importance of intact ecosystems for both humans and wildlife.

The legacy of Megaflyover is a photographic catalogue of a continent of diverse, often vast, ecosystems undergoing unprecedented change. Here, we find a place where levels of the human footprint are consistent with human infrastructure and land uses, but where "wildlands" do not necessarily mean "wildlife." Instead, we find that protected areas are sometimes, but not always, better predictors of wildlife presence than overall levels of human influence as expressed by the human footprint. We find that cultural and political attitudes towards wildlife are key to conserving them, and that with good planning and management, countries like Zambia and South Africa can maintain large populations of wildlife despite high levels of human influence. We find that many ecosystems are nonetheless degraded, offering little hope for supporting livelihoods of people or wildlife populations. Without a doubt, good natural resource management and land use planning are key to the land where people and wildlife can continue to co-exist.

JESSICA L. FORREST
J. MICHAEL FAY
ERIC W. SANDERSON
WILLANDIA CHAVES DIDIER

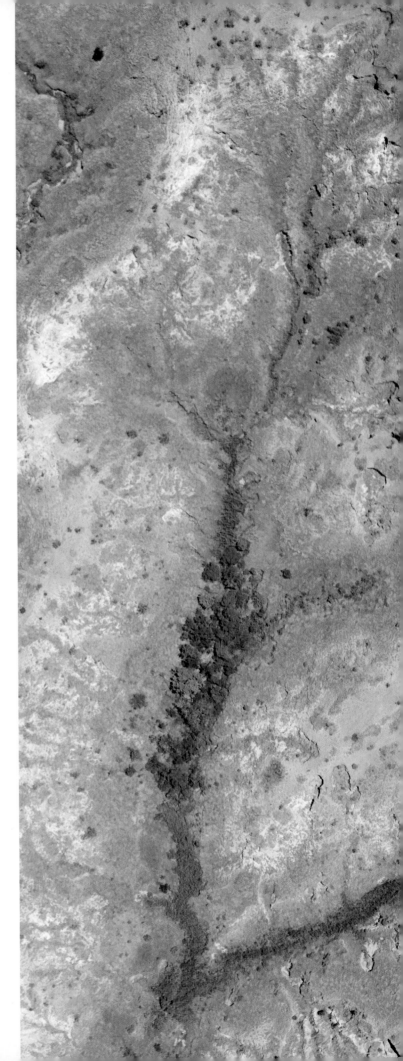

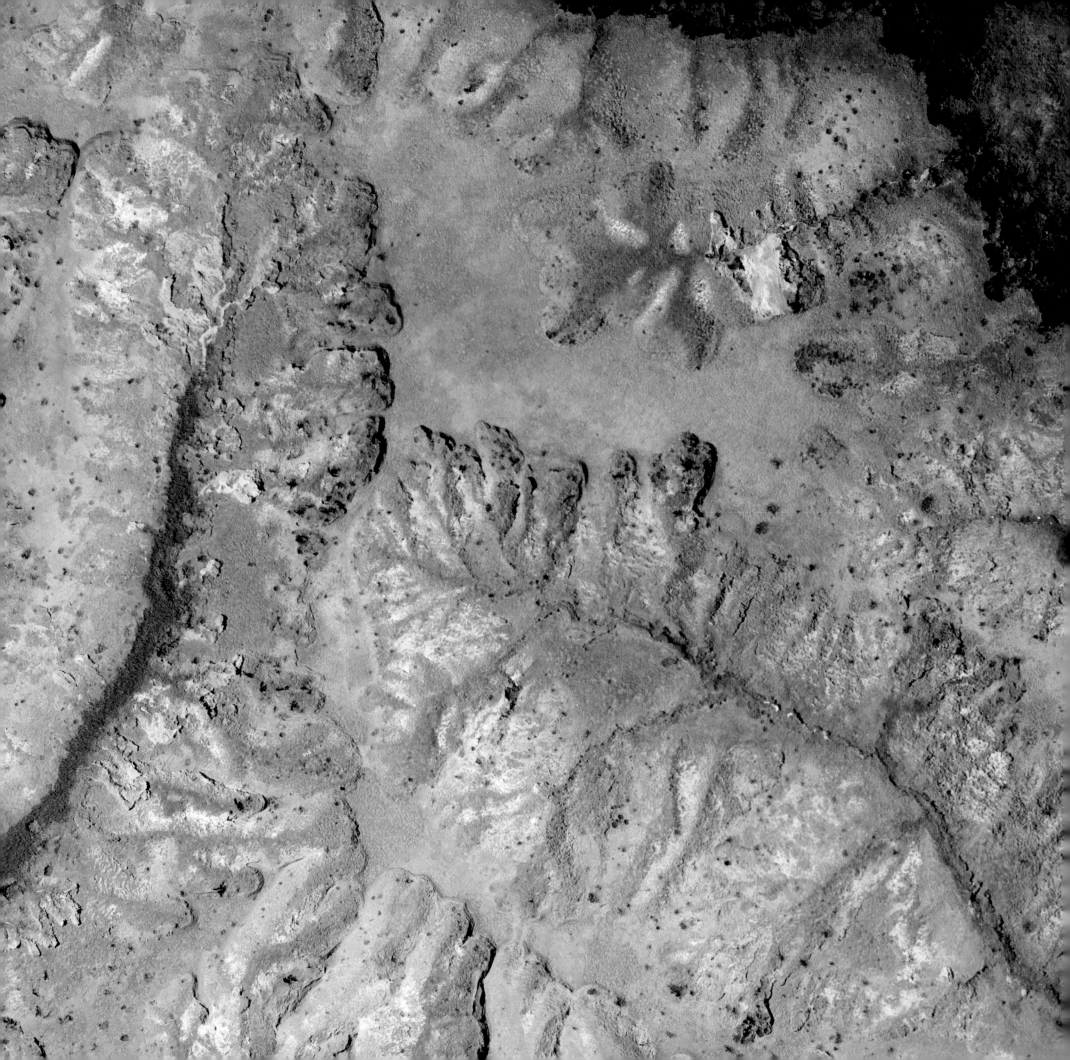

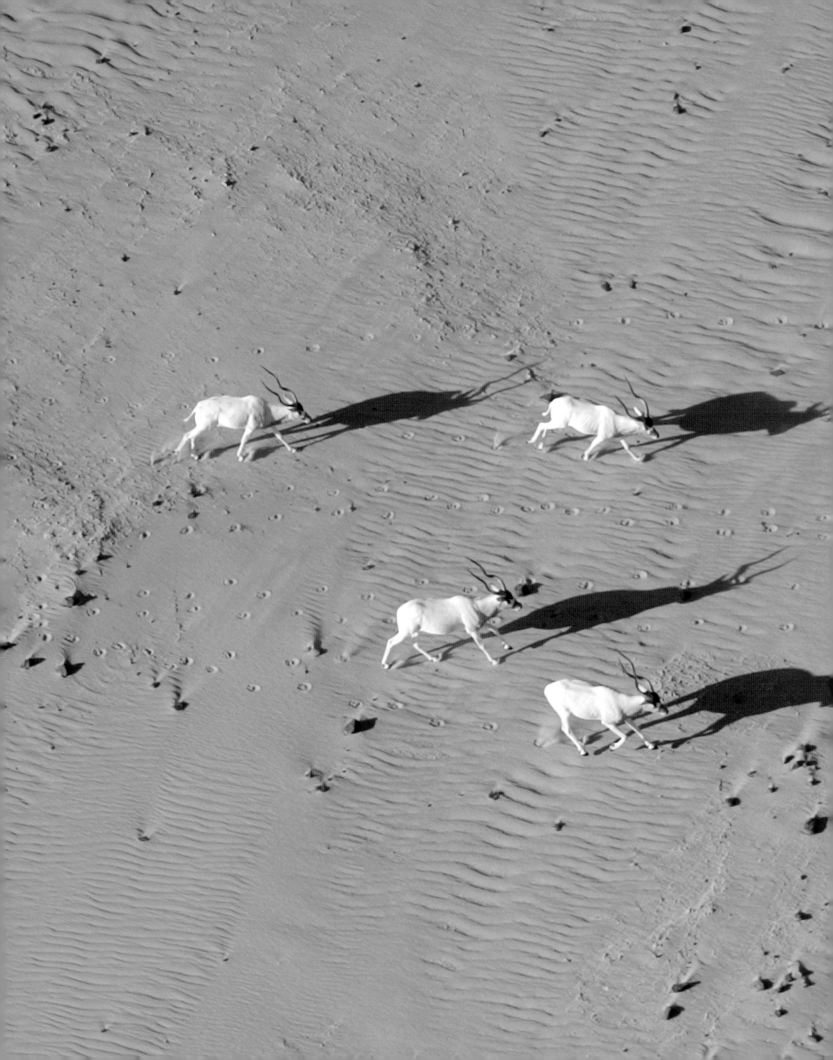

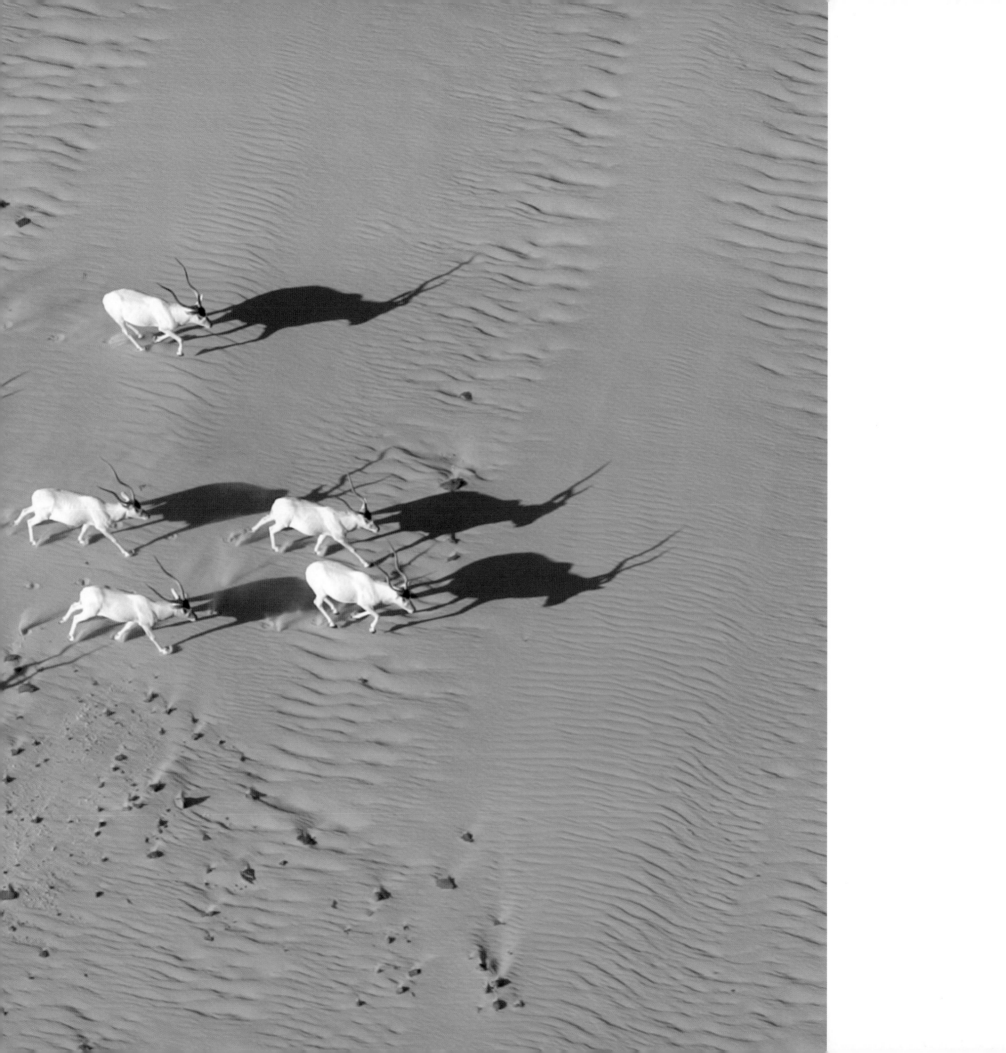

THE LAST OF THE WILD

FOUR REASONS TO PRESERVE WILDERNESS

God's Grandeur

The world is charged with the grandeur of God.
It will flame out, like shining from shook foil;
It gathers to a greatness, like the ooze of oil
Crushed. Why do men then now not reck his rod?
Generations have trod, have trod, have trod;
And all is seared with trade; Bleared, smeared with toil;
And wears man's smudge and shares man's smell: the soil
Is bare now, nor can foot feel, being shod.
And for all this, nature is never spent;
There lives the dearest freshness deep down things;
And though the last lights off the black West went
Oh, morning, at the brown brink eastward, springs—
Because the Holy Ghost over the bent
World broods with warm breast and with ah! bright wings.

GERARD MANLEY HOPKINS (1844-1889)

Why is it that so many people no longer care about the wild? After all, human beings are a species that has daily contact with wild places, plants and wildlife, and it has only been in the last 500 years (essentially only the last 100) that most people—at least in the developed world—have separated themselves from wild things. Do we really forget so quickly?

In order to give the reader a clear parting message, this book ends with personal perspectives from four of the co-authors. As you have read in these pages, the human footprint is incessant-ly striding across our planet with the suffering natural world increasingly underfoot. But it is not too late to correct our path, soften our tread and tidy our trail. What it takes is personal commitment; the individual and the institutions that answer to them are the key. Our personal choices will fuel the process of change. We urge each of you to reflect on the information in this book, to understand the situation we are all creating and to com-mit to the changes you know we must make if the wild is to be recovered and if wild nature is to reclaim its place in our world.

I remember as a boy how much pleasure I took from running with my cousins round my grandparents' old cabin in the Colorado Mountains. My grandma would kick us out of the cabin at breakfast and tell us not to come back until we heard the bell ring; peace and quiet for her, and a 40-acre playground for us with a shady pine forest, hot southerly hillsides and the white columns of aspens with thick grass to roll around in. It wasn't even that wild. You could drive to it. The fish were stocked each spring by truck. Over the years, my grandparents put in electricity, then a phone, then a satellite dish. The wolves and the grizzly bear were gone and so were the periodical fires that used to burn the meadows. There were cattle down the road, up the hill in the national forest and around and over the next mountain. There were Texans too, in their RVs. Across the valley, there was the non-stop echo of big trucks heading up the highway to the pass. Even so, that place, faraway from my regular suburban home, sheltered me for a few weeks each summer and became the place that I still return to when I need to remember what's important in life: Family, nature and a sense of joy. It was a wild place and it was important to me because of the trees and flowers and animals that I knew there.

Now I live in New York City and I know there's nature here too. I like to think of the cityscape in natural terms, like speaking in a different language. Sometimes for me, I see the city streets as big, unusually flat, rock outcrops capping the ground. They keep the mud down and they are great for running and jumping (also, for wheels to roll on), but they leave so little soil showing. The plants must suffer from a lack of room. The sewers are streams, and I still like to watch the water run down the side of the rock-lined streets, rushing as fast as it can into a hole in the ground. I know at the other end of the magic hole there is our answer to wetlands: The sewage treatment plant. At night, I like to think about all the lights downtown, so bright they fill misty skies with a twilight all their own, and the horns and sirens that have replaced the frog calls. I think it must be tough for an owl that flies silently in the dark, listening all the time.

New York City scores 98-100 on the human footprint. It has a lot of human influence. My grandma's cabin scores about 15. That's a lot less. In my job at the Wildlife Conservation Society, which operates from the Bronx Zoo, sometimes I'm lucky enough to visit places that score less than 5, even a few times all the way to zero. I have seen some of the wildest places on Earth and they inspire me time and again.

Why do I care about the last of the wild? I could tell you it is because those places are beautiful (because they are), because they are valuable (because they are), because we don't have a right to destroy them (because we don't.) But the real reason is that it is good for us to let something be. We don't need to leave our footprints on everything. We do need to learn to live within bounds. Let us leave the last of the wild unspoiled.

ERIC W. SANDERSON

I f you read the newspapers about the U.S./Mexico border issues, you could rightly assume that the world has gone mad: Expanded, highly-armed border patrols; illegal immigrants left to die in the desert by their "coyotes" (guides); volunteer "Minutemen" on the frontier; mile-wide "sterilization zones" and impenetrable walls. This is certainly another type of human footprint, and an especially ugly one. And all of this takes place in the Chihuahuan Desert, one of the world-recognized biodiversity "hotspots" and a very important, highly-threatened refuge for wild nature. One could also easily assume that we have, indeed, forgotten our wild roots.

Here's a wholly different perspective. I arrived in Monterrey, Mexico, last week direct from Africa, where our group of associated organizations—The WILD Network—had had serious, tough discussions on how to continue our decades-old, wilderness trail program that has positively affected so many people. Mexico was my next stop. There, I was privileged to participate in and help facilitate one of the most ambitious and important conservation projects in the world: The El Carmen-Big Bend Corridor Initiative. This trans-boundary project between northeast Mexico and Texas involves a host of players: National and state governments, ranchers, *ejidatarios* (communal land farmers), many conservation organizations (local and international), a major international corporation (CEMEX), and others. Its vision is as inspirational as it is practical and achievable: 10 million hectares (25 million acres) of conservation land under many different ownership regimes, yet with designated core-wilderness zones, re-wilding work well underway and expanding, plus funding on tap to purchase more land, to train local communities, and to create eco-friendly tourism infrastructure. Maybe the world is not as mad as it seems.

I was met at Monterrey airport by Rafael García Zuazua, a man in his early fifties who had just recently left the iron industry to work as a professional volunteer for Agrupación Sierra Madre, a central player in this Corridor Initiative. He will monitor reintroduced pronghorn antelope, work with networks of ranchers and *ejidatarios*, and will—he said with some passion—do anything else required. He had a vehicle, already donated, to help him negotiate the vast Chihuahuan Desert landscape, and was trying hard to raise funding to secure his position. Funded or not, he was on the job. But there's more to his story.

Before we had even cleared the airport, Rafael exuberantly told me he had walked in the African wilderness on one of our programs some 35 years ago. He burst into descriptions about people, places and habitat. I remarked on how well he remembered minute details of that time in Africa. He simply said, *That experience changed my life. That is why now, in 2006, I am very clear on what I must do for conservation.*

Rafael's words, uttered as the soft, early morning sun slanted across the airport and the garrulous, great-tailed grackles chattered away in the trees planted around the car park, are etched in my mind. His experience in Africa many years ago, its relationship to me and its impact on this current initiative in Mexico was "synchronicity" in the finest style.

This experience changed my life… is the phrase that appears over and over again in the thousands of reports we've received from people who have trekked our wilderness trails in Africa. Since 1965, some 45 000 people of all ages, races, and from all walks of life have walked with us in small groups in the Imfolozi, St. Lucía or other wilderness areas. They've slept under the African stars, watched the hippo fight in the rivers, heard the hyena moan, the elephant trumpet and the lion roar. At some point during this experience, often after their first night-watch around the campfire where they have the responsibility of guarding the camp while others sleep, most of them remark simply, *This feels like home.*

Yes, it is home. Aren't we genetically imprinted by wild nature? Millions of years of evolution in the open savannahs, verdant forests and vast, wild landscapes have left us indelibly marked. It may appear that we have forgotten this as we rush into decisions with values more immediately influenced by the most recent few years of industrial development: A mere blink of an eye in our evolutionary history.

But can we actually forget the wild? Or are we just sleeping and in need of a wake-up call? Today, humankind cannot afford to lie in bed much longer.

This experience changed my life… affirms that we cannot forget; and the wake-up call of the wilderness can rouse us from our materialistic dream and reorient us as to our role as stewards of wild landscapes and our fellow wild creatures. *This experience changed my life* also affirms the power of the individual and evokes the question: *What can I do?* The ensuing activity starts with a feeling, is structured by ideas and information, fueled by emotion, and continues as imaginative, long-term, committed work. Piece by piece, step by step, each wilderness can be protected, each area re-wilded, each policy crafted and implemented. It's a complex and daunting task, requiring all our professionalism and all our volunteerism. Then sometimes, the steps gather themselves into a vision, the players unite, something as daring and beneficial as the El Carmen-Big Bend Corridor begins to grow and nature's voice is our own voice once again.

VANCE G. MARTIN

When we think about large pristine landscapes, wilderness areas untouched by human activities, it is easy to forget that many of these wild places are often the home of people who, for millennia, have walked with lighter feet in the wild. In many of the most remote and inaccessible corners of our planet, indigenous peoples still follow traditional lifestyles and eke out their livings in great intimacy with nature. In some places, these indigenous nations are the last line of defense between what we call development and our planet's last remaining wilderness. They haven't forgotten the wild! Their efforts are as inspirational and important as they are difficult.

For example, take the case of the Kayapó indigenous nation of the Brazilian Amazon. I was recently a member of a small party of conservation leaders, journalists, film-makers and photographers invited to a large "leadership summit", whose main objective was the unification of this tribal nation to stand up and speak out for the protection of their territory: A vast 30 million acre indigenous reserve in the southern Amazon.

The village of Piaraçu, on the southern fringe of the Kayapó Indigenous Reserve, was the stage for this week-long meeting in which 200 chiefs and warriors discussed the Brazilian government's project to build several hydro-electric dams on the Xingú River and its main tributary, the Iriří. These two rivers and a hundred other smaller tributaries are critical to the survival of the Kayapó.

This meeting was the largest gathering ever of Kayapó leaders, and it was the culmination of years of tribal organization and political alliance-building to form a united front comprising all the peoples of the Xingú Valley, both indigenous and otherwise, whose livelihoods are threatened by the proposed dams and other forms of environmentally destructive development. The first step towards this grand diplomatic scheme was to mend strained relations, end old tribal feuds and build new trust within other indigenous groups in the Xingú region. This was accomplished by means of sustained leadership and diplomacy over several years and through the creation of alliances with non-indigenous settlers in the region, who are also opposed to the dams. It is through this unified front that the plan to mount a large demonstration against the dam scheme is being formed.

Other subjects of discussion included the denouncing of increased pollution of the Xingú River by massive soy bean plantations, cattle ranching and the clearance of large areas of forest near the tributaries of the river. The chiefs demanded that the state regulate these activities to prevent the degradation of the riverine ecosystem on which their survival depends. Finally, the concern about increased insecurity of their territorial boundaries was widely discussed. Invasions of Kayapó areas have peaked in intensity and this has forced the tribal communities to take decisive action, even resorting to violence in order to keep the intruders at bay. The most important of these actions has been the establishment of guard posts along the borders of Kayapó territories. Each community has taken responsibility for the section of the border that passes through its area of the reserve and men have been deployed to stand guard and sound the alarm when invasions take place.

Megaron Txukarramãe's, the main leader of the Kayapó nation, closed the meeting by saying: *We Mebegokre Kayapó are aware that the problems that threaten the lives of our communities in the Xingú Valley also threaten other peoples, both indigenous and Brazilian, who also live in the valley. The solution to these problems, which will effectively protect our river and our forest, forms part of a common struggle that we share with all the peoples of the Xingú Valley. Now, following the successful conclusion of the meeting held by all of our own communities, we are entering the next stage of our struggle to form an alliance among all the peoples of the Valley of the Xingú to save our river from dams, pollution and all kinds of destructive development, and to promote alternative forms of production using the capabilities of our local communities to exploit sustainable resources. We call on all the inhabitants of the Xingú Valley to join us in a great demonstration in Altamira against the Belo Monte dam, and the other dams that Eletronorte wants to build throughout our valley, and in favor of the protection and development of our own productive capabilities, our cultures and communities.*

The response to this statement was the victory chant of 200 chiefs and warriors, all beautifully decorated in black and red body paint, feather headdresses and bead necklaces, brandishing their war clubs—from which they're inseparable—in a scene reminiscent of what the Great Plains tribes of the United States must have looked like 200 hundred years ago.

The culmination of the meeting was the creation of a new ritual to strengthen the leadership lines not just down from elders to younger chiefs, but among all the villages. Anthropologist and Kayapó expert, Dr. Terence Turner, who was invited to the summit to witness, record and produce a report on the findings, points out that an indigenous nation's response of this type (political and cultural) to threats made by the dominant governing society demonstrates new possibilities for resistance and self-empowerment by relatively marginal, "weak" peoples. The Kayapó have been able to create a new opposition model that highlights their social and cultural differences and use them as the basis for a brilliant diplomacy that has achieved the support of certain sectors of the government. Furthermore, it has created successful alliances with national and international social movements and organizations and sends a clear message to the government: The Kayapó are ready to use organized social disruption and, if all else fails, even armed struggle, to protect their territory.

It is clear that the Kayapó are brilliant marketers and advocates of their own cause. They know how to successfully gain access to and effectively use national and international electronic and print media. From video and television to print and photo-journalism, they have created an effective network of national and international communications within and among non-governmental organizations and have used them as powerful "weapons of the weak."

When I arrived in Piaraçu I was not sure what my role at this whole meeting would be, but as our small airplane circled one last time over the village in a noisy farewell, I knew exactly why I had been invited to photograph the Kayapó Leadership Summit: To bring their story and their images to the public and to do so in a manner that both dignifies their struggle and efforts, and harnesses support to their cause. Indigenous communities can be great advocates for the conservation of their own territories, and the exemplary case of the Kayapó fills me with hope for the last of the wild and the indigenous people that call it home.

CRISTINA G. MITTERMEIER

I believe that peace of mind is difficult to find in this troubled world, but it is without doubt one of our most important quests, for anxiety—its opposite—leads us into a life of uncertainty and unease.

I find peace in wild, open spaces. The natural world is to me as a temple is to those who have faith. On occasion it does not come upon me immediately; it takes me up to six or seven days to be able to leave the urban life of the likes of Mexico City behind.

I am deeply nostalgic about my early trips to undisturbed places. I used to backpack into the Sierra Madre with my brothers and friends. In those days, more than peace of mind, my spirit was nourished by the unknown, by freedom and my first authentic encounters with the natural world. We would use maps to locate places where there were no roads or trails: No ways through. We were attracted by the absence of humans. In the space of seven or eight days, we would cross several canyons and sleep under the stars. In the most remote parts, my thought processes changed radically. I became much more aware of the danger of an accident or a possible encounter with a snake. Each sip of water was the best of my life; everything was simplified, and the basics of life, like breathing, drinking, eating and resting took on a new dimension. On every trip I discovered myself and my life changed radically.

On one of those trips into the Sierra Madre heartlands of Chihuahua, we came across some very large canid footprints—four and a half inches—, no doubt the tracks of one of the last Mexican wolves. At the time, I did not give the find any great importance. This sub-species has been hunted practically into extinction in Mexico and the south-east of the United States and current efforts to reintroduce this animal into its former territory face a great dilemma: How to find large spaces, with an abundance of prey, where they can roam free without interference from man. But today, few areas have these characteristics.

The wolf is a very significant animal for man, not just because of the lifelong animosity between them, but because of the spirit it represents: Pristine ecosystems with little human presence.

I have to admit that the first time I saw a wolf in the wild, it did not come up to my longstanding expectations of the species. The context of the sighting was somewhat unfortunate, even though it took place in a truly remarkable place like the Denali National Park in Alaska. I found myself in a bus full of tourists, of whom I was, regrettably, but one more. Excitement suddenly broke out on board as a lone wolf was spotted on the road a scant few meters from the bus; its nearness and the lack of warning had taken us by surprise. The telemetry collar hanging from the animal's neck made it look more like a dog, which I found unsettling and it made me wonder whether that first encounter could be counted as a sighting of a totally wild wolf.

Fortunately, my work as a conservationist and photographer has enabled me to travel to many other corners of the planet, to places where the human footprint has not left its mark. My second sighting of a wolf in the wild came in the Tian Shan Mountains, on the border between Kazakhstan and China. Once again, it was a solitary wolf that scared away a herd of Asian ibex that I was trying to photograph; and once again, its presence was too brief to be enjoyed.

You can never be sure what you will see when searching for wild animals. It is patience, and perhaps a little luck, that finally gives you the opportunity to witness something outstanding. In the summer of 2004, my wife and I went back to the Northwest Territories of Canada to see the annual caribou migration. During the last days of out trip, we took an amphibious aircraft across the Nunavut border, the northernmost province, in search of one of the great herds. From the air, numerous trails zigzagged around small and large lakes: Ancient trails, worn into the Canadian tundra over the years by hundreds of thousands of caribous. At dusk, the pilot set us down on the edge of a large lake where one of the herds would probably cross. We walked about two kilometers, picking up the pace so as not to miss the chance to see the heard cross. As we drew close, we saw that the animals were hesitant to go into the water. All of a sudden, as one the caribous began to run in circles. To our surprise, a white wolf had sparked off the stampede; the earth rumbled under the hooves of thousands of animals. It was ten at night and the twilight at that latitude was such that night practically never fell.

Three more wolves appeared and caused the caribous to run towards a little rocky outcrop, probably with the hope that one individual would break a leg. Eventually, they managed it; a hurt young male broke away from the herd and sought refuge in the depths of the lake. It endured the freezing water all night. The wolves paid it no heed and concentrated on chasing some of the young who had become separated from their mothers in the midst of all the confusion. We were slowly caught up in the action. A calf skidded to a halt a scant five meters away from us and took off again; the young wolf in pursuit ran round us once and then got on with the chase. Three hours later, the herd finally decided to cross the lake. On the far side, they found another pack of wolves waiting. Through my telescope, I witnessed the frontal attack of a wolf on a young caribou: A quick attack that brought the animal down alive. Then the wolf disappeared in what was clearly a strategic move, the idea being to cripple as many caribous as possible in order to return later to feed. Thus, the sustenance of the pack was guaranteed for several weeks, even months, to be ready for the next winter.

In our hurry, we had neither brought clothes nor food from the plane. We could never have imagined that we would witness a wolf attack on the herd, let alone that it would last all night and to end at daybreak with a concert of howls. We spent several hours besieged by an enormous number of mosquitoes and whipped by an intense, cold wind which eventually forced us to leave. This unfortunate turn of events did nothing to spoil the experience. I have no words to describe each minute of the drama acted out by the wolves and the caribous. In fact, I do not have a single decent photo of what happened, mainly because the light was very poor; I am actually thankful for that since it enabled me simply to enjoy the spectacle as a mere spectator without having to worry about the focus, the exposure and changing the film.

There is no doubt that that experience was one of the most memorable moments of my life: Such an experience enriches your life and gives it meaning. It could not have happened under other circumstances; so many things had to come together at the same time—my wife, the remoteness of the place, the wild, the wolves, their voices and their looks, the large number of prey, the drama, the fear, death, the cold, the wind, the darkness, the light— for the experience to touch the depths of my soul, to remind me that we, mankind, are also connected to the earth and that in these rituals we discover our roots and our very nature.

It is these experiences that breathe life back into me and enable me, on my return to the whirlpool of civilization, to close my eyes and rediscover peace. What would become of our spirit if these worlds only existed in tales, in descriptions of the past?

Patricio Robles Gil

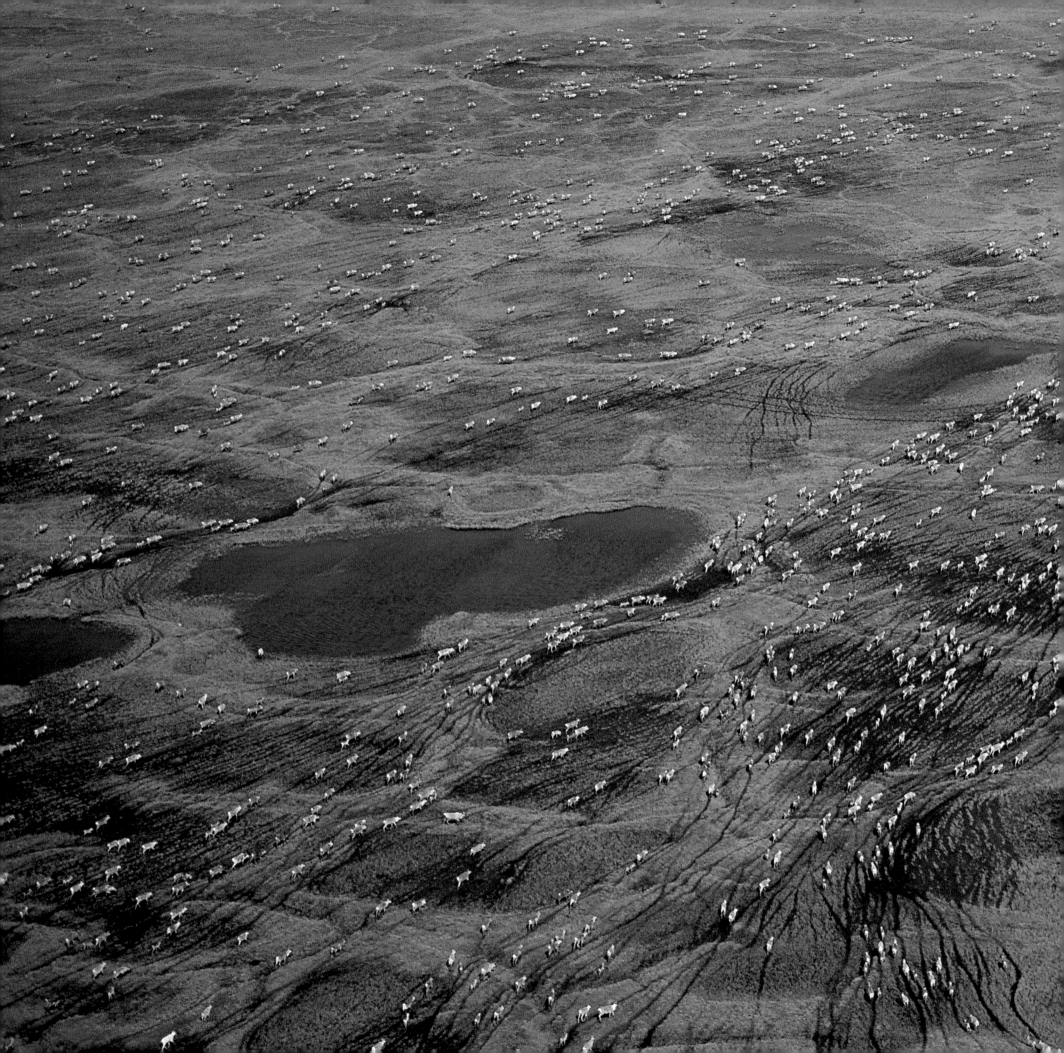

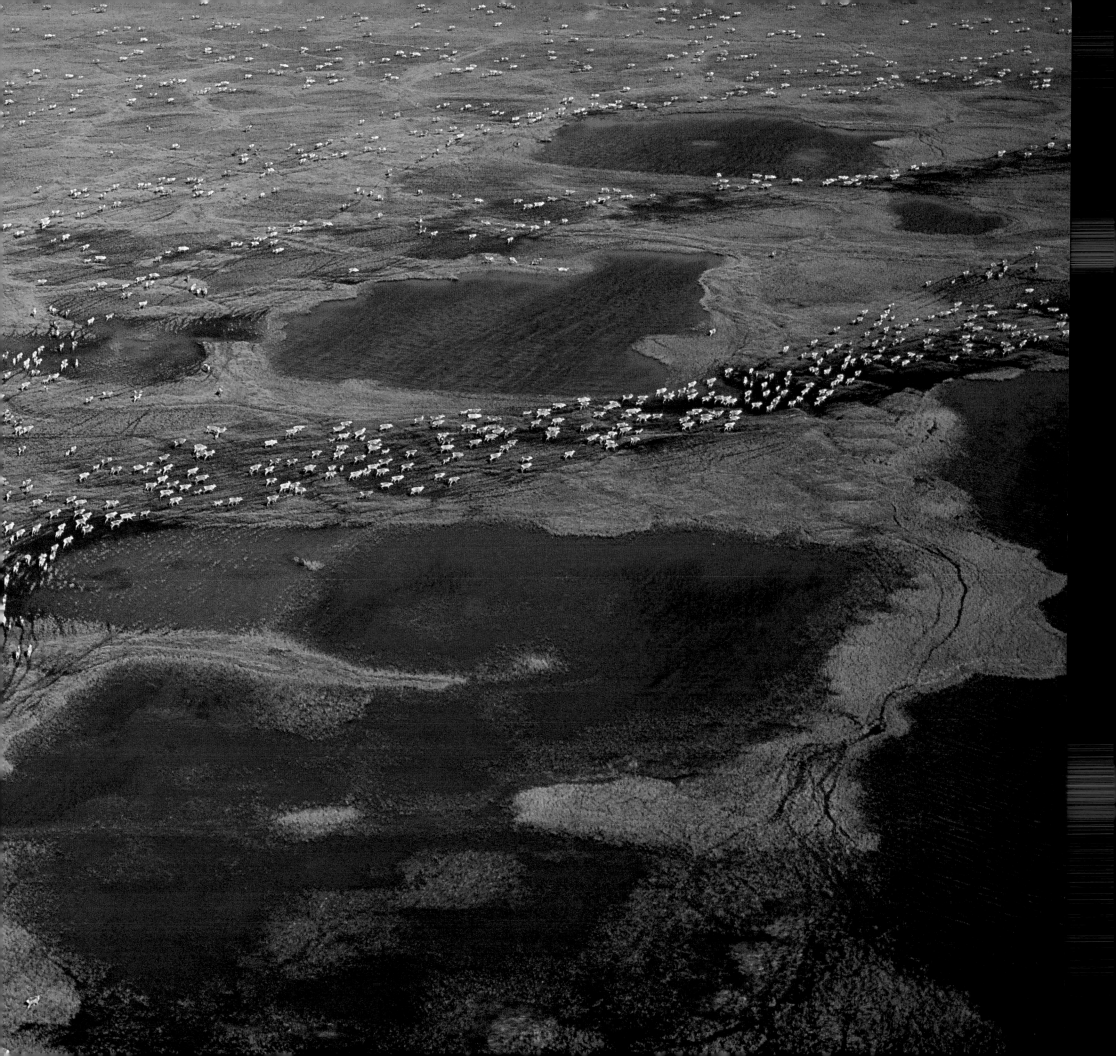

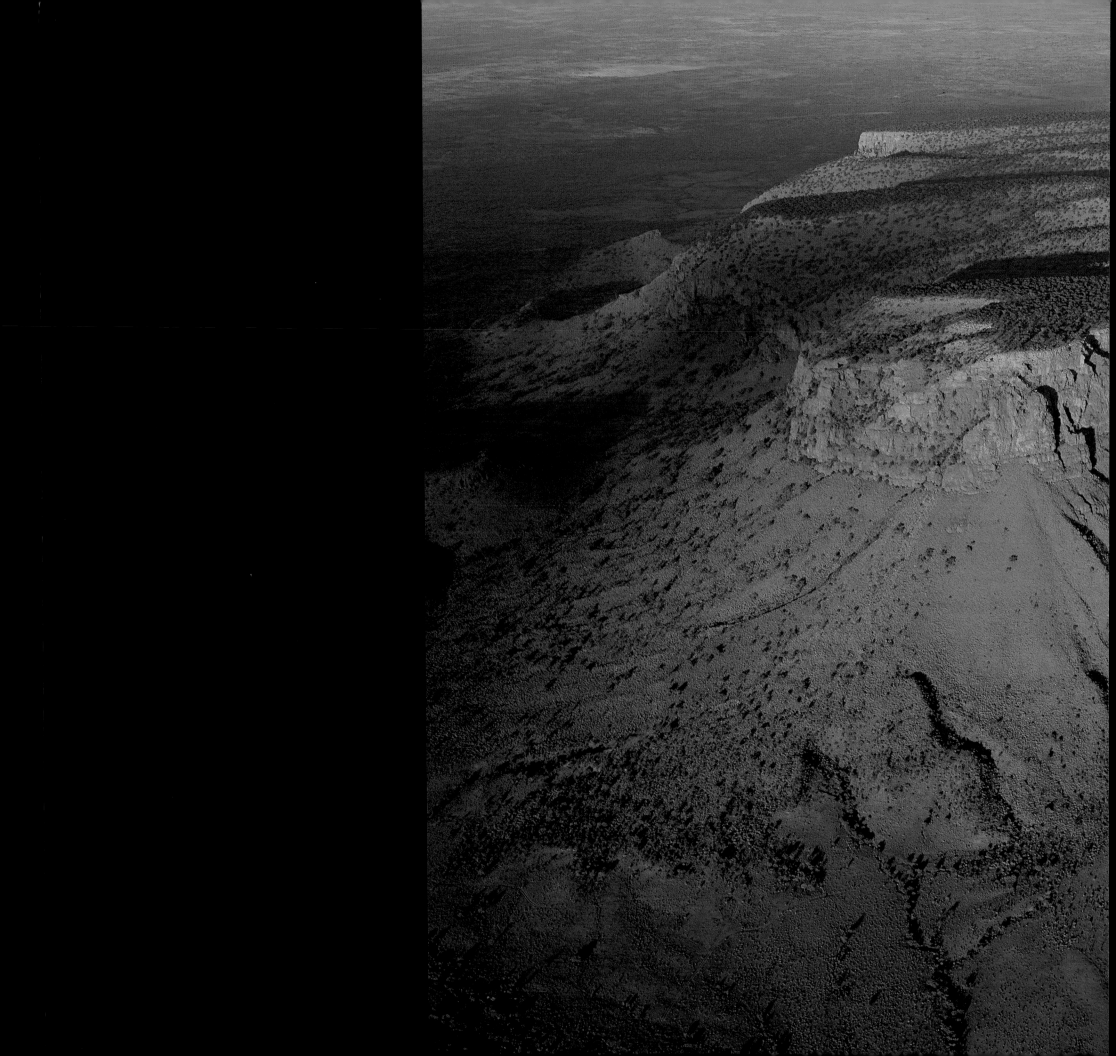

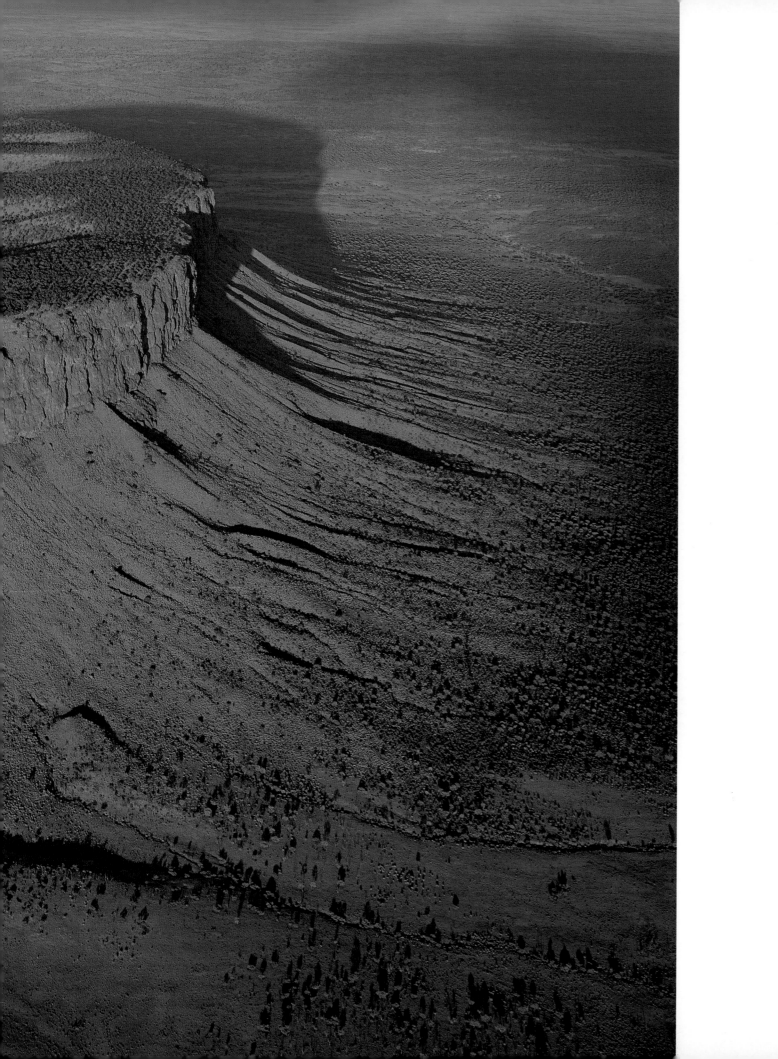

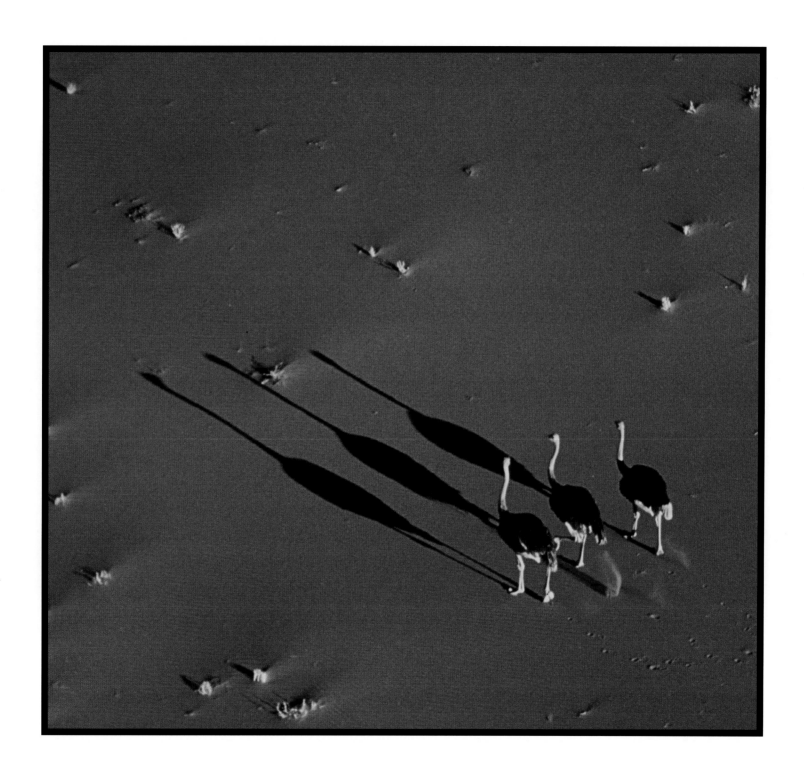

If you telescope time and look back at the expansion of the human footprint in Africa, it has ten...
...sions, epitomized by the elephant's shrinking habitat. People over the last 50 years have invaded f...
...areas, cleared forests, stripped pastures and soils, polluted waters and hastened desertification. Hum...
...n hamlets, villages, towns, cities and mega-cities have acquired a relentless exponential trajectory,...
...nent as a whole has moved from a state of under-population to over-population. It is a familiar litany a...
...et and, in Africa, one measure is the changing status of elephants.

Nevertheless, elephants and other large mammals have survived better in Africa than elsewhere. ...
...was the elephants' greatest threat in the 1970s and 1980s, and cost Africa an estimated half of its ele...
...two decades. Exploitation for ivory diminished after the international 1990 CITES ban on ivory and,...
...definitely still supported at least 402 000 and maybe as many as 650 000 elephants, inhabiting sava...
...forests, wetlands and bushveld. This compares with about one tenth the number in Asia. Destructive...
...could still emerge from newly affluent countries like China that, on a whim of fashion, could r...
...remaining elephant populations in Africa and Asia, but, for now, loss of habitat and growing conflic...
...ng human populations are the main issues.

However, elephants are versatile survivors that give hope for the future of wildife in Africa. Over the a...
...endured catastrophes and weathered countless shifts of climate and habitat. Because of their intellig...
...often stave off population regulation as they vote with their feet for safe places. This may cause loc...
...tion but is often caused by compression by man. They recognize safe places, become stealthy and...
...hide in dense habitats.

By contrast, where mankind's activities are benign, elephants become extraordinarily habituate...
...window to their sentient way of life. Ecotourism nurtured by elephants can provide a supplementar...
...those human beings sharing their range by providing critical political support. Where elephants...
...species can also thrive.

Elephants have a potent grip on the human imagination that may yet prove to be their salvation....
...pools of Nature that may lead to better land use. There is an explosion of education and communica...
...that is too often ignored in dismal representations of the continent as a hot bed of poverty, disease,...
...war. Good news about progress is not news to most of the world. Yet, as educated middle classes gro...
...children now go to school, and improvements in communications and technology bring the outsi...
...mote areas. Like those of the urban west, these children are open to the love of elephants, which lead...
...caring about Nature's bigger issues of biodiversity and conservation. A country's resources belong a...
...city dweller as to the local people who are destroying things.

New technology also gives grounds for some optimism. Remote sensing and radio-tracking eleph...
...us to understand how they make their choices, how they use vital corridors to link ranges, and how...
...their greatest needs in better conservation plans.

Solutions can be found where there is national political will, as demonstrated by Kenya, where e...
...saved by a change of policy in 1989 when 12 tonnes of mainly illegal ivory was burnt to signify an...
...hand trading. Ivory poaching has diminished and if the markets can be kept at bay, this factor can...

Their future can be secured if we engage in better land planning to help both people and wildlife...
...share resources. Key areas, such as corridors, can be given priority in landscape planning, which wil...
...effect of the human footprint in future. The core of protected areas, such as national parks, shoul...
...through thick and thin.

As Jared Diamond remarks, the "same problems of overpopulation, environmental impact and c...
...cannot persist indefinitely". If we can keep enough space for elephants, we can perhaps ultimately...
...collapse as a result of unbridled population expansion and overuse of resources. Our human footpri...
...greatest threat to elephants, but so it is ultimately to ourselves.

With so much of nature's splendor now trodden flat in the human footprint, the plants, the animals, and the hospitality of the habitats they provided, our planet is newly diminished and vulnerable. The urgency of saving what is left is overwhelming.

For the most part, the care and management of Earth's forests, fisheries, its other wildlife, and its incomparable grandeur has been left to the self-serving attentions of their exploiters and few of us have an informed picture of the impoverishing results. Those of us who do feel as though we are hurtling down a mountain side in an overcrowded bus, directionless, with neither brakes nor steering wheel, and that the expanding globalization of resource exploitation is hastening our descent.

Perhaps it is unreasonable to expect that humanity will come to realize that preserving nature is part of preserving itself. But why has not even one major nation made a serious estimate of how many people and wildlife its environment might support, while preserving a desirable quality of life? Why have so few accorded priority to the care and expansion of their irreplaceable national parks and reserves and why do we search in vain among the exhortations of our international leaders for such thinking? It is as though environmental planning is explosive—and inconsequential anyway because the length of its fuse can be no longer than the time to the nearest election.

Fully fifty percent of the world's wetlands have been destroyed in the past century and the amount of Earth's surface afflicted by drought has doubled since the 1970s. In 1998, to protect part of its deteriorating environment, China banned logging over much of its territory, putting 700 000 people out of work. In 2006 however, it purchased logging rights to a major portion of Indonesia's dwindling rainforest, which is among the world's most magnificent and biodiverse. Such solutions for immediate needs make prudent long-term environmental management impossible and impact an ever-smaller resource base. They also impose ever more critical whistle-blowing responsibilities upon environmental organizations and agencies. In the long term, like the continued heavy use of coal by Europe, the U.S. and China, they will affect the planet's carrying capacity for life. Ultimately, we cannot outsource the services of our ecosystems.

To actually shrink the impact of the human footprint from today's devastating boot to a sustainable slipper, and to conserve the beauty and services of nature, it will not be enough to rely upon technological change. It will be necessary to reduce the number of feet and essential to plan specifically and collectively to sustain wild places and wild creatures. It may be that caring for the Earth requires a new kind of "Security Council," one where there is no representation without conservation

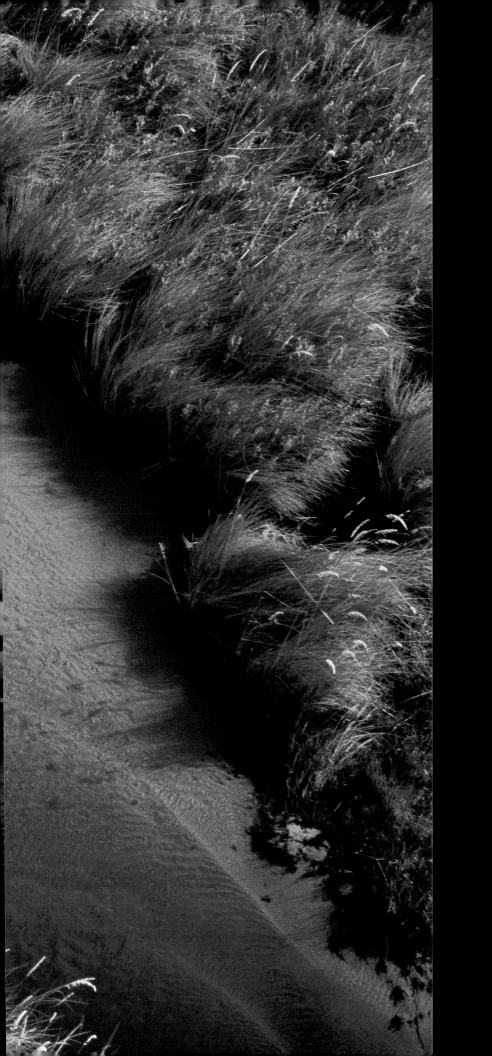

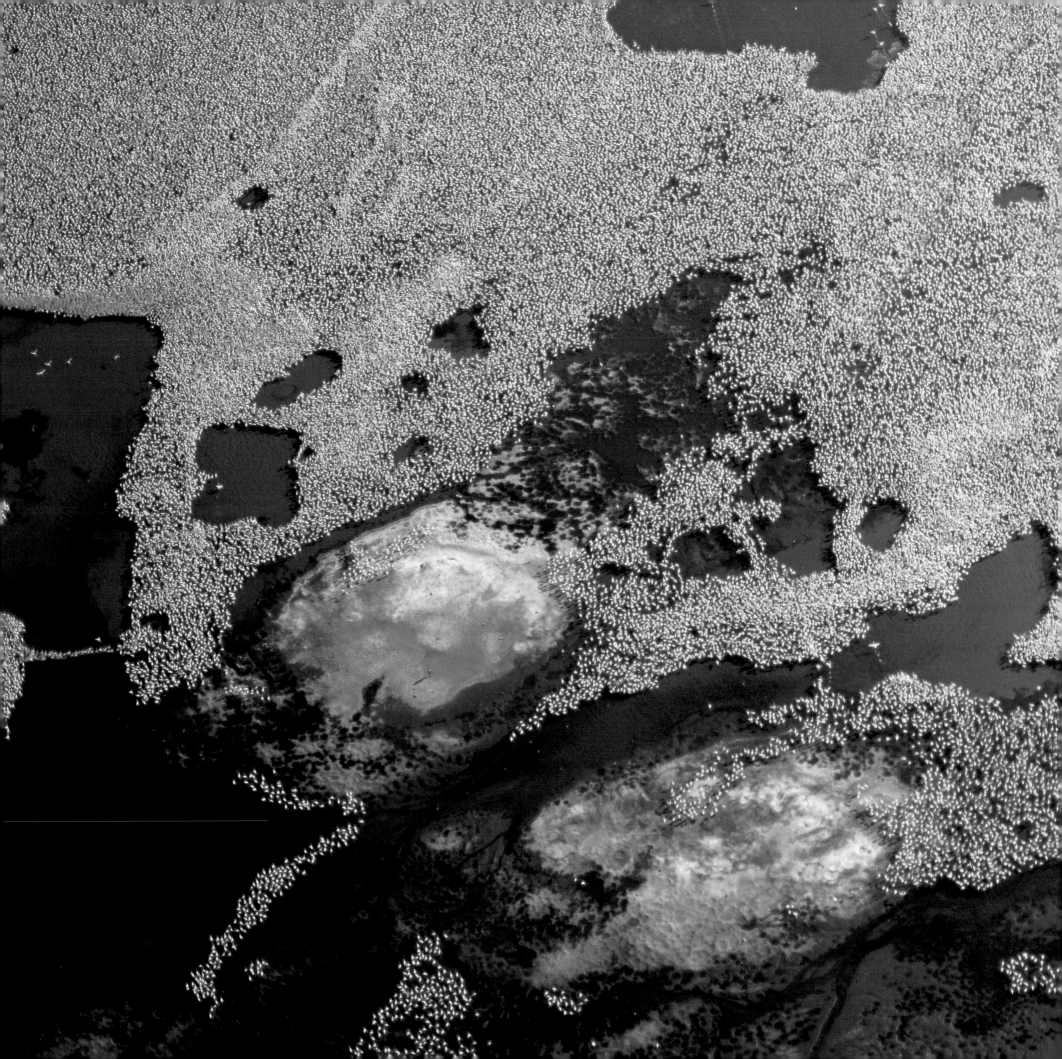

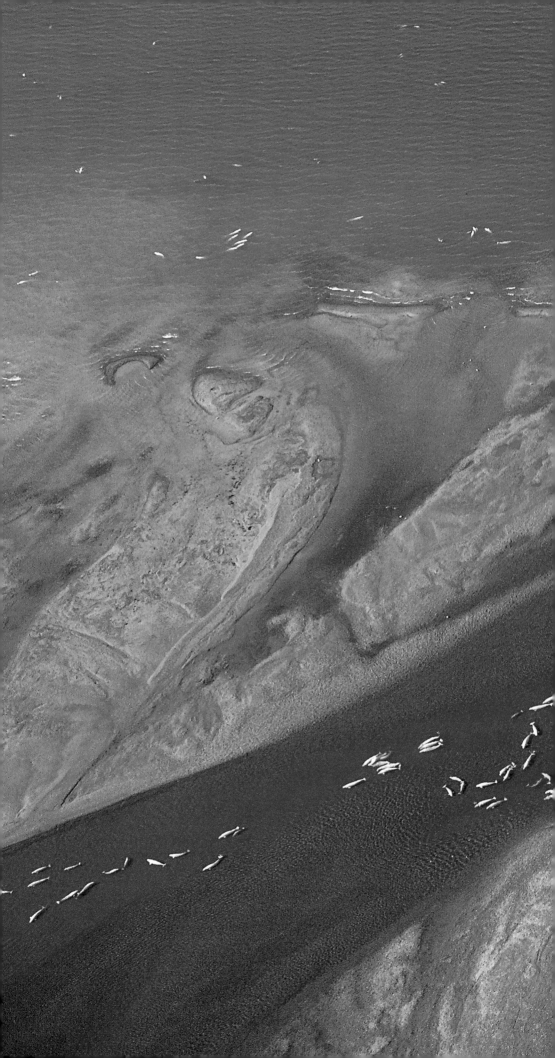

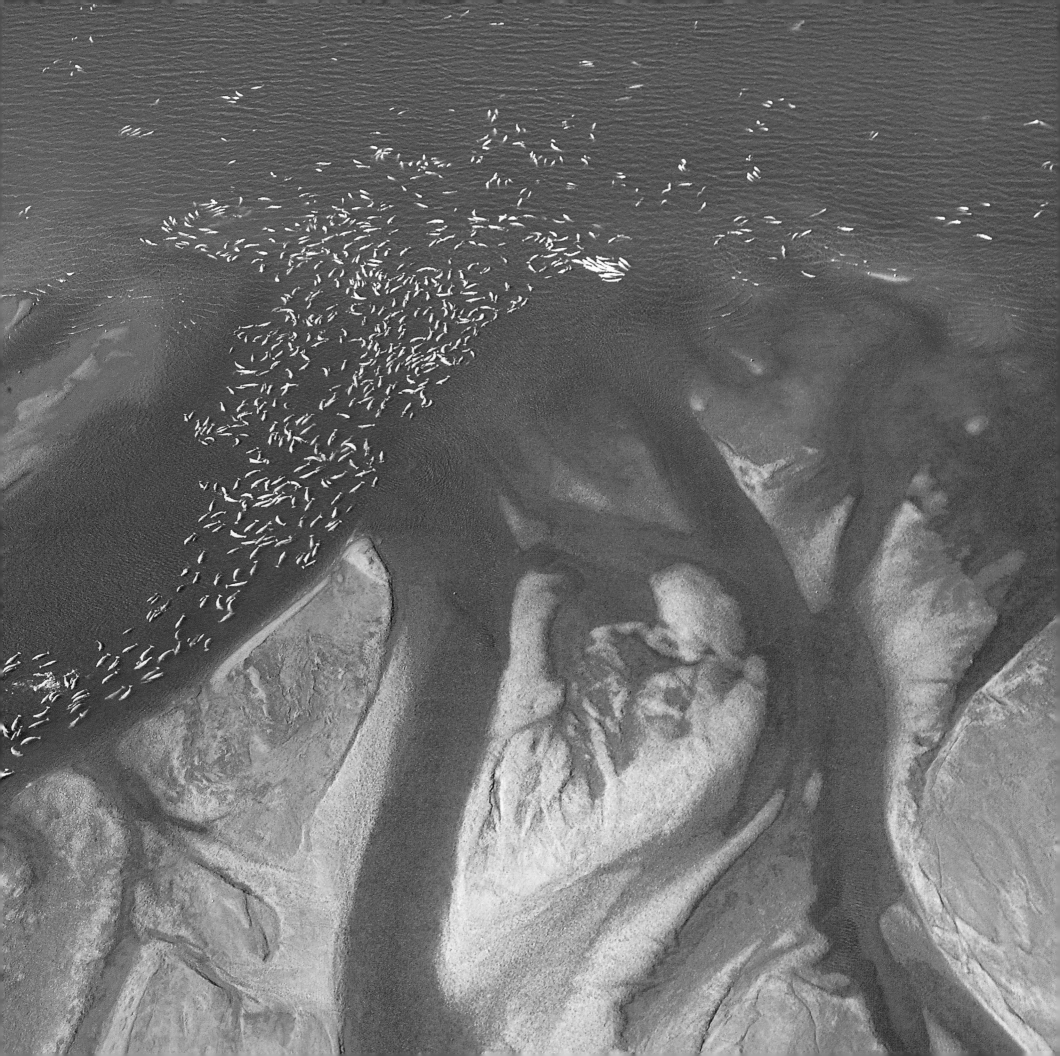

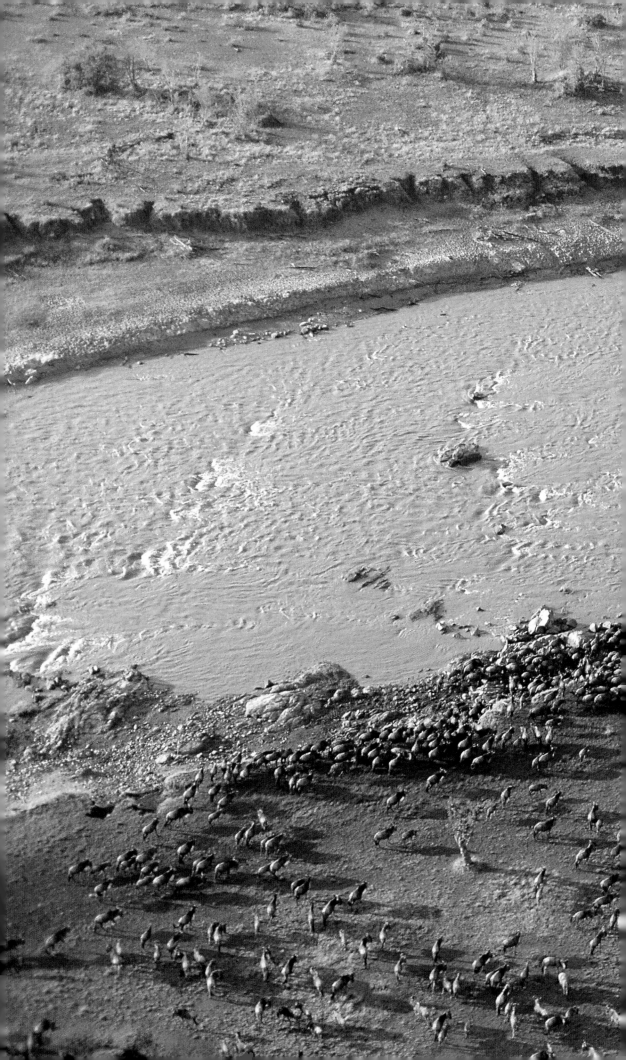

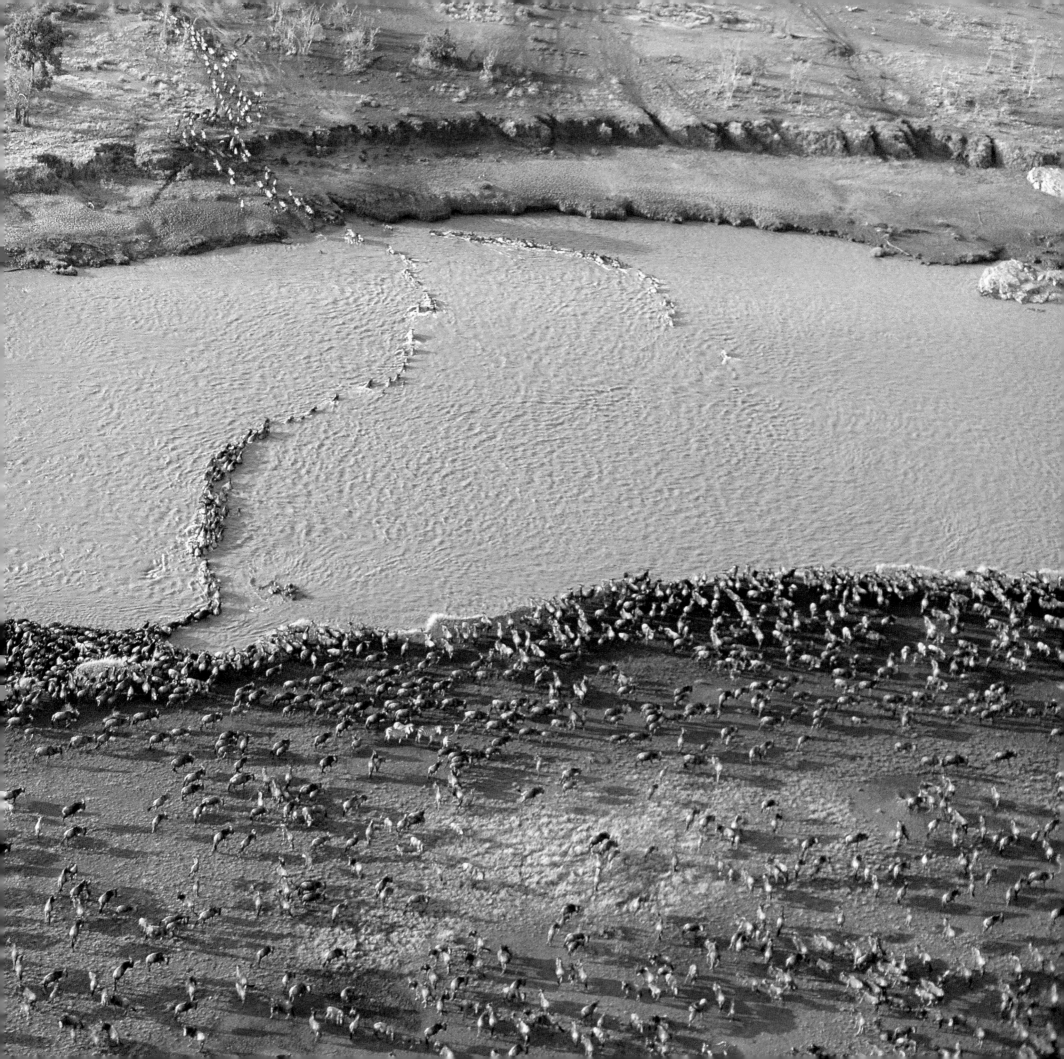

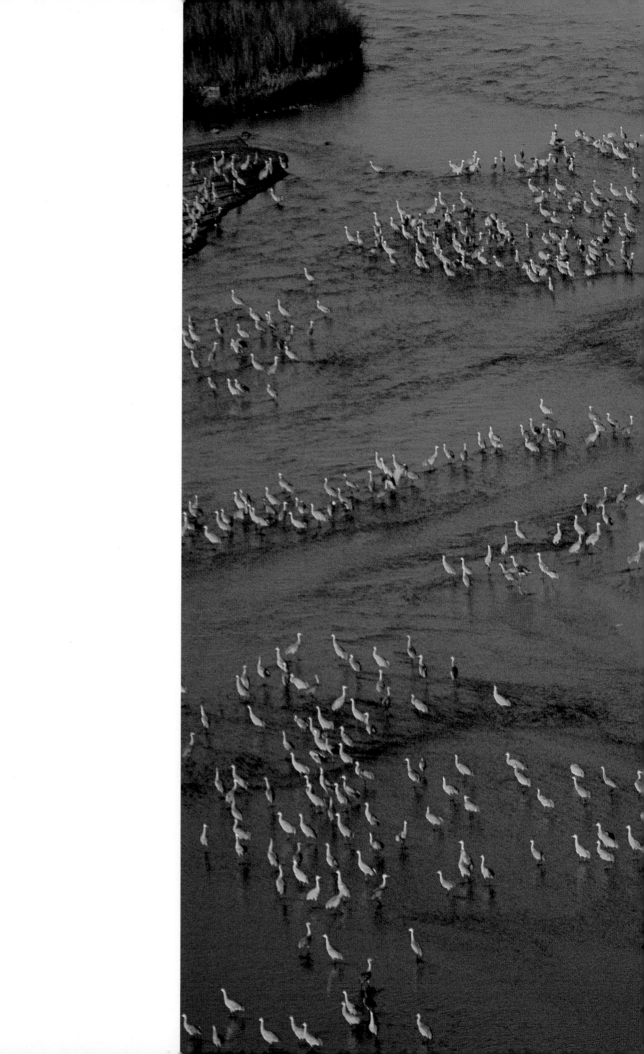

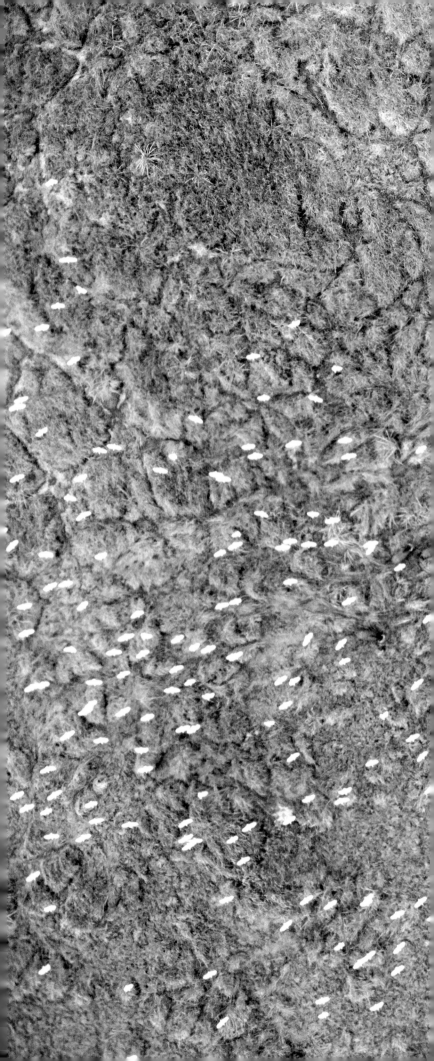

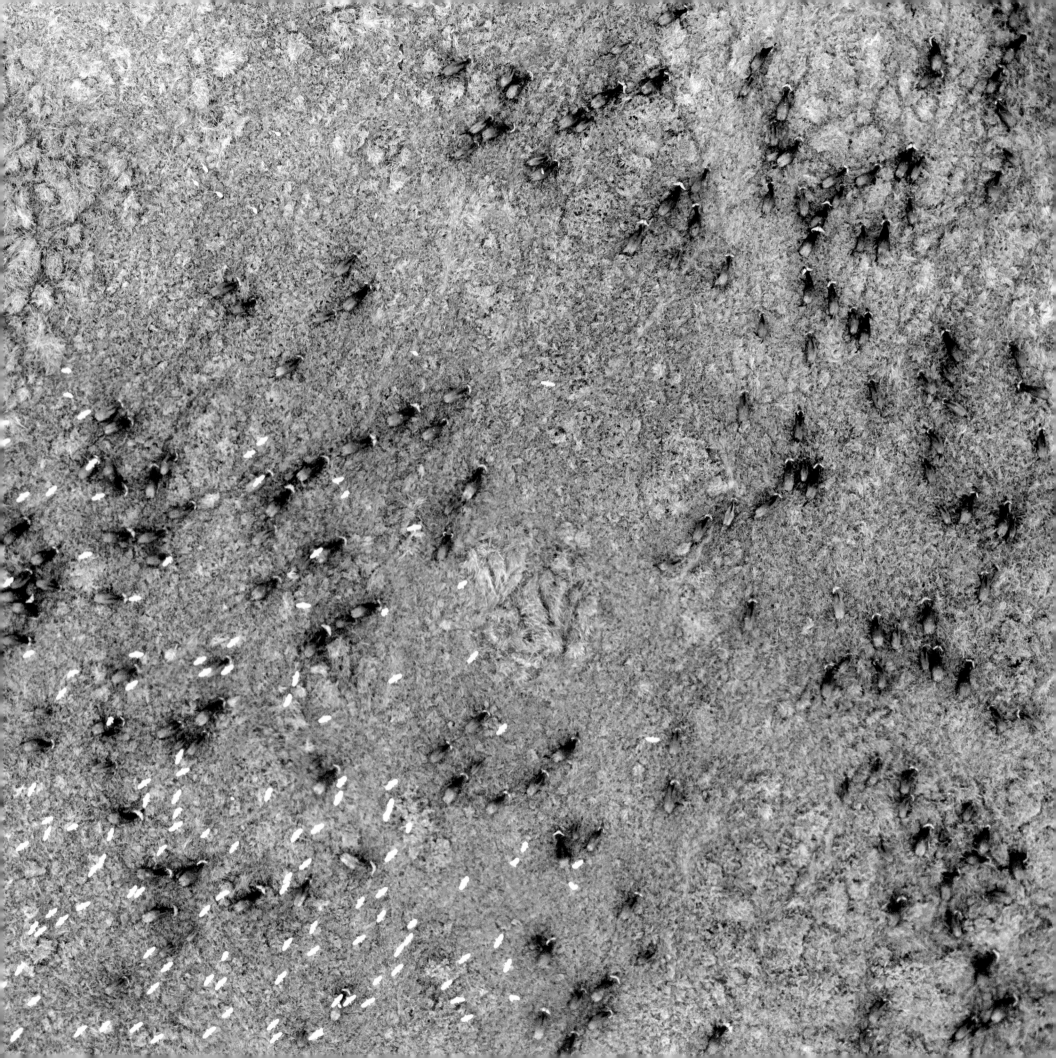

There is no more hiding from it; the human footprint on our climate, as evidenced by greenhouse gases, has already changed the basic physics and chemistry of our planet. The levels of carbon dioxide in our atmosphere are already 37% higher than they were in pre-industrial times. The average global temperature has risen by 0.7 °C with an equal increase to come because of the lag between greenhouse gas accumulation and the build-up of the consequent greenhouse effect.

Sea levels have already risen by four to eight inches, and a rise of one meter is expected by the end of the century simply because of water expansion in response to the temperature increase. In a disturbing related development, elevated CO^2 has led to increased ocean acidity. Arctic ice and most glaciers are in retreat. All tropical glaciers, including the legendary glaciers of Mt. Kilimanjaro, will be gone in less than 15 years.

Inevitably, the first effects are being seen in the natural world. With earlier springs, birds are migrating and nesting earlier, and flowering times are moving forward. The distributions of certain species, like Edith's Checkerspot butterfly in North America, are shifting, sometimes moving to higher altitudes—if they keep shifting upwards, with any further climate change, they could run out of mountain. Opportunistic pests, like the bark beetle forest infestations in Alaska and western Canada, are taking advantage of more favorable conditions. Higher temperatures are also leading to more frequent coral bleaching events and, eventually, increasingly acid seas will have disastrous effects on corals and other organisms that build skeletons of calcium carbonate.

Continuing on this path makes the certainty of a major extinction crisis loom larger and closer. We know from our planet's own geologic history that with increasing climate change, ecological communities will disassemble; different species will move at different rates and directions and ultimately reassemble into novel communities. In the oceans, the shells of some animals will dissolve while they are alive.

What can we do in the face of this awesome challenge? Better environmental practice (e.g. reducing siltation in coastal waters) can ameliorate the impact of a changing climate by reducing and removing other stresses on nature. Restoring and improving the connectivity of nature in landscapes will enhance (as opposed to curtail) opportunities for dispersal. Most important, however, is to recognize that ecosystems are the most sensitive of the concerns enumerated in the Convention on Climate Change. Nature is telling us to take climate change very seriously. It is imperative is to agree on a safe maximum level of greenhouse gas concentrations below levels at which nature would be severely disrupted and to forge the necessary new energy scenario. There is no reason why this cannot be achieved.

THOMAS LOVEJOY

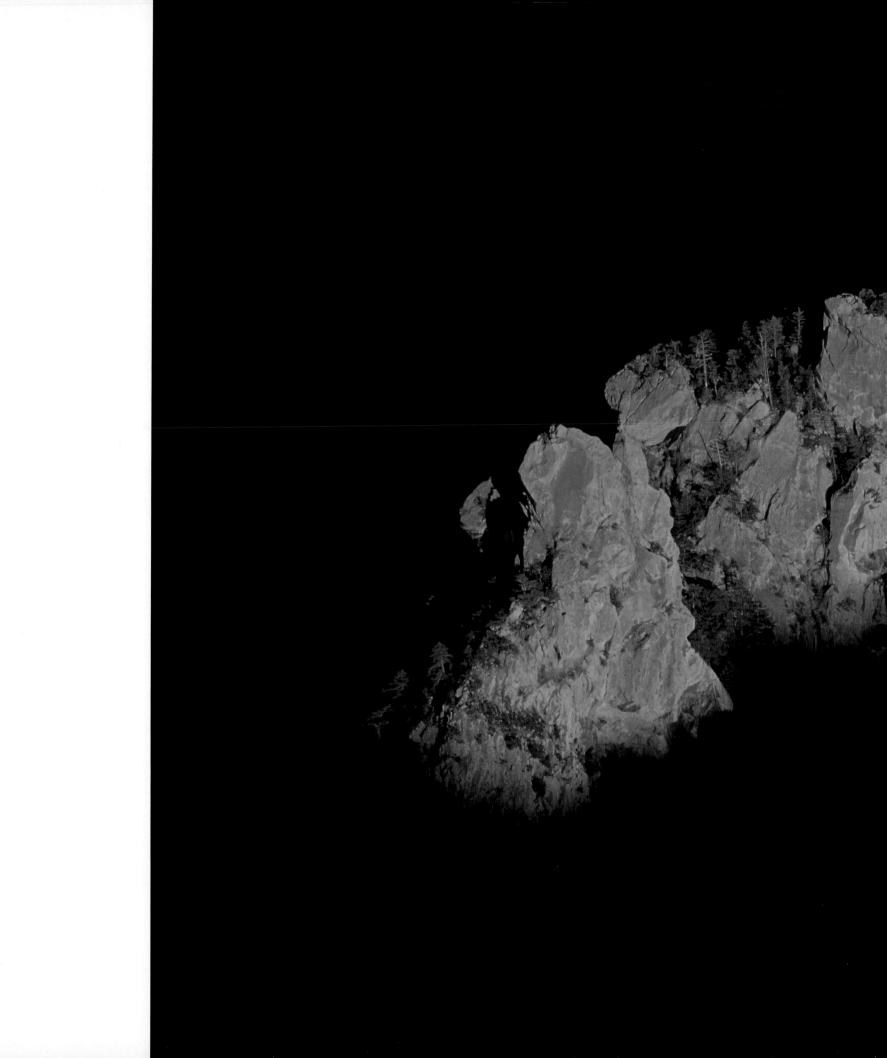

Humankind has pillaged and vandalized nature to such an extent that few places remain unscarred. As the relentless attrition of species continues and ecological processes become disrupted, the small conservation community all too often gropes for solutions without clear thinking. Instead of retaining its traditional focus, that of fighting on behalf of a country's natural heritage, the conservation agenda has almost become an act of apology, its goals surrendered to human desires. Development in the guise of such vague concepts as poverty alleviation and sustainable development, often based more on dogma and faith than on reality, has become an all-encompassing panacea and has diluted the effectiveness of the conservation effort. Such agendas may have logic but lack the knowledge and emotion that only lengthy field experience can provide. Development created our environmental problems and, with the intellectual flights of an ostrich, the proposed solutions tend to be more of the same. Species should not only be commodities to be bought, sold and discarded and to be saved only if we consider them useful at present. All animals and plants lay claim to our concern and respect, whether the transcendent beauty of a tiger or the obscure importance of a soil nematode. Food, health, education, livelihood, clean water and air are all basic to a good quality of life and wholly depend on a healthy environment. But to provide for human well-being is mainly the responsibility of governments, international donor agencies and corporations, not of non-governmental conservation organizations which are increasingly taking on this enormous task.

Many areas have as yet not been degraded in spite of the massive destruction throughout the world. We must decide now, with hard-headed optimism, what to protect and manage before losses become irretrievable. Hot spots, ecoregions and other limited concepts are useful in focusing on areas of high biodiversity, but deserts, tundras, swamps, rivers, woodlands and all other habitats, each with a unique assemblage of species that represent the natural treasures of a country, must not be neglected. Fortunately, some of the world's loveliest and most spectacular places—the Serengeti, the Arctic National Wildlife Refuge and the Virunga volcanoes with their mountain gorillas, to name just three—do have a measure of protection. Yet every country must retain wild places without greed or compromise, caring for them as much as any cultural treasure, to preserve the splendor of its past. However, protected areas cannot survive unchanged as islands in a sea of humanity, especially not in an era of rapid climate change. Plans to manage entire landscapes must be made, plans based on scientific knowledge, including various zones of use from reserves to stewardship in cooperation with communities to assure both livelihood and ecological integrity. Governments have the knowledge and power to develop such comprehensive land-use plans but not the will. As the Koran notes, "Allah loveth not wasters" and, even more emphatically, the Bible asserts, "where there is no vision, the people perish."

Conservation based on science and economics is not enough: Beauty must complement fact. Ethics, esthetics and religious sentiments are part of every culture. The waning of spiritual content in the conservation agenda is of concern. Conservation without moral values cannot sustain itself. Dollar values do not define sacred mountains, ancient forests and the flight of a golden eagle. People find spiritual satisfaction not in shopping centers but in the glory of unbounded nature. Unless we make a covenant with the land, developing a land ethic, to use Aldo Leopold's concept, the future is likely to be one of poverty and bleakness. "Conserve or perish" is the Hindu message in the Bhagavad Gita, and the first principle of Buddhism is to protect all life. Conservation must incorporate into its vision not just ecological wisdom, but also compassion and reverence for life. To achieve this we need new strategies and values for human survival, a change in attitudes, priorities and expectations that will sustain life on Earth. That is the goal of conservation.

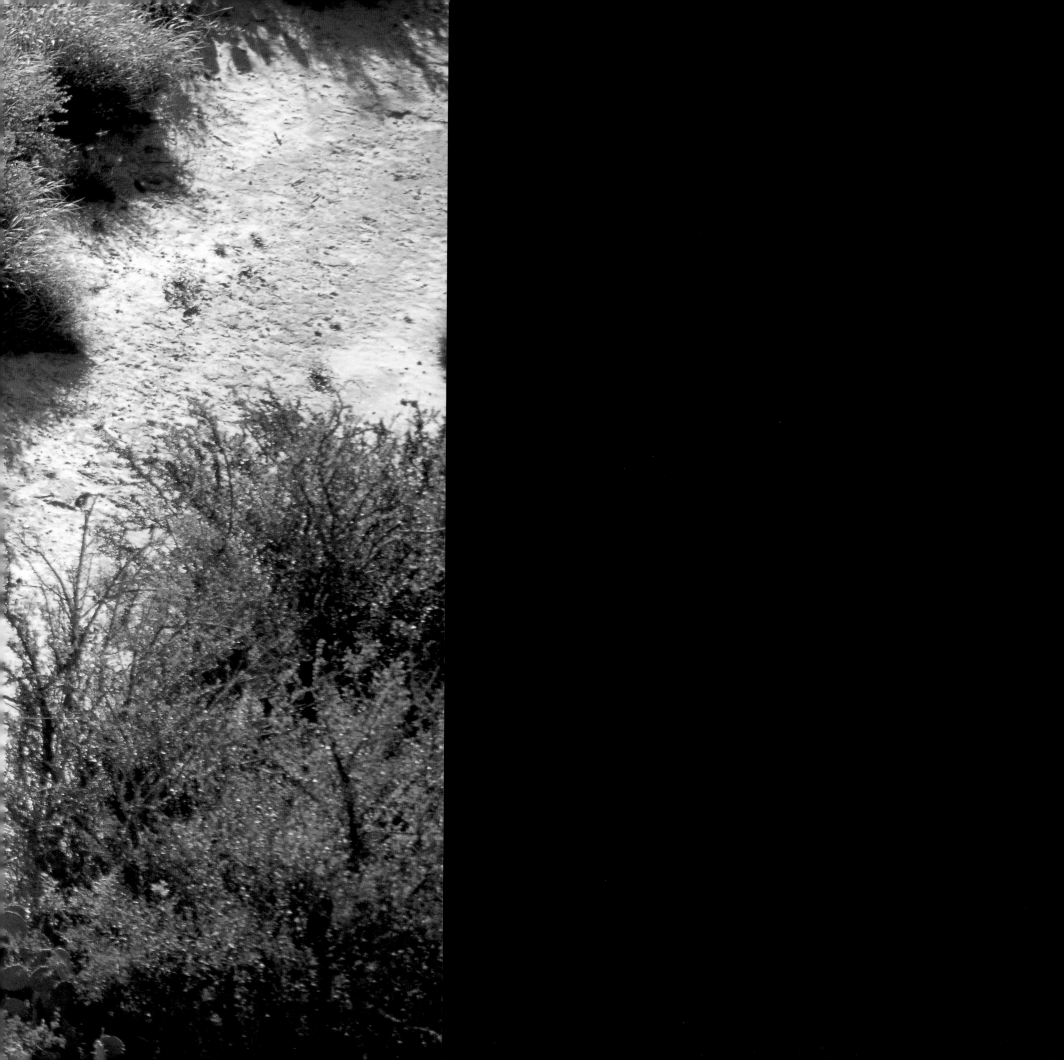

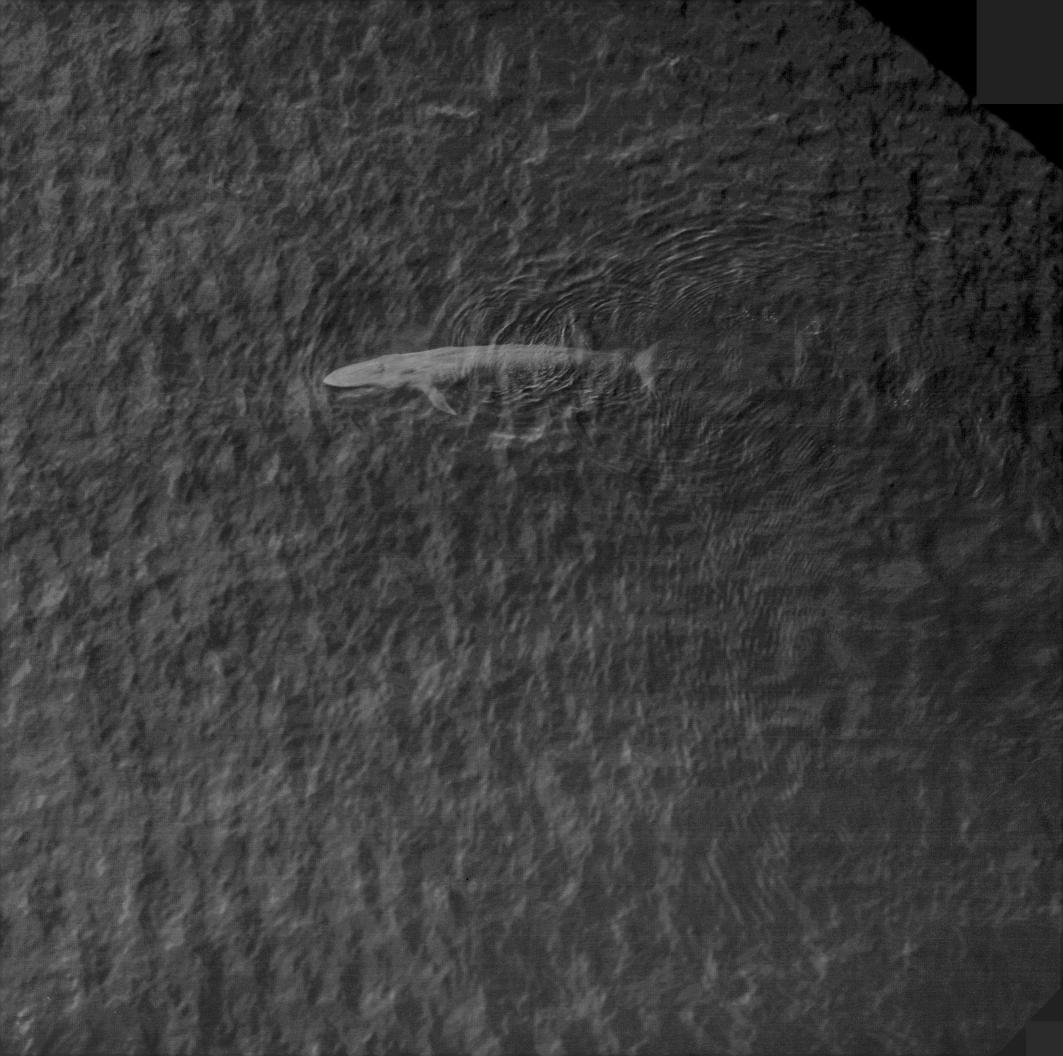

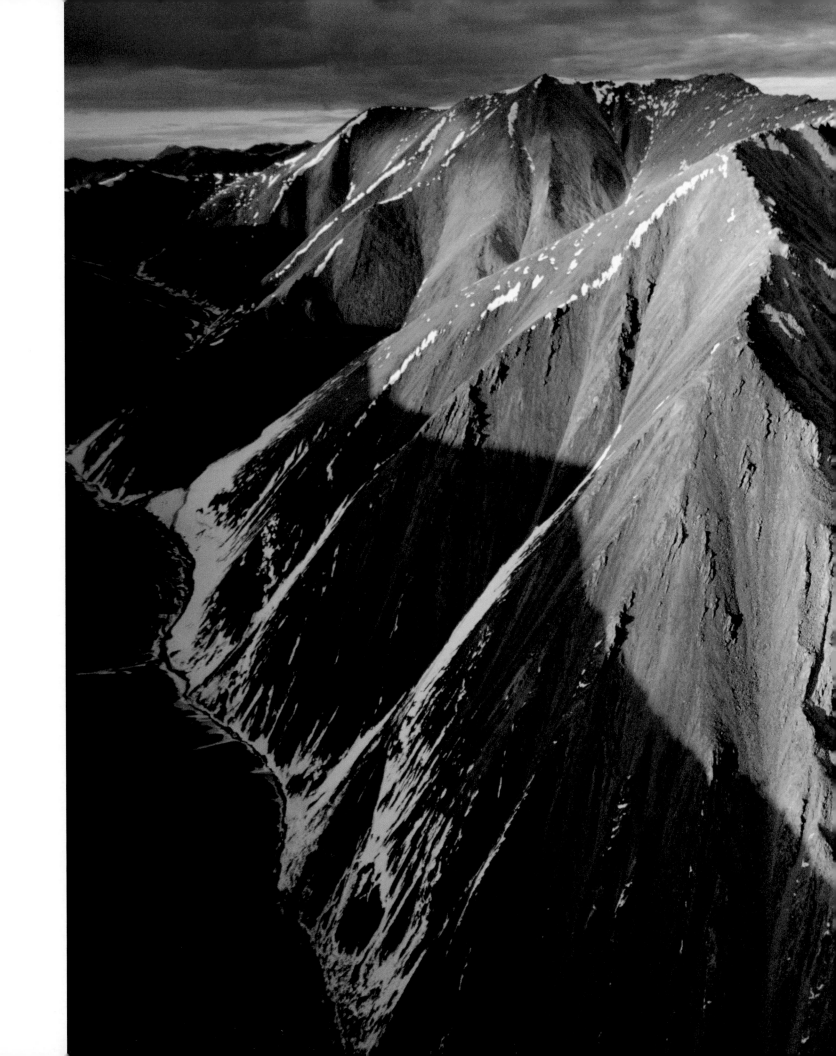

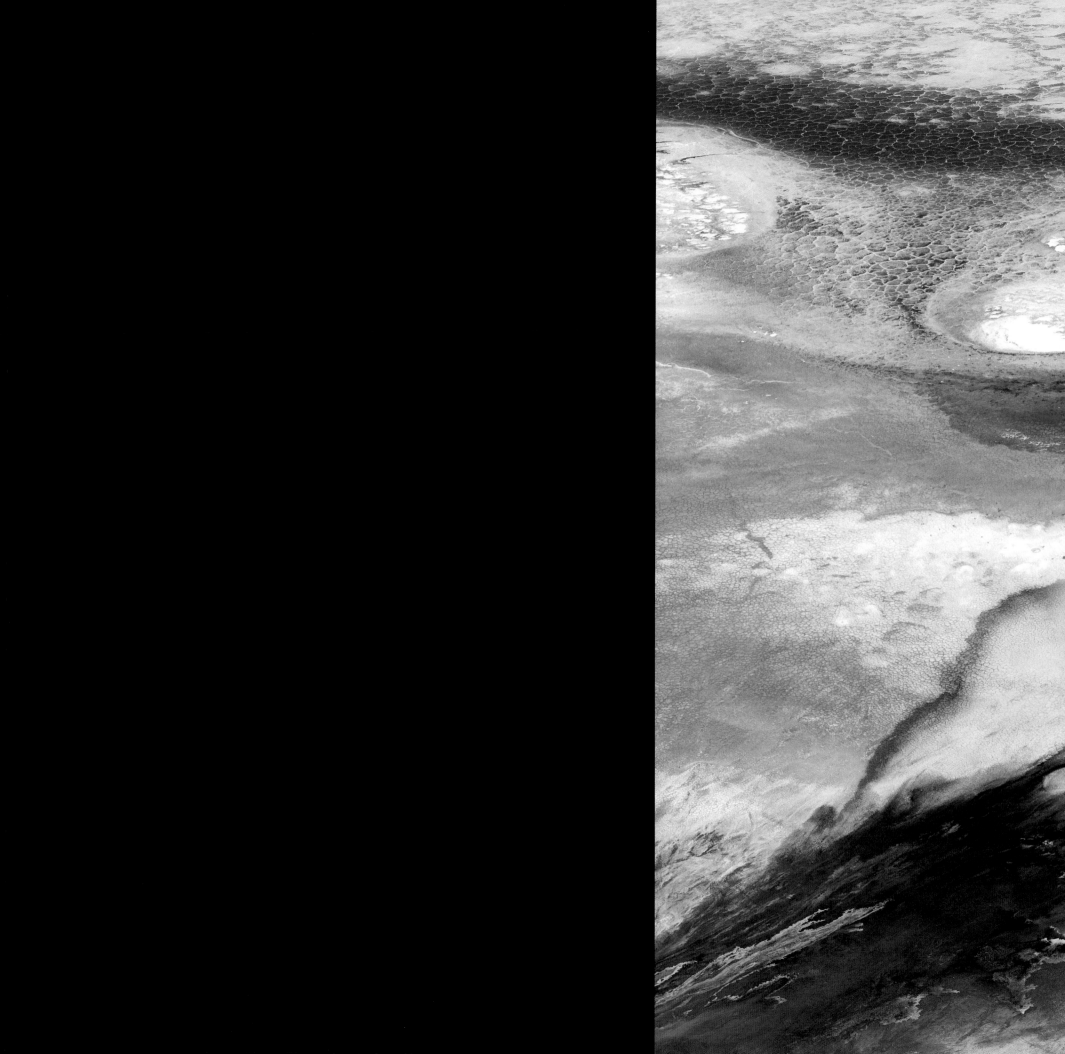

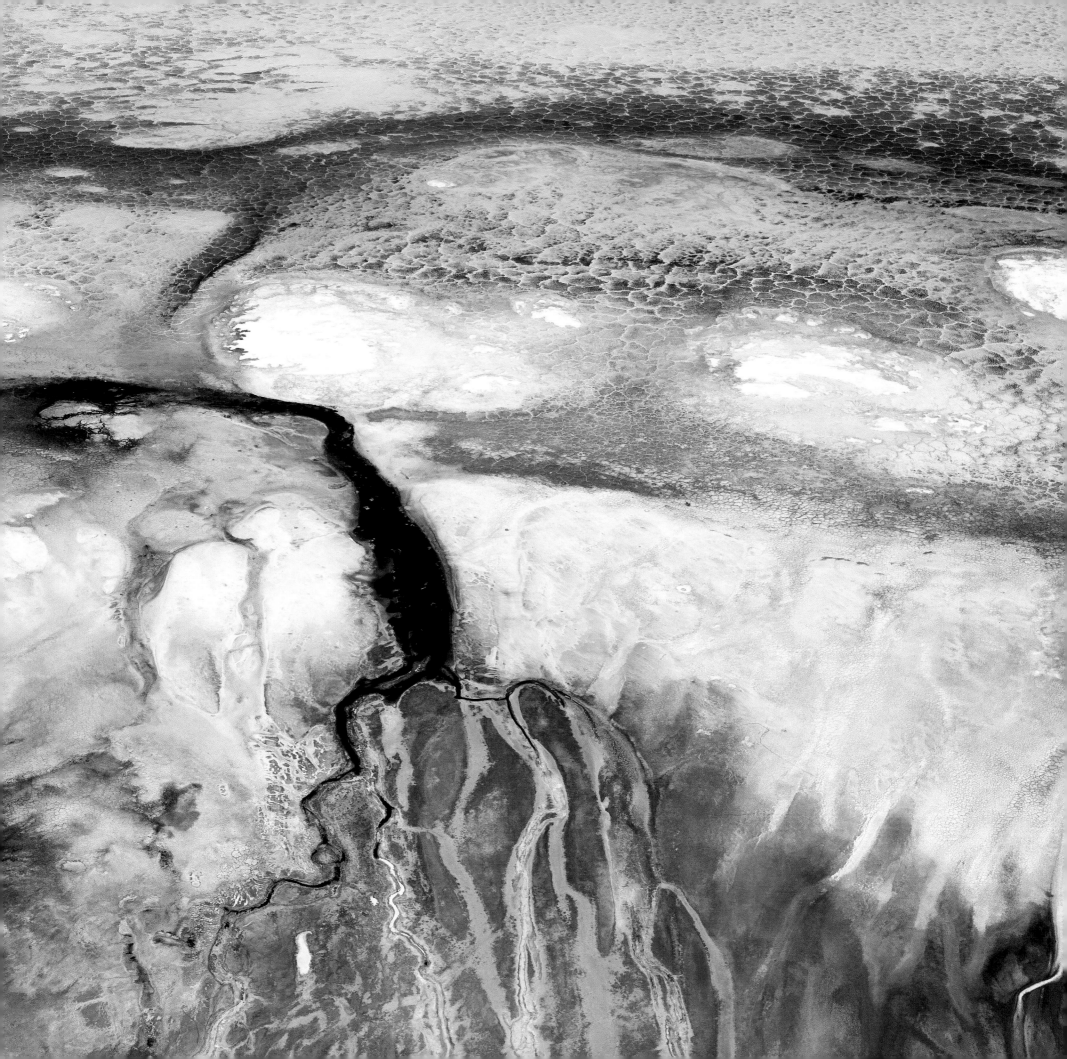

Somerset Level, England. Even in areas heavily impacted by agriculture, gallery forests can play an important role in helping to preserve biodiversity. © Dae Sasitorn/www.lastrefuge.co.uk

The boundary between heavily-logged Targhee National Forest in Idaho, U.S.A. and Yellowstone National Park is clearly visible in this picture. Unfortunately the U.S.D.A Forest Service's multiple use policy often leads to large areas of clear cutting in national forests in the United States. © Peter Essick/Aurora Photos

The U.S. is by far the world's largest producer and consumer of paper. Paper consumption per capita is over six times greater than the world average and about 25% greater than Japan, the world's second largest per capita paper consumer. Feeding this paper appetite chews up trees at an almost incomprehensible rate of 12 trees to produce only one ton of writing paper. Manitoba's Pine Falls log yard, seen here can yield 193 000 tons of newsprint annually, using just a fraction of the 5.2 million cubic meters of timber that its owner, Tembec Industries, harvests from Canada's public lands each year. © Peter Essick/Aurora Photos

Fishing boats near the capital city of Nouakchott, where the population has grown from from 10 000 in 1960 to more than 700 000, partly as a result of drought conditions further inland. Mauritania, Africa. © George Steinmetz

Terraced agriculture in the Virunga Mountains in Rwanda. Extremely high population density places tremendous pressure on Rwanda's protected areas. © George Steinmetz

As an example of its great commitment, CEMEX acquired big extensions of land along the Mexican-U.S. border to protect them in perpetuity and guarantee the connectivity of one of the most significant biological corridors of North America. In the foreground, Maderas del Carmen Flora and Fauna Protection Area in Mexico, and in the background the Adam's Ranch, located between Big Bend National Park and Black Gap Wildlife Management Area in Texas. © Patricio Robles Gil/Sierra Madre

The Rock Islands of Palau seen here, is part of the "Micronesia Challenge" a scheme that will protect 30% of the region's marine areas and 20% of the forests of the countries across Micronesia. A coalition of conservation organizations, including Conservation International, The Nature Conservancy, the Global Environment Facility and the Asian Development Bank, has come together to help six Micronesian nations protect their biodiversity. The region is at the epicenter of the biodiversity extinction crisis and has seen 25 bird species go extinct since the arrival of Europeans 200 years ago. © Michael Pitts/naturepl.com

A solitary lion lies in the sands of the Kalahari near the Moremi Game Reserve in Botswana.
© Robert B. Haas/National Geographic Image Collection

In the Lacandon jungle, in Chiapas, Mexico, at least 23 of the more than 3 400 recorded species of vascular plants there are threatened with extinction. The region also has endemic plants like *Lacandonia schismatica*, described for the first time only 20 years ago. Unlike all other known flowering plants, it has a masculine sexual organ in its center, surrounded by female organs, and its discovery required the classification of a new botanical family. In 1978, 300 000 hectares of the Lacandon jungle became officially protected as the Montes Azules Biosphere Reserve. © Fulvio Eccardi

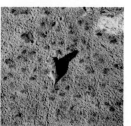

NASA's satellite image of the border between the Mexican states of Tabasco and Chiapas and the northwestern corner of Guatemala, taken in 1989. On the Mexican side we can clearly appreciate the human footprint of deforestation that defines a real line separating the two countries.
© National Aeronautics and Space Administration (NASA)

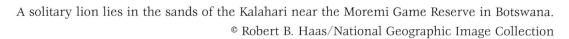

This satellite image of the Mexican southeast and Guatemala, taken in 2002—thirteen years later than the previous image—, shows that, unfortunately, the effects of deforestation on the Guatemalan border have today made the border line, visible in the previous photo, hardly distinguishable.
© National Aeronautics and Space Administration (NASA)

Endangered southern pines, Everglades National Park, Florida, USA. Although this National Park is a World Heritage Site, the park is under significant stress from diversion of water for urban areas, and from pollution and agricultural run-off which is killing wildlife. There are state and federal plans to reengineer the water flow, the best chance for saving the "river of grass." © Getty Images/Stone

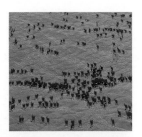

One of the biggest concentrations of ungulates in North America takes place every winter in the surroundings of Jackson Hole, Wyoming when more than 20 000 elks gather together in the National Elk Refuge. © Art Wolfe

Antarctic icebergs, like this one photographed near Adelaide are, in general, much larger and more abundant than Arctic ones. Only one eighth of an iceberg can be seen above the surface, so even seemingly small icebergs can in reality be enormous. Since the end of the last ice age some 12 000 years ago, the Antarctic Peninsula's ice shelves have not experienced as much cracking as we are seeing today. The breakup of the ice shelves is undoubtedly a natural process, but the current size and rate of production of icebergs is alarming scientists, who blame global warming. © Yann Arthus-Bertrand/Altitude

Despite being blessed with one of the highest biodiversity concentrations on Earth, Ecuador also has one of the world's highest rates of deforestation, estimated at over 300 000 hectares or 3% per year. The old-growth forests that once covered these hillsides, north of Quito, were liquidated by the timber industry and cleared for huge African palm plantations, which are currently responsible for the fastest deforestation rate in South America. © Morley Read/www.naturepl.com

Wadi Rum is the result of an enormous topographic upheaval that thrust granite and sandstone outcrops through the surface of the earth millions of years ago. Protected as a Nature Reserve by the Jordanian Royal Society for the Conservation of Nature, Wadi Rum's majestic landscapes harbor a secretive yet diverse array of wildlife. © Latin Stock de México/Corbis

"Today, many Mayan ruins, with their great temples and monuments, still lie surrounded by jungle, far from current human settlement. Yet they were once the sites of the New World's most advanced Native American civilization before European arrival... How could ancient peoples have supported urban societies in areas where few farmers eke out a living today?" from Jared Diamond's book: *Collapse. Why Societies Choose to Fail or Succeed.* In the picture, Yaxchilán Temples and the Usumacinta river, in Chiapas Mexico. Michael Calderwood/Fundación Mexicana para la Educación Ambiental

The rise and fall of Chaco is one of the greatest enigmas in Southwestern prehistory. The fragile and marginal environment, unpredictable rainfall and droughts certainly contributed to the collapse of the Anasazi civilization. Deforestation, salinization, and depletion of soils, however, were caused by an expanding population that could eventually not be supported any further by available resources. The last construction evidence at Pueblo Bonito, in Chaco Canyon, New Mexico dates back to the year A.D. 1170. More disturbing perhaps is the evidence of strife, cannibalism and warfare also found in the site. © Jim Wark

Almost 1 000 years old, the magnificent temples of Angkor Wat in Cambodia are a stunning architectural achievement. Archeologists believe that aside from their political and religious functions, the buildings of Angkor Wat served as an elaborate water management system that, at its height, supported over a million people. A combination of environmental degradation, droughts, and enemy invasions were the probable cause for the collapse of this extraordinary medieval civilization. © Helen Hiscocks/Altitude

This year the world population is expected to reach 6.5 billion people. India alone has 1.1 billion people and despite the recent financial boom the country is experiencing thanks to the expansion of a new Indian middle class, there are between 350-400 million people living below the poverty line, 75% of them in rural areas. © Steve McCurry/Magnum Photos

The pollution caused by the many hills of mine tailings in and around Johannesburg is an unfortunate legacy of South Africa's gold mining industry. © George Steinmetz

Transportation is the source of nearly one third of greenhouse gas emissions in the United States, and mobile sources are among the largest contributors to local air pollutants in urban areas throughout the world. Of all the mass transportation systems, rail travel and freight is the most affordable, energy-efficient and has the slighter infrastructure requirements when compared to air and road travel. The locomotive industry is now moving to more energy-efficient fuels and hybrid engines, which will make it an even more attractive option. © Jim Wark

Roads and power lines, like this one in Arizona, are two major forms of human-made linear clearings that traverse the entire developed world. Edge effect is the name given to the impact caused by the habitat-clearing interface where the power lines are located. The main concerns are habitat fragmentation, ecological changes to the edges of the habitat and health effects to humans, like the increase in the incidence of childhood leukemia that has been linked to the proximity to high voltage power lines. © Jim Wark

Central Park in Manhattan, New York, USA. A recent survey found that over 800 species live in Central Park, proving that biodiversity can persist even in the most urbanized landscapes. Central Park also provides essential relief from the stresses of big city life for millions of people. © Jim Wark

The Sungei Kinabatangan River delta in Sabah, Borneo, harbors a complex mixture of mangrove forest, lowland swamp forest and open reed marsh. This still-largely undisturbed area is critically important for coastal artisan fisheries and also supports significant populations of aquatic birds. © Frans Lanting

The clear waters of the Allen River drain into Lake Chauekuktuli, one of the many large lakes scattered throughout the 640 000 hectares of the Wood-Tikchik State Park in Alaska, the largest state park in the United States. Named for its two separate systems of large, interconnected, clear-water lakes, the park was created in 1978 to protect the area's fish and wildlife breeding. © Robert Glenn Ketchum

Agricultural fields meet the town of Loveland, Colorado in this increasingly-common scene of suburban sprawl in the United States. This type of growth is often fueled by government subsidies and poor federal, state and local planning policies, as well as by a rapid increase in population and migration from cities into suburbs. © Jim Richardson/National Geographic Image Collection

The year 2000 marked a tipping point in Earth's history in which a larger portion of the world population lived in cities than in rural areas. In today's Africa, nearly 40% of the growing population is urban, and by mid-century, most of the remaining rural poor population will be pushed to urban marginalized areas by drought, war or poverty. Nairobi's Kibera slum, a maze of shacks and open sewers where some 800 000 people live, exemplifies the linked crises of rapidly growing urban populations and rapidly deteriorating health conditions throughout Africa. © George Steinmetz

With an approximate area of 2 187 km^2 and a total population of 28 million people, the metropolitan area of Tokyo in Japan, is one of the most densely populated regions in the world, an impressive 6 000 persons per square kilometer. Shinjuku, Tokyo's business district is predominantly made up of administrative buildings, including the city hall, a 243-meter-high structure that was modeled after Notre Dame in Paris. The city burns its waste in giant incinerators and thus emits about 40% of the world's dioxins, a byproduct of burnt plastic that has been linked to several forms of cancer and birth defects. © Yann Arthus-Bertrand/Altitude

The arid lands of Nevada, one of the most inhospitable deserts in the Western Hemisphere, have become the unlikely host to the fastest growing metropolitan area in the United States, the city of Las Vegas. In this crowded maze of new buildings, less than 0.8 hectares of open spaces are devoted for every one thousand residents. © Sarah Leen/National Geographic Image Collection

With almost 100 million inhabitants, affordable housing is one of Mexico's greatest challenges. Given continued rapid growth in the population over age 30, household growth will continue rising through the first decade of the next century, with the number of households increasing by nearly 800 000 per year. To address this demand, the government has created a number of financing mechanisms aimed at aiding workers in the purchase of affordable housing. The National Housing Institute, INFONAVIT, builds low-cost homes under such financing schemes, like these ones in Toluca, Estado de México. © Yann Arthus-Bertrand/Altitude

With a population of 850 inhabitants per square kilometer, Bangladesh is the most densely populated nation in the world, seven times more so than China. Situated on a very fertile but extremely low-lying deltaic plain with some 300 waterways flowing through it, Bangladesh has always had to face up to the devastating flood waters of the great Himalayan rivers, the Ganges and Brahmaputra. During the summer monsoon it is not unusual for a large part of the country, like the town of Dacca, to be under water. Increased deforestation of the Himalayas has caused the flooding to become more serious. © Yann Arthus-Bertrand/Altitude

The ancient city of Jodhpur, also known as the Sun City, was formerly the seat of a princely state named Marwar that in Sanskrit means "Region of Death." Walls painted in shiny blue to refresh the interiors, Jodhpur lies partly in the Thar Desert where the severe climatic conditions of this area make water a very scarce resource and impeded agriculture to flourish as it did in other cities of the state of Rajasthan. However, due to its strategic location and traditional importance, the city serves as a key marketplace for wool and agricultural products. © Yann Arthus-Bertrand/Altitude

The 11 million people who call the Republic of Mali home are among the poorest in the world. Annual per capita income averages about US$ 250, and the majority of the poor people (86%) live in rural areas, like the remote region occupied by the Dogon in Northeastern Mali. This ethnic group, with a total population of about 300 000, lives in a heavily settled area along a 200-kilometer stretch of escarpment called the Cliffs of Bandiagara. Diseases due to poor hygiene are pandemic among the Dogon, and the level of education is extremely low. © Yann Arthus-Bertrand/Altitude

Coastal settlements in the surroundings of Davao city, in the Philippines. One of the most important cities in the Philippines and capital of the island of Mindanao—the second largest and easternmost of the three island groups in the country—, Davao has a land area of 2 443 km^2 and is considered one of the biggest cities in the world. The city has experienced a constant growth in the last ten years that is causing a popular demand for higher capacity infrastructures. © Patricio Robles Gil/Sierra Madre

Brazil is a country where the contrasts between the very wealthy and the very poor are often abysmal. Large slums, or *favelas*, spread for kilometers on end at the edges of the glamorous Rio de Janeiro. Lacking even the most basic services, many of these marginalized communities are breeding grounds of violence and disease. © Yann Arthus-Bertrand/Altitude

Mexico City, one of the biggest population centers of the planet, spreads out for more than 40 km² along the Valle de México where the Aztecs built up the great Tenochtitlan, now buried under this huge city of more than 20 million inhabitants. © Michael Calderwood

Nearly one quarter of the 10 million residents of Rio de Janeiro live in the city's 500 shantytowns, known as *favelas*, which have grown rapidly since the turn of the 20th century and are afflicted by crime and violence. Perched on the city's hillsides, these poor neighborhoods lack basic infrastructure and regularly experience fatal landslides during the heavy-rain season. Approximately 28.5% of Brazil's urban dwellers (41.8 million people) do not have full access to public-water, sewage, and garbage-collection services. © Staffan Widstrand

The global demand for oil palm has fueled the creation of millions of hectares of plantations in Malaysia and Indonesia. This explosive growth has come at the expense of irreplaceable primary forests and endangered species like the orangutan, which has been pushed to the brink of extinction. Roads now travel into areas that just a few years ago were deep in some of our planet's most diverse rain forests.
© Stuart Franklin/Magnum Photos

The great rivers allow the free transit of humans with practically no effort, becoming extraordinary natural highways that provide access to otherwise unattainable natural resources. The cost of logging big trees in the tropics is lowered by throwing the trunks to the river and picking them up hundreds of kilometers downstream, in an area closer to the markets. Bolivia is the world's leader in certified tropical forest and also harbors one of Earth's most important National Parks, Madidi, where illegally logged mahogany trees (*Swietenia macrophylla*) are still commonly found floating downriver on the Rio Madidi. © Andre Bärtschi

In September 1998 torrential rains destroyed one thousand hectares of crops in south Chiapas, Mexico, causing the death of 200 people and 60 million dollars worth of material damages. Seven years later, in 2005, disaster struck again. The rains unleashed by hurricane Stan made rivers overflow and sweep away everything in their path. Ninety bridges and 18 000 houses fell, more than a thousand kilometers of highways were destroyed, and deforested hillsides crumbled into mudslides. © Fulvio Eccardi

Hauling of timber, opening of access routes and the creation of new settlements are some of the most damaging unwanted effects of commercial logging operations. In New Zealand's South Island, sustainable harvesting of red pine, or rimu, is now done using helicopters to avoid unnecessarily damaging the forest.
© Edward Parker/OSF Limited

Lumbering and cattle-raising in the Lacandon jungle have intensified during the last 60 years. To help market forestry products, cattle breeders and people of the oil industry have built highways that have paved the way for numerous towns and communities to mushroom. Over time, these have resulted in a disorderly settlement of all of southeast Mexico. © Fulvio Eccardi

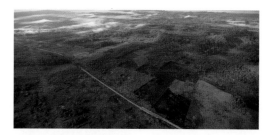

Rondonia, Brazi,l in 1984 and 2001. These pictures show the same area in Rondonia, Brazil, near the Bolivian border at a 17-year interval. The impact of roads, and the deforestation that immediately follows road-building, is clearly visible. © NPA Ltd./www.npagroup.com

Bounded on three sides by the sea, the Dingle Peninsula in Ireland combines in its landscape the ruggedness of rocky outcrops and cliffs with the soft shapes of hills and mountains. The Three Sisters headlands in the background look to the sea on one side and to a maze of country roads that lead past sheep paddocks to *Gaeltacht,* or traditional Irish towns. © Sam Abell/National Geographic Image Collection

Comprised of some 300 islands, one third of them inhabited, the small independent nation of Fiji has been settled by humans for over 2 000 years. It was not until the 17th century, however, that under British rule, the large-scale transformation of its landscapes took place to accommodate a European craving for sugar. Today, sugar cane is the nation's major cash crop and accounts for about 60% of Fiji's exports. Most growers are descendants of the Indian laborers imported by the British. They lease small parcels from native Fijians, who by law own 83% of the nation's land under a communal system. © James L. Stanfield/National Geographic Image Collection

Throughout the American West, a hefty percentage of water supplies (80-95%) are siphoned off from rivers and reservoirs for agricultural uses. The Imperial Valley in California features a half million acres of fruits, vegetables and feedlots that use more water than the cities of Los Angeles and Las Vegas combined. © Gerd Ludwig

The Pantanal region of Brazil is the world's largest contiguous wetland on the planet. The main economic activity in the region has traditionally been cattle ranching. About 95% of the Pantanal is in privately- owned lands and about 80% are used as extensively-managed cattle ranches of zebu, like this herd photographed near the city of Caceres, Mato Grosso, Brazil. © Yann Arthus-Bertrand/Altitude

The neo-volcanic axis is a mountain range that divides Mexico in two halves, north and south. Due to its extraordinary biodiversity and fertile lands, several Mesoamerican cultures flourished amid these mountains. This is the reason why this region today has the highest population density in the country. Great basins like the one of Pátzcuaro lake in Michoacán were formerly important centers of population and agriculture. © Michael Calderwood/Fundación Mexicana para la Educación Ambiental

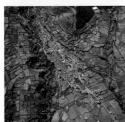

The Sierra Nevada, meaning "Snowy Range," is a dramatic, rugged and extensive mountain range in the region of Andalusia in Spain. Parts of the range have been included in a protected area that encompasses 86 208 hectares of torrential rivers, sheer-sided gorges, stony scree slopes, glacial lakes between snowy summits and, in the foothills of the Alpujarras to the north, a mosaic of cultivated terraces of almond trees, cereal crops, olives, grapes, walnuts, apples and cherries. © Adrian Warren/www.lastrefuge.co.uk

Mount Apo has an elevation of 2 954 meters and is the highest mountain in the Philippines. It is located in the island of Mindanao and overlooks the city of Davao. Declared a national park in 1936, the volcano slopes are home to 270 bird species, of which a hundred are endemic. However, habitat loss due to agriculture and fragmentation of the ecosystems is becoming a serious threat to the conservation of biodiversity in this area. © Patricio Robles Gil/Sierra Madre

Fish breeding basins crowd together in Lake San Isabel, Luzon Island, Philippines. © Guido Alberto Rossi/Altitude

Ecuador harbors portions of two of Earth's biodiversity hotspots, the Tumbes-Chocó-Magdalena and the Tropical Andes, and hosts one of the greatest densities of endemic species in the world. Increased access, colonization, oil and timber exploration, lack of incentives for conservation, insecure land titles and weak public institutions, however, have translated into the highest rate of deforestation of any Amazonian country. Forest cover loss, like the one seen on these deforested hillsides north of Quito, is estimated at 300 000 hectares, or 3% per year. © Morley Read/www.naturepl.com

Agriculture is the lifeblood of the economy in the San Luis Valley in Colorado. Since the 1880s, potatoes have been the main crop in the region, and today, 26 000 hectares are harvested every year. At 2 280 meters of elevation, this is the perfect environment to grow potatoes: the tubers thrive in the warm, bright sunny days and cool nights, and the cold winters mean fewer pests and diseases. In the background are snow-capped Blanca Peak and the Great Sand Dunes National Park. © Jim Wark

Millions of hectares of tropical forest have succumbed to clearings for cattle-raising in order to satisfy the global demand for meat. In Mexico alone less than 5% of this rich ecosystem remains. In the picture we can see a herd of Braha zebu in Tamaulipas, in the coastal plains of the Gulf of Mexico. © Patricio Robles Gil/Sierra Madre

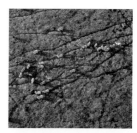

On some of the most densely populated regions of our planet, like the island of Java, cultivation has extended into the ocean. Uneven plots of seaweed form a living checker board in the shallow waters off east Bali. This crop is a global commodity exported worldwide and used as a food thickener in a wide variety of products. © Alexandra Boulat/VII Photo

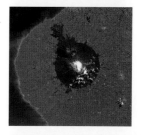

In the shape of a near-perfect cone, Taranaki, seen here in a satellite image, last erupted in the mid-18th century. The mountain and its immediate surrounds form Egmont National Park, New Zeland. The park, established in 1900, is dominated by the dormant volcano. The lush rainforest that covers its foothills is in stark contrast to the surrounding pasture farmlands. This region is exceptionally fertile, thanks to generous rainfall and the rich volcanic soil. © NPA Ltd./www.npagroup.com

Although Yunnan is one of the largest provinces in China, the mountainous terrain allows only about 6% of the land to be arable. The wide climatic variations, however, assure the province a variety of crops with rice being the principal crop, and corn (maize) an important second. © Panorama Stock-Archivo Digital

Experts have been predicting the end of the oil age for more than 100 years, but even today no one knows for sure how much oil is left in the ground. California's South Belridge field, for example, a massive operation with over 10 000 wells, has produced over a billion barrels of oil, but its output has begun declining. © Sarah Leen/National Geographic Image Collection

Coal bed methane is considered a cleaner form of energy than traditional oil or coal. Extraction, however, requires a tremendous amount of highly salty groundwater to be released into the surface, with serious effects on land, rivers and wildlife. The U.S. government owns the mineral rights under private lands in many states. This separation of surface and subsurface ownership, known as "severed estates" allows the government to drill under private grazing lands without their owners' consent; a highly contentious issue in the Powder River Basin area along the Montana-Wyoming border, where large coal bed methane deposits are found. © Joel Sartore

Will they drill or will they not? As Americans continue to debate the fate of the Arctic National Wildlife Refuge and their own determination on the future of energy for America, the Caribou herds cling on to their ancestral migrating routes across the Alaskan tundra by an ever-diminishing thread of hope. The Porcupine Caribou Herd (named after the Porcupine River) numbers approximately 123 000 animals, and generally spends the summer months on the Coastal Plain. © Joel Sartore/National Geographic Image Collection

The Svinafesljokull glacier has been retreating dramatically in recent years, leaving behind rocky debris (terminal moraine) and meltwater ponds. Southeast Iceland. March 3, 2005. © James Balog

The Glen Canyon dam no longer provides efficient water regulation or significant hydropower, and now that water levels in Lake Powell are down more than 60% due to a recent drought, conservationists are calling for lowering the artificial lake further to restore the spectacular Glen Canyon and its wildlife. © Michael Melford/National Geographic Image Collection

Renewable energy companies are beginning to gather momentum, especially in Europe. These companies are dedicated to generating electricity using sustainable, environmentally-friendly resources. Didcot power plant in England, UK, for example, replaces a portion of the coal used in electricity generation with biomass products such as wood waste, switch grass and residues from the olive oil and palm oil industries. This process, known as biomass co-firing is a move in the right direction to lessen the global demand on fossil fuels. © Dae Sasitorn/www.lastrefuge.co.uk

Wind generators, like these ones in Altamont Pass, California, are blamed for the death of thousands of birds every year. Interestingly, windmills are not the only cause of bird mortality in the United States. A recent report shows the estimated annual avian collision mortality to be 60 to 80 million in vehicle collisions, 100 million to 1 billion in collisions with buildings, and 174 million on power lines. Wind-generated electricity reduces the use of other energy sources, and as tragic as it may be, the small number of birds killed in wind turbines is far outweighed by wind's role in reducing greenhouse and air pollutant emissions. © Kevin Schafer

Australia is richly endowed with both non-renewable energy resources such as coal and natural gas, and renewable energy resources such as solar, tidal and wind power. Most of its electricity today, about 77%, is produced with coal. Interestingly, Australian coal burns cleaner by world standards, so electricity is produced without very much sulfur dioxide being emitted. Melbourne, seen here at night, is the second largest city in Australia, with a population of over 3 million people. The city is committed to reducing its carbon emissions to zero by 2020 through a variety of strategies including conservation and carbon trading. © Bill Bachman

As they retreated from Kuwait in the closing stages of the First Gulf War in 1991, Iraqi troops set over 600 oil wells on fire. More than one billion barrels of oil were burned before the fires could be extinguished. Despite a black, oily rain that fell as far afield as Afghanistan, Saddam's "Scorched Earth" policy didn't have the ecological impact it was originally feared it might; the public health consequences, on the other hand, were significant. Left: © McKinnon Films/OSF Limited. Right: © National Aeronautics and Space Administration (NASA)

One of the last refuges of tropical forests of North America is located less than 200 kilometers from the border between Mexico and the state of Texas, in the U.S. The Sierra de Tamaulipas, besides hosting six species of felines, has remained almost unperturbed during the last decades and recently has been declared a protected area, covering a surface of 300 000 hectares. © Patricio Robles Gil/Sierra Madre

Of the eight species of baobabs that exist in the world, six are endemic to the island of Madagascar. Characterized by having massive and bizarre swollen trunks and branches that give them the appearance of "upside down trees," baobabs are also found in Australia, and Africa but have their center of diversification in Madagascar, where they are most abundant on the western slopes of the island. © Latin Stock de México/Corbis

Military macaws (*Ara militaris*). Parrots and macaws are still victims of very intense illegal traffic to satisfy the pet demand. These activities together with habitat loss are the main threats for the military macaw, whose distribution ranges from Argentina to Northern Mexico and whose conservation status is *Vulnerable* according to the IUCN. In Mexico, this species has a refuge in El Cielo Biosphere Reserve (in the picture) where flocks of more than 50 couples can be seen. © Patricio Robles Gil/Sierra Madre

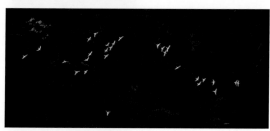

Whooping crane (*Grus americana*). Among the fourteen crane species that we find in the world, nine of them have been classified under a risk category according to the IUCN. Emblematic birds that were venerated by several ancient cultures face today the threats of extinction. The whooping crane (*Grus americana*) is endangered because of the reduced population size, although the efforts of conservationists raised their numbers to 200 individuals. © Tom Mangelsen

Pronghorn antelope (*Antilocapra americana*). Before the arrival of the first European settlers to North America the population of pronghorns was estimated to be up to 40 million. By 1920, there were less than 2 000 animals divided in five subspecies. Baja California pronghorn (in the picture) was one of the most threatened subspecies, with less than a 100 individuals. An important conservation effort led by the directors of the Vizcaino Biosphere Reserve allowed the population to duplicate in five years by means of a captive breeding facility. © Patricio Robles Gil/Sierra Madre

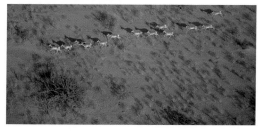

Despite aggressive efforts since the 1940s to protect the Amur or Siberian tiger (*Panthera tigris altaica*), this species remains listed as Critically Endangered, according to the Red List of the IUCN. The total population is estimated at less than 250 mature individuals and it continues to decline due to poaching and habitat destruction. © Michael Nichols/National Geographic Image Collection

Desert bighorn sheep (*Ovis canadensis*). Populations of the desert bighorn sheep have suffered a great decline due to fragmentation of their habitat, illegal hunting and the spread of domestic cattle diseases. The effort for their recovery has brought together government agencies and conservation groups from both Mexico and the U.S. with great results. The highlights of this initiative include the populations in the Chihuahuan desert, the Texas program and the successful recovering of the species in Coahuila, Mexico, carried out by CEMEX, Unidos para la Conservación and Agrupación Sierra Madre. © Patricio Robles Gil/Sierra Madre

Honolulu, Hawaii's largest city with a population of almost 1 million people, approximately 73% of Hawaii's total, sits in the shadow of Koolau Range, one of the state's last remaining refuges for some of the most endangered bird species on the planet. Earth's most remote archipelago is a biodiversity hotspot that harbors more than a third of the birds and plants in the U.S. As a result of human activities, the Hawaiian Islands have lost 50% of their native avian species. This process has accelerated during the past 200 years, and of the remaining 40 endemic species, 70% currently are endangered. © Chris Johns/National Geographic Image Collection

The terrible devastation caused by the Tsunami reinforced the need for protection of coastal zones. In some places intact coral reefs, mangrove forests, wetland areas and other natural areas could have served as natural buffers and lessened the destruction. Banda Aceh shore, Indonesia, June and December 2004. © Courtesy of GlobeXplorer and DigitalGlobe

Together with the Amazon and the island of New Guinea, the Congo Basin is one of the three largest Wilderness Areas identified by Conservation International. In the vast Congo wilderness, large forest clearings like the ones seen in the Mbeli Bai are notable because they were actually cleared by elephants looking for salt. After loggers killed the elephants, the vegetation reverted to the kind favored by gorillas, which can often be seen calmly feeding in such natural clearings. © Michael Nichols/National Geographic Image Collection

New Britain, Papua New Guinea. Although Papua New Guinea is still considered a tropical wilderness area, rapid deforestation and destruction caused by large mining operations could transform the region into a Biodiversity Hotspot in the next decades. © Patricio Robles Gil/Sierra Madre

Winding deep into the heart of the Amazon, the Itaquai River of Brazil has so far been spared the fate of some of the more easily accessible parts of this vast ecoregion. Mining for gold, oil exploration, exploitation of rubber and timber, forest clearing for cattle ranching and soy bean plantations have all contributed to the tragic demise of less fortunate portions of this still massive wilderness.
© Nicolas Reynard/National Geographic Image Collection

Elephants are an enduring symbol of everything that is wild about Africa. Poaching and habitat loss throughout their vast range, however, nearly wiped out entire populations. It was thanks to protected areas like Amboseli National Park, seen in this photograph, and to a worldwide ivory-trade ban, that elephant populations were able to recover. Today, expanding numbers of elephants and growing human populations are creating a whole new set of challenges in which conflict between farmers and elephants that roam outside of protected areas and into the surrounding countryside play out a tragic drama. © George Steinmetz

We need to think on a large scale to create living landscapes and seascapes that address multiple changing needs and concerns as wildlife and people continue to spill over and across ecological and political borders. In the picture we see a human settlement in the transboundary protected area of Laguna Madre, in the Gulf of Mexico. © Patricio Robles Gil/Sierra Madre

Hugging the coasts of Mexico, Belize, Guatemala, and Honduras, the Mesoamerican Reef is the longest coral reef system in the Western Hemisphere and one of the healthiest. Covering over 1 000 kilometers of shallow Caribbean waters, the buffering effect from sea waves provided by the reef once supported a protected navigable seaway that nourished important commercial and cultural links within the Maya world. The Mesoamerican Caribbean Coral Reef Systems Initiative is a joint effort by all the countries in the region to protect this large transboundary resource. © Kevin Schafer

Aerial photographs and satellite imagery are powerful tools available for the analysis of the changes that the human footprint has taken over time. This satellite image shows plumes of pollution caused by mining tailings. Aside from being toxic, the tailings also cause erosion as they flow downriver. Shanghai, China. © ESA 2004

In a recent Rapid Assessment scientific expedition by Conservation International, the Chiquitano dry forest of Eastern Bolivia, a globally outstanding region in terms of its biological distinctiveness, was declared "the largest remaining tract of relatively undisturbed tall dry forest in the Neo-tropics, if not the entire world." This important ecosystem will soon be bisected by a gas pipeline known as the Cuiabá project. In order to minimize the predictable environmental problems associated with energy projects, a financial conservation mechanism has been created by the two companies involved, Enron and Shell, along with several conservation organizations, including WCS, to find a sustainable development plan for the region. © Willy Kenning

"We were aiming for Midongy du Sud (Midongy-South) National Park [...] Once we reached the park, we couldn't enter because it was shrouded in a dense cover of clouds. We were able to skirt the western flank all the way down, where we witnessed remnants of the original tall closed canopy tropical forest that covered this land until recently. From the satellite pictures I've seen, Madagascar continues to loose forest cover. This park had a few incursions of slash and burn, but only a few—a testament to the idea that management can work?"
Mike Fay, Midongy du Sud National Park, Madagascar. October 2, 2004. © Mike Fay

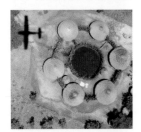

"We headed to Dar es Saalam and spent the night in Arusha [...] We were to stay with a guy named Daudi [...] His business is tourism and he brings clients to isolated places all over Tanzania, showing them what getting close and deep into an ecosystem is all about. It pains Daudi greatly to think that very shortly the world is going to lose its hunters and gatherers. They have no physical stake on the land [...] Hunters and gatherers are universally losing their space to those who have more aggressive tendencies, much greater numbers, and superior physical and technical capacity." Mike Fay, Boma and family compound, Serengeti Park, Tanzania. October 30, 2004. © Mike Fay

"Madagascar seems carpeted with people, rice paddies, and environmental degradation. Here it is difficult to go a minute without seeing extensive land use. There is something wrong. If Madagascar concentrated its rice production and managed the rest of the land so that natural ecosystems could reestablish themselves, I venture to say that they could feed themselves and have a country that looked like a tropical paradise, with all the economic benefits and long-term human benefits that that entails. It's called having your cake and eating it, too."
Mike Fay, Rice paddies in Madagascar. October 2, 2004" © Mike Fay

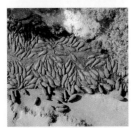

"To call the Katuma a river at this time is generous. It is more like a meandering band of sand with the occasional moist spot [...] We looked over the ledge and there below us, embedded in the bank, were seven motionless, dry, gray forms—hippos that looked like they were sculpted in mud [...] Each hippo only gets enough space to keep the bottom half of his body wet [...] Sometimes one hippo will seem to be taking too much room. There is a spat and pandemonium breaks out, but it is quickly suppressed because none of these animals has the energy to fight."
Mike Fay, Hippos in Katavi National Park, Tanzania. October 24, 2004. © Mike Fay

"Below me was a landscape that had been impacted by humans for at least a couple of hundred years, if not much longer. It showed signs of severe erosion. I wondered when in history humans had destroyed this forest and what had become of them. Today, the landscape contains only the occasional settlement and well-worn cattle trails. The folks who changed this vegetation from forest to eroded clear-cut are long gone. Now, this place can support only a small human population."
Mike Fay, Madagascar Sub-humid Forest Ecoregion, October 1, 2004. © Mike Fay

"It is hard to imagine that a large mammal that existed in herds of hundreds in more than one country in this desert 30 years ago is fast going extinct. Its cohabitant, the scimitar-horned oryx, is already said by many scientists to be extinct in the wild. What blows me away is that the world seems to be complacent about the fact that most of the large mammal fauna of the Sahara Desert will probably go extinct in our lifetimes if we do nothing to save them." Mike Fay, Addax (*Addax nasomaculatus*) in Sahara Desert, December 5, 2004.
© Mike Fay/National Geographic Image Collection

Superlatives define Wadi Rum. Once described by English colonel T.E. Lawrence, better known as Lawrence of Arabia as "immense and resounding divine," this largest of Jordan's deserts is an ancient wilderness that has been trekked by traders and inhabited by Bedouins for many centuries. It is modern travelers, however, that are now creating some serious challenges for this magnificent area. The growing pressure from visitors, including littering and illegal hunting, and the impacts of popular off-road vehicles, are seriously damaging the fragile desert ecology. © Annie Griffiths Belt/National Geographic Image Collection

Dipterocarp trees, like this flowering one photographed in the Danum Valley of Sabah in Borneo, are the most important canopy trees in the rainforests of South East Asia. This group is particularly significant in the island of Borneo where the family reaches its center of diversity. Dipterocarps account for 80 – 90% of the canopy and emergent trees in the lowland rainforests of Sabah. Of the 284 species of dipterocarp occurring in Borneo, approximately 180 are found in Sabah. © Frans Lanting

Among the results of El Carmen-Big Bend Conservation Corridor Initiative between Mexico and the U.S. it is worth highlighting the designation of the first wilderness area in Latin America —20 000 hectares inside the CEMEX properties— located at the northern end of the Maderas del Carmen Protected Area. In the picture we see the mesas and cliffs of El Carmen that for years have avoided the footprint of industrial man and now, thanks to the commitment of CEMEX, have been protected to perpetuity. © Patricio Robles Gil/Sierra Madre

The 2.6-million-hectare Xingu Indigenous Reserve, where the village of Kendjam is located, is home to some 6 000 people of the Kayapo Indian nation, the legal owners of the land. Although it is necessary to fly for more than two hours over unbroken rain forest to arrive in this remote area, the Kayapo have to constantly patrol and defend the boundaries of their territory from intrusions by loggers, cattle-ranches, and soybean plantations, which are constantly pushing the boundaries of this magnificent reserve. Indigenous nations, like the Kayapo, are playing increasingly prominent roles in the conservation of their own homelands. © Cristina Mittermeier

Aerial views allow us to see the millenary paths of the caribous in their annual migration along the Canadian tundra. One of their most recent threats is global warming, that causes important changes in this sensitive ecosystem and affects the food availability for the animals, a factor of greater importance when raising the calves. © Michio Hoshino/Minden Pictures

Mt. Conner in Australia's Northern Territory is the most easterly of central Australia's giant monoliths, which include Ayers Rock (known as Uluru by local Aborigines) and the Olga Rocks. Rising above the desert plain in the southwestern Northern Territory, these giants have tremendous spiritual and cultural significance for the Aborigine population of this vast wilderness area. More than a quarter of the population of the northern territory is Aborigine. © Jean-Paul Ferrero/Auscape

Known as Canada's *Matterhorn,* Mount Assiniboine has an elevation of 3 610 m and is located in British Columbia, in the spectacular wilderness setting of Canada's share of the Rocky Mountains, the backbone of North America. Often referred to as one of the world's leading landscape-scale conservation efforts, the Yellowstone to Yukon Conservation Initiative seeks the long-term protection of this ecological linkage and has grown from an innovative idea to a powerful on-the-ground reality. © Florian Schulz/Visions of the Wild

On its 2 410-km run from the Guiana highlands to the Atlantic ocean, the Orinoco River divides Venezuela into two very different realities. The north, with its already fragmented ecosystems is where 90% of the country's population lives. In contrast, the wild south still harbors vast biological and mineral resources and is where most conservation efforts need to focus to prevent irresponsible exploitation from damaging what has been identified as one of Earth's last remaining wilderness areas. © Robert Caputo/Aurora Photos

The wild and tropical northern half of Australia starts to heat up sometime in late October. Rolling thunderheads of towering cumulus clouds and a hot, steamy, sauna-like climate herald the arrival of the wet season and then, around Christmas, give or take a few weeks, the Australian monsoon, with its heavy rains and occasional cyclone hits. © Randy Olson/National Geographic Image Collection

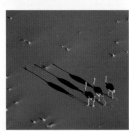

Meaning "sand flat" in Afrikaans, the Sossusvlei region of Namibia is a desert wonderland. Red and orange-colored dunes extend as far as the eye can see and the eerily denuded landscape defies the very existence of wildlife. And yet, gemsbok, oryx and even ostriches can occasionally be seen feeding on the sparse vegetation. © Robert B. Haas/National Geographic Image Collection

Extending for 2 500 kilometers, the Ural Mountains of Russia meander from the hot Kazakh steppes to the frozen coast of the Arctic Ocean. Covered with mixed forests, the highest peaks emerge like ancient islands from the surrounding taiga. The most important part of this vast wilderness is the 7 213 km^2 Pechora-Ilych Zapovednik, or strict protected area, which was formed in 1930 to protect this fragile boreal ecosystem. The Pechora River, seen here, is one of the few rivers in Europe that remain still undisturbed. © Konrad Wothe/Minden Pictures

The Caldera of the Uzon Volcano is located in Kronotsky Strict Nature Reserve on Russia's Kamchatka Peninsula and is part of the Volcanoes of Kamchatka, a UNESCO World Heritage Site. Steep rock cliffs up to 800 meters rim the giant basin of the Caldera that extends for more than a hundred square kilometers. Fumaroles emitting steam and gases make Uzon's Caldera a very distinctive ecosystem in the middle of one of the wildest regions on Earth. © Igor Shpilenok

The Great Limpopo Transfrontier Park, at 3 600 000 hectares, is the largest park in South Africa. and at its heart lies Kruger National Park. One of the park's greatest challenges is the management of its swelling elephant population. From near extermination for the ivory trade before the park was established to a population so large it has been necessary to cull it annually to prevent the elephants from destroying the park and from starving, elephant management to keep the population at a carrying capacity of 7 500 animals remains a difficult and controversial issue. © Gerald Cubitt

Made up of over 400 species of coral, the Great Barrier Reef is the largest coral reef system in the world. Stretching for an amazing 2 300 kilometers along Australia's northeastern coast, it is quite simply the largest living structure on the planet, and the only one visible from space. Protected since 1975 as the Great Barrier Reef Marine Park and recognized as a World Heritage Site, the delicate corals are highly susceptible to coral bleaching due to temperature increases. As is the case with all of our planet's reefs, climate change is widely considered to pose the greatest long-term threat to this remarkable natural wonder. © Theo & Sabine Allofs

Wilderness is evident in many remote corners of the Earth, in the inaccessible mountains or in the beauty of waterfalls, which represent one of the most wonderful spectacles of nature, like the Tamul cascade in the Sierra Madre Oriental in San Luis Potosí, Mexico. © Patricio Robles Gil/Sierra Madre

Living in one of the most extreme weather conditions on earth, the wolves of Ellesmere Island in the Canadian Arctic are too far to be directly threatened by the human footprint. However, indirect effects such as the climate change can disturb the balanced cycles that have reigned for thousands of years in their habitat. © Jim Brandenburg/Minden Pictures

The state of Mato Grosso in Brazil is one of the last wild frontiers on the continent. However, it is quickly becoming the soybean and beef capital of the world. In recent years, agro-industry in the region has experienced explosive growth, especially in beef and soybean production. Between 1998 and 2002 soy production grew by approximately 60% and the cattle herd nearly doubled from 26.2 million in 1991 to 51.6 million in 2001. The Brazilian government estimates that roughly 20 million hectares of rainforest has been cleared over the past 10 years, and that the vast majority of the land was converted to cattle pasture. © Staffan Widstrand

The Okavango River originates in the uplands of Angola and flows into Botswana's Kalahari Desert spreading over the sandy landscape and forming an immense and wondrous inland delta of lagoon and labyrinthine channels, palm-fringed islands and fertile floodplains. Large herds of animals, like the buffalos seen here, roam over flood plains, salt pans and marshy deltas across this magnificent ecosystem.
© Robert B. Haas/National Geographic Image Collection

The Great Desert of Altar—with thousands of square kilometers of deserts and sand dunes—is probably the most arid place in North America. The first settlers in Southern California had to go through these hostile lands, which they named *Camino del Diablo* (The Devil's Path) for its drinking water scarcity. Not finding water holes in the sierra, many of them died of thirst in one of the most pristine and wildest landscapes of the continent. © Patricio Robles Gil/Sierra Madre

It is known as The Great River by the Tlingit people of the Pacific coast, who have traveled on it for thousands of generations. The Stikine River originates in the Cassiar and Stikine Mountains of northwestern British Columbia and drains a 51 000 km^2 basin before crossing the border into the United States on the Alaska Panhandle and discharging into the Pacific. Its main tributary, the Iskut River joins it 11 km upstream from the Alaska border and accounts for about 25% of the river's flow. This river system is considered one of the most endangered in North America. © Sarah Leen/National Geographic Image Collection

Covering some 15 000 hectares, the Chaco National Park was established in 1954 to preserve a sample of the Gran Chaco—a large biome that covers a vast extent of northern Argentina, northwestern Paraguay and southeastern Bolivia. Palm savannas, thorn forests and grasslands dot the landscape of this wild region that was described by the first Spanish who first arrived here as "inhospitable." Outside of the protected areas, rampant overgrazing, oil exploration and human population growth threaten to permanently transform the rugged scenery of this beautiful region. © Willy Kenning

The hippopotamus population of the Okavango River delta in Botswana has come increasingly under pressure. These charismatic animals have all but disappeared from the western delta, where the majority of people live, and there seem to be far fewer hippos than the habitat should be able to support. Hippos are extremely important to the nature of the Okavango and they are known to play a critical role in the hydrology of the delta. There is no doubt that the form and function of this entire ecosystem depends on healthy populations of these large mammals. © Robert B. Haas/National Geographic Image Collection

The awesome force of glaciers like Russell and Moraines in the Yukon Territories, Canada, can carve imposing valleys and flatten wide swaths of land. The rock and soil that is picked up and transferred by such forces creates new landscapes through the constant ebb and flow of the melting and retreating glaciers. © Latin Stock de México/Corbis

The great central desert of Baja California is home to one of the most valuable floral treasures of the Mexican biota, the Cirio or Bojuum Tree (*Idria columnaris*), a rare desert species measuring several meters in height and whose shape reminds us of a huge carrot covered with tiny leaves. Their silhouettes give an odd character to the landscape of this peninsula. © Patricio Robles Gil/Sierra Madre

The Cape fur seal (*Arctocephalus pusillus pusillus*) is the only breeding pinniped found in southern Africa and the only marine mammal still being legally-slaughtered in large numbers. The seals mate and give birth on Kleinsee beach, South Africa but are also found in large numbers in neighboring Namibia, where they compete with that nation's fishing industry. The government has authorized an increase in the number of seals to be culled from 5 000 bulls and 65 000 pups in the 2005 season, to 6 000 bulls and 85 000 pups, which will be clubbed to death between July and November 2006. © David Doubilet

Jagged edges clue us as to how Australia broke away from the ancient Gondwana supercontinent about 100 million years ago. A crater found under the Antarctic ice sheet reveals the place where a giant meteor crashed unto Earth, causing an impact so powerful that the large chunk of land we recognize today as Australia, broke off and began drifting north, pushed away by the expansion of a rift valley into the eastern Indian Ocean. © Cary Wolinsky/National Geographic Image Collection

Known as the river that never reaches the sea, the Okavango River flows instead into the Kalahari Desert creating a fantastic mosaic of swamps and grasslands that supports hundreds of varieties of birds, fish and mammals, including zebras, lions, elephants, hippos and giraffes, like the herd seen here. Fanning out over 16 000 km^2 during the wet season to form the largest inland delta in sub-Saharan Africa, the river slowly thins down, and then, like a glimmering mirage, it disappears.
© Robert B. Haas/National Geographic Image Collection

Split by the Alpine Fault, Tai Poutini/Westland National Park in New Zealand is a place of dramatic contrasts. To the east, mountains rise abruptly into steep, forested slopes traversed by deep, impassable gorges. High above, permanent snowfields feed myriad glaciers, including the impressive Balfour glacier, seen here. The park extends from snow-capped mountains, rimu forests, and tussock grasslands to coastal lakes, rivers and wetlands; and from the highest peaks of the Ka Tiritiri o Te Moana/Southern Alps to the remote beaches of the wild West Coast. © Colin Monteath/www.hedgehoghouse.com

El Salto del Ángel measuring more than 900 meters is the world's highest waterfall and is located in one of the most remote areas of the Venezuelan savanna. Its famous plateau rock formations called *tepuis* are so ancient and inaccessible that they host flora and fauna endemic to each of them.
© Patricio Robles Gil/Sierra Madre

Lake Nakuru in Kenya shelters nearly 370 bird species, including the lesser flamingo and the greater flamingo, of which 1.4 million have been counted on the site. Its location on a rocky volcanic substrate, weak flow, intense evaporation and low depth give it a high soda content, that favors the formation of blue-green algae, microorganisms, and small crustaceans, which provided the basic diet of flamingos. However, chemical products used in river farming and the water runoff from the nearby city of Nakuru have gradually polluted the lake waters. © Tom Mangelsen

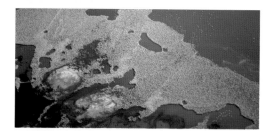

The Namib Rand Nature Reserve harbors a vivid and varied mosaic of all the natural beauty of the Namib desert. Steep mountain ranges, vast savannas, imposing sand dunes of deep red hues, and clay pans. Herds of wildlife, like the zebras seen here, sprint across plains sprinkled with "fairy circles"—circular, concave depressions that are devoid of vegetation and are often surrounded by a fringe of tall grass. Despite 25 years of research, scientists are still puzzling over what causes these grass-ringed bald spots. © George Steinmetz

Water scarcity in desert ecosystems or the rugged topography of some mountains makes preservation of the wilderness easier. But sometimes the quest for new sources of energy has opened new paths for the development of resources and expansion of the human footprint, as in the Vizcaíno Biosphere Reserve in Baja California where the Energy Department of Mexico opened a new geothermal power station in the volcanoes Las Tres Vírgenes and El Azufre, both in the picture. © Patricio Robles Gil/Sierra Madre

The short Arctic summer brings hundreds of beluga whales (*Delphinapterus leucas*) into Cunningham Inlet in Canada to nurse their young and to molt in the warm water at the mouth of the Cunningham River. For a few precious weeks, the river becomes a breathtaking natural spectacle of frolicking white whales. © Günter Ziesler

Habitat fragmentation among different ecosystems has limited the freedom of wild species to roam in search of new food sources or reproduction areas. An interesting example of the connectivity of ecosystems is the return of the black bear (*Ursus americanus*) to southwestern Texas after a forty-year absence. This came about, on the one hand, due to growing populations in the Mexican mountains, protected under a private ranching scheme, and on the other hand, due to protection of the existing biological corridors between both countries, allowing young bears to re-conquer their former territories across the Rio Grande. © Patricio Robles Gil/Sierra Madre

Covering much of the central Namib desert, the Namib-Naukluft National Park in Namibia is one of Africa's largest protected areas and one of the most beautiful and powerful landscapes on Earth. Its isolation, remoteness and our own vulnerability in such a harsh environment, makes a visit to this area an almost spiritual experience. The slow-shifting sands of the Soussuvlei dunes, some of the largest and oldest in the world, are one of the most awesome sights on our planet. © George Steinmetz

Arnhem Land, on the rooftop of Australia is a very important Aboriginal territory. The highly-seasonal monsoon climate that characterizes this region also drives most ecological processes. Rainfall quotas of 1 000 to 1 600 mm a year, feed the vast wetlands and inundated paperback forests (*Melaleuca* spp.) that dominate the region. The western Arnhem Land massif is the headwaters of many large rivers. Tall waterfalls mark the path of many of these rivers as they leave the massif. The lowland reaches of these rivers are highly sinuous as they traverse the flat floodplains, and their banks are broken seasonally to extend over large annual swamplands. © Bill Bachman

One of the features that distinguish the forests of northern Congo from other parts of the central African wilderness area is the existence of hundreds of forest clearings, called "bais", which attract high concentrations of large mammals, including gorillas, elephants, buffalos, and bongos. The remote Capital Bai, seen here, is a large mineral-rich clearing that attracts large numbers of forest elephants. © Michael Nichols/National Geographic Image Collection

Over the past 50 years, the population of emperor penguins (*Aptenodytes forsteri*) in Antarctica has declined by 50%. An abnormally long warm spell in the Southern Ocean during the late 1970s has been blamed for this decline. Although it is impossible to determine if this warming trend was caused by climate change or was a natural climatic variation, what is certain is that today the Antarctic ice sheet is losing up to 152 km^3 of ice annually due to warmer temperatures. © Tui De Roy/Roving Tortoise

The blue wildebeest (*Connochaetes taurinus*) is a key species of the Serengeti-Mara region in East Africa. Outside the Serengeti and Masai-Mara protected areas, the herds face land clearing for agricultural production and competition for food with Masai cattle. Poaching both within and outside the reserves is also a problem. © Joan Root/SAL-OSF Limited

Montserrat, a Catalonian name literally meaning "jagged mountain" is the name given to the beautiful pink peaks of this mountain in Barcelona, Spain. The mountain, which was declared a natural park in 1989, has great spiritual and religious significance in the region and even served as a symbol of the Catalonian opposition to the Franco regime. © Klaus D. Francke/Bilderberg

"High horns, low horns, silence, and finally a pandemonium of trumpets, rattles, croaks, and cries that almost shakes the bog with its nearness, but without yet disclosing whence it comes" were the evocative words used by Aldo Leopold to describe the intense wildlife spectacle of thousands of sandhill cranes (*Grus canadensis*) arriving by the thousands to the Platte River in the midwestern USA. The flocks spend several weeks resting and feeding on the extensive corn fields of the region before returning to their breeding grounds in the north. © Tom & Pat Leeson

Stretching along the coast of Namibia, the Namib is the world's oldest desert and also the most spectacular one. Endlessly reshaped by the relentless winds, giant dunes, some over 300 meters high, adorn the landscape. © Gerald Cubitt

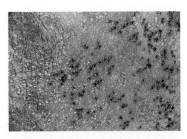

"When we broke through the clouds, I spotted the most gigantic patch of green and water I have ever seen. This delta is a few hundred kilometers long and wide—bigger than Florida's Everglades. At the edge of the swamp, we spied a group of sable antelope. A few minutes later we were over a rich, green mixture of papyrus and phragmites reeds. In the distance, I spotted a patch of dark black on the horizon against the verdant green: buffalo. We buzzed on over and before we reached the spot, a flock of white birds exploded from the patch of black: egrets." Mike Fay, September 9, 2004. Zambezi Delta in Mozambique. © Mike Fay

Created in 1937 to safeguard the magnificent mountain wilderness, Los Glaciares National Park is the second largest park in Argentina. The giant ice cap that gives it its name is the largest one outside of Antarctica, and it feeds 47 large glaciers, of which only 13 flow towards the Atlantic Ocean. With an annual income of over 1 million dollars, Los Glaciares is one of Argentina's major tourist attractions and one of the most important sources of revenue in the region. © Willy Kenning

One of the most recent and interesting conservation stories in Mexico took place in this island, Espíritu Santo, in the Gulf of California. Several private groups of civil organizations joined forces—first time ever on such a large scale—and bought the island from a group of communal land owners. They donated it to the Mexican nation so as to protect the island and its wilderness in perpetuity, and prevent the construction of resorts being promoted by some tourism developers. © Patricio Robles Gil/Sierra Madre

The Linyanti River winds through the arid landscape forming a natural border between Namibia and Botswana. The Linyati Wildlife Reserve, located on the Botswanan bank of the river, is fringed with swamps and slow-flowing lagoons where large herds of animals, like elephants (*Loxodonta africana*), converge during the dry winter months. © Frans Lanting

One of the few places on Earth that can still be called a true wilderness is the strikingly beautiful Kamchatka Peninsula. Part of the "Ring of Fire," Kamchatka is one of the most active volcanic regions on Earth. Of the over 100 volcanoes found here, over a dozen are active. Some of the dormant ones, like Maly Semyachik Volcano, whose crater is filled with azure-colored acidic water, are truly stunning. With a depth of 120 and 500 meters in width, the water is so acidic, it simply corrodes metal and eats away at clothes. © Igor Shpilenok

After the recent natural disasters caused by hurricanes and tsunamis, wetlands have been revalued not only for their importance in maintaining global fisheries but because of their role as buffer zones in the event of natural disasters. © Patricio Robles Gil/Sierra Madre

Mountain summits are sacred for many cultures and people. Though not rich in biodiversity, they are regions where man has not yet left his footprint. That is why humans must show great respect in their attempts to conquer them. © Patricio Robles Gil/Sierra Madre

One of the most famous *tepuis* or table top mountains in the world, Mount Roraima, in Venezuela rises above the clouds. The *tepuis* in this region are known for their large numbers of endemic species. © Adrian Warren/www.lastrefuge.co.uk

Mozambique's southern province of Maputo is home to the Maputo Elephant Reserve. Bordering South Africa and Swaziland, the reserve is part of the Lubombo Transfrontier Conservation Area, an international conservation project. Until 1995 Maputo was ravaged by war and for over a decade the park was left completely unprotected. Much of the wildlife was poached shamelessly, including many ungulates, like the reedbuck (*Redunca arundinum*) seen here. Sadly, all of the rhinoceros in the park perished and only 200 elephants survived. © Chris Johns/National Geographic Image Collection

At the northern end of the mountain ranges the landscapes are as beautiful as they are remote. The high summits are flanked with valleys where the great glaciers are born. In Kenai's peninsula, in Alaska, we see, standing out like knives, several peaks that have probably never been conquered by man and where we should guarantee no footprint will be left in the future. © Patricio Robles Gil/Sierra Madre

The construction of high-fence enclosures destined to the genetic breeding of game species in search of bigger trophies is causing severe habitat fragmentation in northern Mexico and southern United States, impeding the free roaming of wild species and interfering in the natural dispersion of populations. In the picture we see a white-tailed deer through the Tamaulipan shrub. © Patricio Robles Gil/Sierra Madre

The loud screeching of scarlet macaws (*Ara macao*) is one of the most emblematic sounds of the American tropical forests. This couple of macaws flies over the canopy at Montes Azules Biosphere Reserve in Chiapas, Mexico. The colorful, noisy flocks of these birds represent one of the greatest wildlife spectacles. Unfortunately, illegal trading and habitat loss caused by deforestation is threatening the existence of wild parrots and parakeets. One such case is the Indigo macaw (*Andorhynchus leari*), considered to be extinct in the wild. © Martin H. Price

The elaborate and beautiful sandstone landscapes found in the states of Utah, Arizona and Colorado in the United States, can only be described as nature's artwork. These awe-inspiring formations were created by the patient layering of thousands of tiny grains of quartz that settled into the bottom of oceans, lakes and rivers over several millennia. When our planet's climate changed and the hardened sediments were exposed, the forces of wind and water shaped them into the colorful and evocative formations we can find today in the deserts of the American southwest. © Frans Lanting

Marine mammals are as fascinating as they are diverse, and our relationship with them is full of contrast. Commercial hunting still is a common practice, even when in the past we have seen how it put the blue whale at great risk and drove its population to a situation from which it has not yet recovered. However, marine-mammal watching around the world has proven to be, if developed carefully, a sustainable alternative with low impact on the environment. © Patricio Robles Gil/Sierra Madre

The limited precipitation in the Arctic causes some islands to have plateau edges with sheer cliffs that create inaccessible coastlines. Some of these cliffs, located in areas adjacent to productive marine waters provide an excellent protected nesting habitat for colonies of seabirds like these ones at the edge of Lancaster Sound, Canada. © Robert Glenn Ketchum

One of the biggest threats to the North American wilderness is the creation of small breeding facilities for species with hunting value. Animals like the desert bighorn sheep, flagship species of the great desert mountain ranges, are subject to this kind of management. By moving this activity out of the fences into the wild we are promoting the fair chase, increasing the bighorn sheep's hunting value by providing a wilderness experience, and creating a sustainable alternative for the management of this species. © Patricio Robles Gil/Sierra Madre

Ellesmere Island is as far north as one can travel into the Canadian Arctic. Incised by fjords and ice shelves, this large and fragile wilderness is home to small herds of muskoxen and caribou, while its surrounding waters harbor narwhals, seals and polar bears. Considered one of the most remote places on the planet, Ellesmere was once inhabited by Paleo-Eskimo people, but now has no permanent human dwellings and is only visited by adventurers during the Arctic Summer months. © Jim Brandenburg/Minden Pictures

Situated on the rugged coast of the state of Maine in northeastern United States, Acadia National Park encompasses over 18 800 hectares of granite mountains, forests, woodlands, lakes and ponds, and extends all the way to the rugged ocean shoreline. In order to preserve this magnificent landscape the United States Congress created the park in 1929. Today this protected area hosts over two million visitors a year and protects over 273 species of birds, seven species of reptiles, eleven species of amphibians and forty species of mammals. © Michael Melford/National Geographic Image Collection

The amazing coloration of the delta in Lake Natron, Tanzania, is the result of the very high levels of evaporation it experiences. As water evaporates during the dry season, salinity levels increase and salt-loving organisms, like cyanobacteria, begin to thrive. The red pigment in the bacteria produces the deep red colors found in the deeper parts of the lake while the orange colors are found in the shallower areas. In 2001 the government of Tanzania identified the lake as a Ramsar Wetland of International Importance, an intergovernmental treaty meant to protect wetlands. © Mike Fay

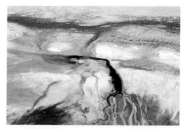

Torres del Paine National Park was declared a UNESCO Biosphere Reserve in 1978. It lies in the heart of the Cordillera del Paine, a small but spectacular range in the Chilean Patagonia. These gigantic granite monoliths were shaped by the forces of the glacial age and are one of the most iconic landscapes of the Patagonian wilderness. © Peter Essick/Aurora Photos

The plains of Botswana are the backdrop for large herds of Cape buffalo (*Syncerus caffer caffer*), often numbering in the hundreds. The females and their offspring make up most of the herd while males spend most of their time in bachelor groups. When approached by a predator, the entire herd, always alert to possible attacks by lions, leopards or wild dogs, can flee in a fantastic stampede of dust and hooves. © Frans Lanting

"With a stroke of a pen, the president can not only accomplish the single largest act of conservation in American history, but he can inspire the American public on the broader importance of our ocean and coastal environments," was the statement made by a senior United States administration official on the occasion of proclamation of America's newest and largest park in Hawaii. With a total area of 363 000 km^2, the Northwestern Hawaiian National Monument, created this year by President George W. Bush, is larger than all other American national parks combined. © Sterling Zumbrunn

Polar bears (*Ursus maritimus*) like this one photographed in Hudson Bay, Canada are confined to the Arctic Circle where temperatures are increasing at the rate of 1.2 degrees Celsius per decade. The ice sheet is becoming dangerously thin and, in some places, disappearing completely forcing the bears to swim increasingly larger distances across open sea—up to 100 kilometers—to find food. Hypothermia and exhaustion are causing a rising number of polar bears to drown. Populations decrease has prompted scientists to upgrade their conservation status from "least concern" to "vulnerable." © Norbert Rosing/National Geographic Image Collection

The Iriri River, a major tributary of the mighty Xingu, feeds a lush and productive landscape and the lives of thousands of Kayapo Indians in the Amazon. However. five huge hydroelectric dams are planned on the Xingu River, and there are plans to complete the second half of a 1 770 kilometers paved highway. As we close the last page of this book, let's reflect on the necessary boundaries to protect the last of the wild from human trampling. Will we stand for a higher moral highground?, or will all hope of an enlightened society that can coexist with nature drown along with the Xingu basin? © Russell A. Mittermeier

INTRODUCTION

Berry, W. 1982. Getting Along with Nature. Home Economics. North Point Press, New York.

Intergovernmental Panel on Climate Change. 2001. Climate Change 2001: Synthesis Report. UNEP/WMO. Available at: http://www.ipcc.ch/

Millennium Ecosystem Assessment. 2006. Living Beyond Our Means: Natural Assets and Human Well-being (Statement of the MA Board). Available at: http://www.millenniumassessment.org/en/Products.aspx

Pew Oceans Commission. 2003. America's Living Oceans: Charting a Course for Sea Change. Pew Charitable Trusts. Available at: http://www.pewtrusts.com/pdf/env_pew_oceans_final_report.pdf

Sanderson, E.W., M. Jaiteh, M.A. Levy, K.H. Redford, A.V. Wannebo and G. Woolmer. 2002. The Human Footprint and the Last of the Wild. *BioScience* 52(10):891-904. Also see www.wcs.org/humanfootprint

1. POPULATION

Carnevale, E., C. Stauffer, A. Gelbard and K. Darvich-Kodjuri. 1999. *World Population: More than Just Numbers*. Population Reference Bureau, Washington, D.C.

Center for International Earth Science Information Network (CIESIN), Columbia University; United Nations Food and Agriculture Programme (FAO), and Centro Internacional de Agricultura Tropical (CIAT). 2005a. Gridded Population of the World: Future Estimates, 2005 (GPW2005): Population Grids. Palisades, NY: Socioeconomic Data and Applications Center (SEDAC), Columbia University. Available at: http://sedac.ciesicolumbia.edu/gpw (22 December 2005).

Center for International Earth Science Information Network (CIESIN), Columbia University; United Nations Food and Agriculture Programme (FAO), and Centro Internacional de Agricultura Tropical (CIAT). 2005b. Gridded Population of the World: Future Estimates, 2015 (GPW2015): Population Grids. Palisades, NY: Socioeconomic Data and Applications Center (SEDAC), Columbia University. Available at: http://sedac.ciesin.columbia.edu/gpw (22 December 2005).

Center for International Earth Science Information Network (CIESIN), Columbia University; United Nations Food and Agriculture Programme (FAO), and Centro Internacional de Agricultura Tropical (CIAT). 2005c. Gridded Population of the World: Future Estimates, 2005 (GPW2005): Population Density Grids. Palisades, NY: Socioeconomic Data and Applications Center (SEDAC), Columbia University. Available at: http://sedac.ciesin.columbia.edu/gpw (22 December 2005).

Center for International Earth Science Information Network (CIESIN), Columbia University; United Nations Food and Agriculture Programme (FAO), and Centro Internacional de Agricultura Tropical (CIAT). 2005d. Gridded Population of the World: Future Estimates, 2015 (GPW2015): Population Density Grids. Palisades, NY: Socioeconomic Data and Applications Center

(SEDAC), Columbia University. Available at: http://sedac.ciesin.columbia.edu/gpw (22 December 2005).

Cohen, J.E. 1995. *How Many People Can the Earth Support?* W.W. Norton, New York.

Food and Agriculture Organization. 1997. *State of the World's Forests 1997*. Food and Agriculture Organization of the United Nations, Rome.

Gorenflo, L.J. 2002. *The Evaluation of Human Population in Conservation Planning: An Example from the Sonoran Desert Ecoregion*. Publications for Capacity Building. The Nature Conservancy, Arlington.

Gorenflo, L.J. 2006. Human demography, land use, and conservation in the Apache Highlands Ecoregion, U.S.–Mexico Borderlands. In R. Cincotta, L.J. Gorenflo and D. Macgeean (eds.), *Demographic Ecogeography: Relationships Between Human Population Dynamics and Biological Diversity*. Springer, Berlin.

Gorenflo, L.J. and K. Brandon. 2006. *Living in the Gaps: The Human Dimensions of Expanding the Global Protected Area System*. Center for Applied Biodiversity Science, Conservation International, Washington, D.C.

McKee, J. 2003. *Sparing Nature. The Conflict between Human Population Growth and Earth's Biodiversity*. Rutgers University Press, New Brunswick.

Pimm, S.L., G.J. Russell, J.L. Gittleman and T.M. Brooks. 1995. The Future of Biodiversity. *Science* 269:347-350.

United States Bureau of the Census. 2005. Population Clock. Available at: http://www.census.gov/ (1 January 2006).

United Nations Population Division. World Population Prospects: The 2004 Revision Population Database, 2005. Available at: http://esa.un.org/unpp (Accessed 02 June 2005).

2. HUMAN ACCESS

Auzel, P. and D.S. Wilkie. 2000. Wildlife Use in Northern Congo: Hunting in a Commercial Logging Concession. In: J.G. Robinson and E.L. Bennett (eds.), *Hunting for Sustainability in Tropical Forests*. Columbia University Press, New York, pp. 413-426.

Bennett, E.L. and M.T. Gumal. 2001. The inter-relationships of commercial logging, hunting, and wildlife in Sarawak, and recommendations for forest management. In: R.A. Fimbel, A. Grajal and J.G. Robinson (eds.), *The Cutting Edge: Conserving Wildlife in Managed Tropical Forests*. Columbia University Press, New York, pp. 359-374.

Chin, C.L.M. 2002. *Hunting Patterns and Wildlife Densities in Primary and Production Forests in Upper Baram, Sarawak*. Master's thesis, Universiti Malaysia Sarawak.

Elkan, P.W., S.W. Elkan, A. Moukassa, R. Malonga, M. Ngangoue and L.D. Smith. In press. Managing Threats from Bushmeat Hunting in a Concession in the Republic of Congo. In: C. Peres and W. Laurence (eds.), *Emerging Threats to Tropical Forests*.

Griffin, P.B. and M.B. Griffin. 2000. Agta Hunting and the Sustainability of Resource Use in Northeastern Luzon, Philippines. In: J.G. Robinson and E.L. Bennett (eds.), *Hunting for Sustainability in Tropical Forests*. Columbia University Press, New York, pp. 325-335.

Johns, A.G. 1997. *Timber Production and Biodiversity Con-

servation in Tropical Rain Forests*. Cambridge University Press, Cambridge.

Millennium Ecosystem Assessment. 2005. *Ecosystems and Human Well-Being: Synthesis*. Island Press, Washington D.C.

Robinson, J.G. 1994. Carving Up Tomorrow's Planet. *International Wildlife*, 24:30-37.

Robinson, J.G., K.H. Redford, and E.L. Bennett. 1999. Wildlife Harvest in Logged Tropical Forests. *Science*, 284:595-596.

Robinson, J.G. and E.L. Bennett. 2000. Carrying Capacity Limits to Sustainable Hunting in Tropical Forests. In: J.G. Robinson and E.L. Bennett (eds.), *Hunting for Sustainability in Tropical Forests*. Columbia University Press, New York, pp. 13-30.

Rumiz, D.I., D.S. Guinart, N.R. Solar and J.C.F. Herrera. 2001. Logging and Hunting in Community Forests and Corporate Concessions: Two Contrasting Case Studies in Bolivia. In: R.A. Fimbel, A. Grajal and J.G. Robinson (eds.), *The Cutting Edge: Conserving Wildlife in Managed Tropical Forests*. Columbia University Press, New York, pp. 333-358.

Stearman, A.M. 2000. A Pound of Flesh: Social Change and Modernization as Factors in Hunting Sustainability Among Neotropical Indigenous Societies. In: J.G. Robinson and E.L. Bennett (eds.), *Hunting for Sustainability in Tropical Forests*. Columbia University Press, New York, pp. 233-250.

Wilkie, D.S., J.G. Sidle, G.C. Boundzanga, P. Auzel and S. Blake. 2001. Defaunation, not Deforestation: Commercial Logging and Market Hunting in Northern Congo. In: R.A. Fimbel, A. Grajal and J.G. Robinson (eds.), *The Cutting Edge: Conserving Wildlife in Managed Tropical Forests*. Columbia University Press, New York, pp. 375-399.

3. LAND USE

Boocock, C.N. 2002. Environmental Impacts of Foreign Direct Investment in the Mining Sector in Sub-Saharan Africa, *OECD Global Forum on International Investment*. Conference on Foreign Direct Investment and the Environment. Lessons to be Learned from the Mining Sector. Organization for Economic Co-operation and Development, Paris, p. 35.

Brandon, K. 2000. Moving Beyond Integrated Conservation and Development Projects (ICDPs) to Achieve Biodiversity Conservation. In: D.R. Lee and C.B. Barrett (eds.), *Tradeoffs or Synergies? Agricultural Intensification, Economic Development and the Environment*. CAB International, Wallingford.

Calhoun, A.J.K. and M.W. Klemens. 2002. Best Development Practices: Conserving Pool-Breeding Amphibians in Residential and Commercial Development in the Northeastern United States. MCA Technical Paper No. 5, Metropolitan Conservation Alliance, Wildlife Conservation Soceity, Bronx, New York.

Folke, C., S. Carpenter, B. Walker, M. Scheffer, T. Elmqvist, L.H. Gunderson and C.S. Holling. 2004. Regime Shifts, Resilience, and Biodiversity in Ecosystem Management. *Annual Review of Ecology and Systematics*, 35:557-581.

Forman, R.T.T., D. Sperling, J.A. Bissnette, A.P. Clevenger, C.D. Cutshall, V.H. Dale, L. Fahrig, R. France, C.R. Goldman, K. Heanue, J.A. Jones, F.J. Swanson, T. Turrentine and T.C. Winter. 2003. *Road Ecology*. Island Press, Washington, D.C.

Hansen, A.J., R.L. Knight, J.M. Marluff, S. Powell, K. Brown, P.H. Gude and K. Jones. 2005. Effects of Exurban Development on Biodiversity: Patterns, Mechanisms, and Research Needs. *Ecological Applications*, 16:1893-1905.

Hilty, J.A., A.M. Merenlender, W.Z. Lidicker, Jr. 2006. *Corridor Ecology: The Science and Practice of Linking Landscapes for Biodiversity Conservation*. Island Press, Washington, D.C.

Johnson, E. and M.W. Klemens (eds.). 2005. *Nature in Fragments: The Legacy of Sprawl*. Columbia University Press, New York.

Rodrigues, A.S.L. *et al.* 2004. Global Gap Analysis: Priority Regions for Expanding the Global Protected-Area Network, *BioScience* 54(12):1092-1100.

UN-Habitat. 2001. State of the World's Cities, 2001. United Nations Centre for Human Settlement (Habitat) Publications Unit, Nairobi.

Wilcove, D., M. Bean, R. Bonnie and M. McMillan. 1996. *Rebuilding the Arc: Toward a More Effective Endangered Species Act for Private Land*. Environmental Defense Fund, Washington, D.C.

4. ENERGY

Archer, C. and M.Z. Jacobson. 2005. Evaluation of Global Wind Power, *Journal of Geophysical Research*, Vol. 110. Available at: http://www.stanford.edu/~lozej/2004JD005462.pdf.

Berger, J. 2004. The Last Mile: How to Sustain Long Distance Migration in Mammals. *Conservation Biology*, 18:320-329.

Bund, M. and A. Weir. 2005. The Seven Myths of Nuclear Terrorism / Current History. Available at: http://bcsia.ksg.harvard.edu/BCSIA_content/documents/BunnWier.pdf

Cameron, R.D., W.T. Smith, R.G. White and B. Griffith. 2005. Central Arctic Caribou and Petroleum Development: Distributional, Nutritional, and Reproductive Implications. *Arctic*, 58:1-9.

Chernobyl Children's Project International. 2005. Available at: www.chernobyl-international.org

Feiveson, H. 2001. The Search for Proliferation-Resistant Nuclear Power, *F.A.S. Public Interest Report*, Federation of American Scientists, Vol. 54, No. 5. Available at: www.fas.org

Ferguson, C.D., W.C. Potter, A. Sands, L.S. Spector and F.L. Wehling. 2004. *The Four Faces of Nuclear Terrorism*, Center for Nonproliferation Studies, first edition.

Keshner M.S. and R. Arya. 2004. *Study of Potential Reductions Resulting from Super-Large-Scale Manufacturing of PV Modules*, National Renewable Energy Lab, NREL/SR-520-36846, October 2004. Available at: www.nrel.gov/ncpv/thin_film

Lovins, A. and H. Lovins. 1981. *Brittle Power, Energy Strategy for National Security*, prepared for the Civil Defense
Preparedness Agency. Available at: www.rmi.org/sitepages/pid1011.php

Lovins, A. 2005. Energy Efficiency, *Encyclopedia of Energy, A Taxonomic Overview*, Vol. 2, Elsevier Academic Press.

NAS. 2003. Cumulative Environmental Effects of Oil and Gas Activities on Alaska's North Slope. The National Academies Press.

Noss, R.F., C. Carroll, K. Vance-Borland and G. Wuerthner. 2002. A Multicriteria Assessment of the Irreplaceability and Vulnerability of Sites in the Greater Yellowstone Ecosystem. *Conservation Biology*, 16:895-908.

Patzek, T.W. and D. Pimentel. 2005. Thermodynamics of Energy Production from Biomass, invited manuscript, *Critical Reviews in Plant Sciences*. Available at: http://petroleum.berkeley.edu/papers/-patzek/

Rockström J., L. Gordon, C. Folke *et al.* 1999. Linkages Among Water Vapor Flows, Food Production, and Terrestrial Ecosystem Services. *Conservation Ecology*, 3:5. Available at: www.consecol.org/vol3/iss2/art5

St. Louis, V.L., Kelly C.A., Duchemin E., et al. 2000. Reservoir surfaces as sources of greenhouse gases to the atmosphere: a global estimate. *BioScience* 50: 766–75.

The World Commission on Dams. 2000. A New Framework for Decision-Making: The Report of the World Commission on Dams. An Overview. November 16/2000.

UNDP. 2000. *World Energy Assessment: Energy and the Challenge of Sustainability*, United Nations Development Programme. Available at: www.undp.org/seed/eap/activities/wea

UN/SADC, Chernobyl. Info. 2005. A partnership of the United Nations and the Swiss Agency for Development and Cooperation. Available at: http://Chernobyl.info

Van Beers, C. and A. de Moor. 2001. *Public Subsidies and Policy Failures*, Edward Elgar Publishers, 2001. See also, A. de Moor, *Building a Grand Deal to Phase Out Harmful Energy Subsidies*, INFORSE-Seminar, Sustainable Energy for Europe, Nov. 29, 2002. Available at: www.inforse.dk/europe/ppt_docs/Subsidies-Andre.ppt.

Williams, R.H. 2001. Nuclear and Alternative Energy Supply Options for an Environmentally Constrained World: A Long-Term Perspective, prepared for the Nuclear Control Institute Conference Nuclear Power and the Spread of Nuclear Weapons: Can We Have One Without the Other? Washington, D.C., April 2001. Available at: www.nci.org/conf/williams/williams.pdf

Zweibel, K. 2005. The Terawatt Challenge for Thin Film PV. In: J. Poortmans and V. Archipov (eds.), *Thin Film Solar Cells: Fabrication, Characterization and Applications*. John Wiley, 2005.

5. THREATENED BIODIVERSITY

Baillie, J.E.M., C. Hilton-Taylor and S.N. Stuart (eds.). 2004. *2004 IUCN Red List of Threatened Species. A Global Species Assessment*. IUCN, Gland, Switzerland, and Cambridge, U.K.

BirdLife International. 2004. State of the World's Birds 2004–Indicators for Our Changing World. BirdLife International, Cambridge.
Bisby, F.A., J. Shimura, M. Ruggiero, J. Edwards and C. Haeuser. 2002. Taxonomy, at the Click of a Mouse. *Nature*, 418:367.

Butchart, S.H.M., A.J. Stattersfield, L.A. Bennun, S.M. Shutes, H.R. Akçakaya, J.E.M. Baillie, S.N. Stuart, C. Hilton-Taylor and G.M. Mace. 2004. Measuring Global Trends in the Status of Biodiversity: Red List Indices for Birds. *Public Library of Science Biology*, 2(12):e383.

Eken, G., L. Bennun, T.M. Brooks, W. Darwall, L.D.C. Fishpool, M. Foster, D. Knox, P. Langhammer, P. Matiku, E. Radford, P. Salaman, W. Sechrest, M.L. Smith, S. Spector and A. Tordoff. 2004. Key Biodiversity Areas as Site Conservation Targets. *BioScience*, 54(12):1110-1118.

Gaston, K.J. 1996. Species-range-size Distributions: Patterns, Mechanisms, and Implications. *TRENDS in Ecology and Evolution*, 11(5):197-201.

Gaston, K.J., R.L. Pressey and C.R. Margules. 2002. Persistence and Vulnerability: Retaining Biodiversity in the Landscape and in Protected Areas. *Journal of Bioscience*, 27 (Suppl. 2):361-384.

Lennon, J. J., P. Koleff, J.J.D. Greenwood and K.J. Gaston. 2004. Contribution of Rarity and Commonness to Patterns of Species Richness. *Ecology Letters*, 7:81-87.

Margules, C.R. and R.L. Pressey. 2000. Systematic Conservation Planning. *Nature*, 405:243-253.

Pressey, R.L., I.R. Johnson and P.D. Wilson. 1994. Shades of Irreplaceability – Towards a Measure of the Contribution of Sites to a Reservation Goal. *Biodiversity and Conservation*, 3:242-262.

Ricketts, T.H., E. Dinerstein, T. Boucher, T.M. Brooks, S.H.M. Butchart, M. Hoffmann, J.F. Lamoreux, J. Morrison, M. Parr, J.D. Pilgrim, A.S.L. Rodrigues, W. Sechrest, G.E. Wallace, K. Berlin, J. Bielby, N.D. Burgess, D.R. Church, N. Cox, D. Knox, C. Loucks, G.W. Luck, L.L. Master, R. Moore, R. Naidoo, R. Ridgely, G.E. Schatz, G. Shire, H. Strand, W. Wettengel and E. Wikramanayake. 2005. Pinpointing and Preventing Imminent Extinctions. *Proceedings of the National Academy of Sciences, USA*, 102(51):18497-18501.

Rodrigues, A.S.L., J.D. Pilgrim, J.F. Lamoreux, M. Hoffmann and T.M. Brooks. 2006. The Value of the IUCN Red List for Conservation. *TRENDS in Ecology and Evolution*, 21(2):71-76.

Rondinini, C., S.N. Stuart and L. Boitani. 2005. Habitat Suitability Models and the Shortfall in Conservation Planning for African Vertebrates. *Conservation Biology*, 19(5):1488-1497.

Sanderson, E.W., M. Jaiteh, M.A. Levy, K.H. Redford, A.V. Wannebo and G. Woolmer. 2002. The Human Footprint and the Last of the Wild. *BioScience*, 52(10):891-904.

Wilson, K., R.L. Pressey, A. Newton, M. Burgman, H. Possingham and C. Weston. 2005. Measuring and Incorporating Vulnerability into Conservation Planning. *Environmental Management*, 35(5):527-543.

6. THE GLOBAL IMPERATIVE OF WILDERNESS

Allnutt, T., E. Wikramanayake, E. Dinerstein, C. Loucks, R. Jackson, D. Hunter and C. Carpenter. 2002. Composition of the Alpine Himalayan Protected Areas Network and its Contribution to Biodiversity Conservation. In: E. Wikramanayake, E. Dinerstein, C.J. Loucks, D. Olson, J. Morrison, J. Lamoreux, M. McKnight and P. Hedao (eds.), *Terrestrial Ecoregions of the Indo-Pacific: A Conservation Assessment*. Island Press, Washington, D.C., pp. 131-135.

Bryant, D., D. Nielsen and L. Tangley. 1997. *The Last Frontier Forests: Ecosystems and Economies on the Edge*. World Resources Institute, Washington D.C. Available at: http://www.wri.org/wri/ffi/lff-eng/index.html

Hannah, L., D. Lohse, C. Hutchinson, J.L. Carr and A. Langkerani. 1994. A Preliminary Inventory of Human Disturbance of World Ecosystems. *Ambio*, 23:246-250.

Margules, C.R. and R.L. Pressey. 2000. Systematic Conservation Planning. *Nature*, 405:243 - 253.

Marris, E. 2005. Tsunami Damage Was Enhanced by Coral Theft. *Nature*, 436:1071.

McCloskey, M.J. and H. Spalding. 1989. A Reconnaissance-level Inventory of the Amount of Wilderness Remaining in the World. *Ambio*, 8:221-227.

Millennium Ecosystem Assessment. 2005. *Ecosystems and Human Well-being: Synthesis*. Island Press, Washington, D.C.

Pounds, J.A., M.R. Bustamante, L.A. Coloma, J.A. Consuegra, M.P.L. Fogden, P.N. Foster, E. La Marca, K.L. Masters, A. Merino-Viteri, R. Puschendorf, S.R. Ron, G.A. Sánchez-Azofeifa, C.J. Still and B.E. Young. 2006. Widespread Amphibian Extinctions from Epidemic Disease Driven by Global Warming. *Nature*, 439:161-167.

Ricketts, T.H., E. Dinerstein, T. Boucher, T.M. Brooks, S.H.M. Butchart, M. Hoffmann, J.F. Lamoreux, J. Morrison, M. Parr, J.D. Pilgrim, A.S.L. Rodrigues, W. Sechrest, G.E. Wallace, K. Berlin, J. Bielby, N.D. Burgess, D.R. Church, N. Cox, D. Knox, C. Loucks, G.W. Luck, L.L. Master, R. Moore, R. Naidoo, R. Ridgely, G.E. Schatz, G. Shire, H. Strand, W. Wettengel and E. Wikramanayake. 2005. Pinpointing and Preventing Imminent Extinctions. *PNAS*, 102(51):18497-18501.

Rodrigues, A.S.L., H.R. Akçakaya, S.J. Andelman, M.I. Bakarr, L. Boitani, T.M. Brooks, L.D.C. Fishpool, G.A.B. Fonseca, K.J. Gaston, M. Hoffmann, J.S. Long, P.A. Marquet, J.D. Pilgrim, R.L. Pressey, J. Schipper, W. Sechrest, S.N. Stuart, L.G. Underhill, R.W. Waller, M.E.J. Watts and X. Yan. 2004a. Global Gap Analysis: Priorities for Expanding the Global Protected Area Network. *BioScience*, 54:1092-1100.

Rodrigues, A.S.L., S.J. Andelman, M.I. Bakarr, L. Boitani, T.M. Brooks, R.M. Cowling, L.D.C. Fishpool, G.A.B. Fonseca, K.J. Gaston, M. Hoffmann, J.S. Long, P.A. Marquet, J.D. Pilgrim, R.L. Pressey, J. Schipper, W. Sechrest, S.N. Stuart, L.G. Underhill, R.W. Waller, M.E.J. Watts and X. Yan. 2004. Effectiveness of the Global Protected Area Network in Representing Species Diversity. *Nature*, 428:640-643.

Sarkar, S. 1999. Wilderness Preservation and Biodiversity Conservation: Keeping Divergent Goals Distinct. *BioScience*, 49:405-412.

Stuart, S.N., J.S. Chanson, N.A. Cox, B.E. Young, A.S.L. Rodrigues, D.L. Fischman and R.W. Waller. 2004. Status and Trends of Amphibian Declines and Extinctions Worldwide. *Science*, 306:1783-1786.

Travis, J. 2005. Scientists' Fears Come True as Hurricane Floods New Orleans. *Science*, 309:1656-1659.

7. LIVING LANDSCAPES

Dudley, N., M. Hockings and S. Stolton. 2004. Options for Guaranteeing the Effective Management of the World's Protected Areas. *Journal of Environmental Policy and Planning,* 6:131-142.

Groves, C.R., D.B. Jensen, L.L. Valutis, K.H. Redford, M.L. Shaffer, J.M. Scott, J.V. Baumgartner, J.V. Higgins, M.W. Beck and M.G. Anderson. 2002. Planning for Biodiversity Conservation: Putting Conservation Science into Practice. *BioScience*, 52:499-512.

Kramer, R., C.P. Van Schaik and J. Johnson. 1997. Last Stand: Protected Areas and the Defense of Tropical Biodiversity. Oxford University Press, New York.

Redford, K.H., P. Coppolillo, E.W. Sanderson, G.A.B. Fonseca, E. Dinerstein, C. Groves, G. Mace, S. Maginnis, R.A. Mittermeier, R. Noss, D. Olson, J.G. Robinson, A. Vedder and M. Wright. 2003. Mapping the Conservation Landscape. *Conservation Biology*, 17:116-131.

Sanderson, E.W., M. Jaiteh, M.A. Levy, K.H. Redford, A.V. Wannebo and G. Woolmer. 2002a. The Human Footprint and the Last of the Wild. *BioScience*, 52:891-904.

Sanderson, E.W., K.H. Redford, A. Vedder, P.B. Coppolillo and S.E. Ward. 2002b. A Conceptual Model for Conservation Planning Based on Landscape Species Requirements. *Landscape and Urban Planning*, 58:41-56.

Sanderson, E.W., D.S. Wilkie, P.B. Coppolillo, S. Strindberg, S. Stone and A. Vedder. 2001. Umbrella species. *Conservation Biology in Practice*, 2:4-5.

Terborgh, J. 1999. *Requiem for Nature*. Island Press, Washington, D.C.

Wildlife Conservation Society. 2001. Bulletin 2: The Landscape Species Approach –A Tool for Site– Based Conservation. Bronx, New York. Available at: http://wcslivinglandscapes.com/bulletins (accessed April, 2006)

Wildlife Conservation Society. 2002. Bulletin 3: The Roles of Landscape Species in Site-based Conservation. Bronx, New York. Available at: http://wcslivinglandscapes.com/bulletins (Accessed April, 2006).

Wildlife Conservation Society. 2004. Technical Manual 1: Participatory Spatial Assessment of Human Activities –A Tool for Conservation Planning. Bronx, New York. Available at: http://wcslivinglandscapes.com/bulletins (Accessed April, 2006).

8. AFRICA MEGAFLYOVER

Adams, J.S. and T.O. McShane. 1992. *The Myth of Wild Africa*. W.W. Norton & Company. New York.

Ceballos G. and P.R. Erlich. 2002. Mammal Population Losses and the Extinction Crisis. *Science*, 296(5569):904-907.

Coppolillo, P., M. Demment, B. Mbano, S. Bergen and J. Forrest. 2006. *Current Wetlands Management Practices in the Usangu Sub Catchments: A Review of Drivers, Pressures, State, Impacts and Responses*. Presented to the Wildlife Division of the Ministry of Natural Resources and Tourism. WCS Rungwa Ruaha Program.

Millenium Ecosystem Assessment (MA). 2004.

Olson D.M., E. Dinerstein, E.E. Wikramnayake, N.D.Burgess, G.V.N. Powell, E.C. Underwood, J. D'Amico, I. Itoua, H.E. Strand, J.C. Morrison, C.J. Loucks, T.F. Alnutt, T.H. Ricketts, Y. Umikokura, J.F. Lamoreux, W.W. Wettengel, P. Hedao, K.R. Kassem. 2001. Terrestrial Ecoregions of the World: A New Map of Life on Earth. *Biological Conservation*, 51(11):933-938.

Sanderson E.W., M. Jaiteh, M.A. Levy, K.H. Redford, A.V. Wannebo and G. Woolmer. 2002. The Human Footprint and the Last of the Wild. *BioScience*, 52(10):891-904.

Sitati N.W., M.J. Walpole, R.J. Smith, N. Leader-Williams. 2003. Factors Affecting Susceptibility of Farms to Crop Raiding by African Elephants: Using a Predictive Model to Mitigate Conflict. *Journal of Applied Ecology*, 40(4):667-677.

UN Population Division of the Department of Economic and Social Affairs of the United Nations Secretariat (UN Population Division). 2005. World Population Prospectus, the 2004 Revision. Highlights. United Nations, New York. Available at: http://www.un.org/esa/|population/publications/WPP2004/wpp2004.htm (Accessed March, 2006).

Van Dyke F.G., R.H. Brocke, H.G. Shaw, B.B. Ackerman, T.P. Hemker, F.G. Lindzey. 1986. Reactions of Mountain Lions to Logging and Human Activity. *Journal of Wildlife Management*, 50(1):95-102.

Wackernagel M., L. Onisto, A.C. Linares, I.A. López Falfán, J. Méndez García, A.I. Suárez Guerrero, M.G. Suárez Guerrero. 1997. Ecological Footprints of Nations. How Much Nature Do They Use? – How Much Nature Do They Have? Available at: http://www.ecouncil.ac.cr/rio/focus/report/english/footprint/

World Resources Institute (WRI). 2005. The Wealth of the Poor: Managing Ecosystems to Fight Poverty. UNDP, UNEP, World Bank, WRI. Washington, D.C.

PRODUCTION
Agrupación Sierra Madre, S.C.

GENERAL COORDINATION   *Ana Ezcurra*

EDITORIAL REVISION AND CORRECTION   *Ian Gardner*   *Carole Bullard*

GRAPHIC DESIGN   *Juan Carlos Burgoa*   *Patricio Robles Gil*

PHOTOGRAPHS COMPILATION   *Roxana Vega*

CONTENTS SUPERVISION   *Jaime Rojo*

TECHNICAL SUPPORT   *Elena León*

PRINTING SUPERVISION   *Carolin Stransky*

DIGITAL ADAPTATION OF THE MAPS   *Renato H. Flores*
From images provided by Wildlife Conservation Society/CIESIN – Columbia University

ISBN 968-6397-99-X

Printed in Japan by Toppan Printing Co., on acid free paper.

Suggested citation for this book:
Sanderson, E.W., P. Robles Gil, C.G. Mittermeier, V.G. Martin, and C.F. Kormos. 2006. *The Human Footprint: Challenges for Wilderness and Biodiversity*. CEMEX-Agrupación Sierra Madre-Wildlife Conservation Society, Mexico, 324 pp.

THE HUMAN FOOTPRINT is a trademark registered to the Wildlife Conservation Society.

The authors would like to thank the following people for their various contributions to this book. For their assistance with the introduction, we thank Dr. Thomas Brooks, Michael Hoffmann and Daniel Juhn from Conservation International. We are thankful to Mark Denil, from Conservation International's GIS lab, for providing us with several valuable suggestions on map design. Leanne Miller and Karyn Tabor, both from CI's Regional Analysis program in the Center for Applied Biodiversity Science were of invaluable help in locating maps and satellite photographs. A special thanks to Tim Bean of WCS for his hard work in the production of maps. The authors of the Human Access chapter would like to thank John G. Robinson of the Wildlife Conservation Society for his comments on a draft of this paper. Thanks as well to Paddy Rees of The WILD Foundation for her editorial assistance and to Jill Lucena, Doan Nguyen, Ella Outlaw and Sterling Zumbrunn of Conservation International for all their help during the long months of production. And also to Tiffany Johnson, Samantha Strindberg, Timothy O'Brien, Wildlife Conservation Society Africa–Science and Exploration, and Living Landscapes Programs, and to National Geographic Society. Agrupación Sierra Madre in turn would also like to thank the following people and institutions for their help and assistance in various aspects relating to the production of this book: Michael Calderwood, Sue Cedarholm, Exequiel Ezcurra, Fundación Mexicana para la Educación Ambiental, Francisco J.M. Gutiérrez, Sandy Lanham, Claudia Lucotti, National Aeronautics and Space Administration (NASA), Raúl Pérez Madero, Thomas Mangelsen, Gina Martin, Enrique Martínez, Dolores Mestre de Robles Gil, María Antonieta Morales de Yarrington, Rodolfo Ogarrio, Martin Price, Patricia Rojo, Roberto Saldívar, and Tomás Yarrington.